SEXUALITY AND PSYCHOANALYSIS

Sexuality and Psychoanalysis

Edited by

Edward T. Adelson, M. D.

BRUNNER/MAZEL, *Publishers* New York

Published by
BRUNNER/MAZEL, INC.
64 University Place, New York, N.Y. 10003

MANUFACTURED IN THE UNITED STATES OF AMERICA

Library of Congress Cataloging in Publication Data

Main entry under title:

Sexuality and psychoanalysis.

"Presented at the sixth symposium organized by the Society of Medical Psychoanalysts."
Includes bibliographical references.
1. Sex (Psychology)—Congresses. 2. Psychoanalysis—Congresses. I. Adelson, Edward T., ed. II. Society of Medical Psychoanalysts.
BF692.S435 616.6 73-94007
ISBN 0-87630-095-6

Preface

THE PAPERS IN THIS VOLUME were presented at the Sixth Symposium organized by the Society of Medical Psychoanalysts. It is the tradition of the Society to arrange triennial symposia on salient topics of psychoanalysis. For the Sixth Symposium the Society chose the topic *Sexuality and Psychoanalysis Revisited.*

Sexuality and psychoanalysis have been interrelated from the beginning. I shall not repeat here the history of this relationship, since I do so in the introductory chapter. Our knowledge of the physiology, anatomy, biochemistry, and psychology of sexuality has increased tremendously since Freud's time, and the last fifteen years have witnessed an explosion in this field. The research of Masters and Johnson, Stoller, and Money, Sherfey's papers on female sexuality, the revolution caused by the pill, the change in attitude of many psychoanalysts about sexual variations, and changes in the concepts of masculinity and femininity have to be incorporated into psychoanalytic theory and practice. We believe the theories of psychoanalysis should be consistent with the new facts discovered by other disciplines.

We therefore invited scientists in the vanguard of research on sexuality to participate in this Symposium. In addition, psychoanalysts who use this new knowledge in their work have enriched the Symposium with their experience. Dr. Irving Bieber, for example, has sagaciously arranged for a new translation of S. Lindner's paper on "Thumbsucking," so that the reader may ascertain firsthand whether Lindner's article confirms or refutes Freud's deduction about the sexual character of thumbsucking. The quality of the papers, as well as of the discussion and the response of the audience, continues the high standards set by the Society's previous symposia.

We believe this book may answer many old questions in psychoanalysis and raise new ones. We are proud to offer this volume to psychoanalysts and other professionals in the fields of psychoanalysis and sexuality.

ACKNOWLEDGMENTS

This symposium is the result of the work of many members who gave generously of their special skills and competences. In all, we are thankful for their prodigious efforts.

However, special commendation and appreciation are here expressed to Drs. Harry Kosovsky and Moses Naftalin, former presidents of the Society of Medical Psychoanalysts, without whose generous support and encouragement the task of organizing this Symposium would have been more arduous.

Mrs. Dorothy Harte, our executive secretary, gave invaluable assistance in planning and running the Symposium, for which we are indeed grateful.

Contents

Contributors

EDWARD T. ADELSON, M.D.—Assistant Clinical Professor of Psychiatry, Cornell University Medical College, New York, N.Y.

IAN ALGER, M.D.—Visiting Associate Clinical Professor of Psychiatry, Albert Einstein College of Medicine, Bronx, New York, and Training Psychoanalyst, New York Medical College.

SILVANO ARIETI, M.D.—Clinical Professor of Psychiatry, New York Medical College.

JULES R. BEMPORAD, M.D.—Director, Pediatric Psychiatry, Babies Hospital, Columbia-Presbyterian Medical Center, New York, and Faculty Member, Psychoanalytic Division, New York Medical College.

IRVING BIEBER, M.D.—Clinical Professor of Psychiatry, New York Medical College.

EWALD W. BUSSE, M.D., SC.D.—J. P. Gibbons Professor of Psychiatry and Chairman of the Department of Psychiatry, Duke University Medical School, Durham, North Carolina.

MIO FREDLAND, M.D.—Assistant Clinical Professor, Department of Psychiatry, Cornell University Medical College, New York, N.Y.

EDRITA FRIED, Ph.D.—Associate Professor of Psychiatry, Albert Einstein Medical College, Bronx State Hospital, Bronx, N.Y.

ELEANOR GALENSON, M.D.—Associate Professor of Clinical Psychiatry, Albert Einstein College of Medicine, Bronx, N.Y.

ALVIN I. GOLDFARB, M.D.—Associate Clinical Professor of Psychiatry, The Mount Sinai School of Medicine of the City University of New York.

HENRY GREENBAUM, M.D.—Associate Clinical Professor of Psychiatry, New York University School of Medicine.

EDWARD J. HORNICK—Department of Psychiatry, Albert Einstein College of Medicine, Bronx, N.Y.

CHARLES L. IHLENFELD, M.D.—Associate Attending Department of Medicine, Lutheran Medical Center, Brooklyn, N.Y.

MICHAEL G. KALOGERAKIS, M.D.—Associate Clinical Professor, New York Medical College.

HELEN SINGER KAPLAN, M.D., Ph.D.—Director, Sex Therapy and Education Program, New York Hospital-Cornell Medical Center.

CLARICE J. KESTENBAUM, M.D.—Director of the Division of Child Psychiatry, St. Luke's Hospital Center, New York, N.Y.

SHEILA KLEBANOW, M.D.—Clinical Assistant Professor of Psychiatry, New York Medical College, formerly Associate in Psychiatry, Mount Sinai School of Medicine.

S. LINDNER—

DONALD T. LUNDE, M.D.—Department of Psychiatry, Stanford University, School of Medicine, Stanford, California.

WILLIAM T. MC KINNEY, JR., M.D.—Associate Professor of Psychiatry, University of Wisconsin Medical School, Madison, Wisconsin.

JOHN MONEY, M.D.—Professor of Medical Psychology and Associate Professor of Pediatrics, Department of Psychiatry and Behavioral Sciences and Department of Pediatrics, Johns Hopkins University School of Medicine and Hospital, Baltimore, Maryland.

PETER B. NEUBAUER, M.D.—Clinical Professor of Psychiatry, State University of New York, Downstate Medical College.

ALFRED H. RIFKIN, M.D.—Clinical Associate Professor of Psychiatry, New York University School of Medicine, and Associate Clinical Professor of Psychiatry, New York Medical College.

CLIFFORD J. SAGER, M.D.—Clinical Professor of Psychiatry, Mt. Sinai School of Medicine, CUNY; Psychiatric Director, Jewish Family Service, New York.

NATALIE SHAINESS, M.D.—Lecturer in Psychiatry, College of Physicians and Surgeons, Columbia University, New York

JAMES TOOLAN, M.D.—Associate Professor, Department of Psychiatry, University of Vermont Medical School.

RICHARD G. VAN GELDER, Ph.D.—Director, Division of Mammalogy, The American Museum of Natural History, New York.

SEXUALITY AND PSYCHOANALYSIS

Introduction

EDWARD T. ADELSON, M.D.

THE CONCEPT OF THE SEXUAL ORIGIN of mental disorders is generally attributed to Freud. However, the theory that sexual disturbances cause mental disorders goes back to Hippocrates. While Freud gave an extensive history of dream theory, he failed to do this in respect to the sexual etiology of the neuroses, and, in fact, failed to acknowledge the theories of Greisinger (1), the eminent internist and psychiatrist of the 19th century and the creator of the concept of Ego, who believed the sexual organs were responsible for hysteria. Feuchtersleben (2), another distinguished psychiatrist of the same era, taught that hysteria was caused by the societal treatment of women because it emphasized "the sexual sphere and sanctioned the feelings and impulses related to it."

Havelock Ellis (3), Krafft-Ebing (4), Erb (5), and Rohleder (6), all contemporaries of Freud, believed that masturbation produced neurosis in those constitutionally disposed to neurosis. A partial explanation for Freud's oversight may be the fact that Freud was primarily a neurologist at the beginning of his career and had no psychiatric training. He may also have repressed any knowledge that others had attributed mental illness to sexual disturbances and masturbation.

The idea that sexuality and mental illness are interrelated is ancient. The term hysteria, which means "wandering womb" in Greek, was first used by Hippocrates. In ancient Rome, Galen (7), and other Roman physicians emphasized the theory that sexual abstinence is the principal etiology of hysteria. Galen had noted that hysteria occurred mostly in virgins and widows.

When Christianity evolved, the pagan idea of sex as something natural was contested. Early priests and other ecclesiastical writers contradicted the natural character of sexuality. Questions of lust pervaded the writing and thinking of this time, and a distinction between evil erotic pleasures and sexual union for procreation evolved. The early Christians regarded abstinence as a virtue and saw no ill effects from it. This was primarily the result of the work of St. Paul, who said, "It is better to marry than to burn, but it is best not to marry at all." The early Christians believed that the second coming of Christ was imminent and that they would have all the pleasures in heaven; therefore it was not necessary to have secular pleasures on earth.

St. Augustine (8) agreed that sexual union was justified only as a means of procreation. He said that carnal pleasures were the work of unholy spirits and recommended severe punishment for hysterics, "to wrest the demon from the body." Under the influence of early Christian preachings and admonitions, many hysterics admitted having sexual intercourse with the devil.

During the Middle Ages, with the exception of Irish monastics and Byzantine scholars, knowledge of Greek and Roman philosophers and physicians disappeared from Western Europe. The tradition of the ancients, however, remained alive among the Mohammedans and the Jews who lived in Spain, North Africa, and Turkey. In the 9th to 11th centuries, at least one hundred books dealing with sexual intercourse in all its aspects were written. One of the most prominent of these authors was Maimonides (9) (1135-1204). He was born in Cordova, Spain, but because of a change of dynasties he fled, first to Morocco and then to Egypt. He was physician to Sultan Saladin, who defeated Richard the Lion-Hearted. He wrote *On Sexual Intercourse,* a treatise on the medical aspects of sexual intercourse. Maimonides believed that the need for sexual intercourse varied among individuals, that a happy sexual life was essential for a happy life, and that abrupt abstinence produced emotional illness. He attributed melancholia to an abrupt cessation of sexual intercourse.

The Christian bias against sexual pleasure was continued in the *Malleus Maleficarum* (10), published in 1489. Kramer and Sprenger stated that any kind of sexual relations that evoked pleasure, even in marriage, was caused by the devil.

Dr. Oskar Diethelm (11), Professor Emeritus of Psychiatry at the Cornell University Medical College, has investigated the history of "sexual excitement," and has brought to light papers published from the late 16th century to the 18th century. In one of these papers, Forestus (12), in 1590, wrote that *furor uterinus* was caused by excess love.

Pinel (13), an 18th century French physician, wrote that there was more to hysteria than mere somatic manifestations. He believed in a psychogenic basis for disease and held that some of the factors involved in the origin of hysteria were a predisposition to emotional instability, stimulation by voluptuous conversation or literature, abuse of sexual pleasure, or deprivation after a long period of sexual enjoyment.

Feuchtersleben (2), a 19th century German psychiatrist, thought that the greater incidence of hysteria in females versus males was a result of societal cultivation of women which gave "a preponderance to the sexual sphere and sanctions the feelings and impulses related to it." He maintained that married women are most predisposed to hysteria because they have "both the want of exercise in those sexual functions intended by nature for use and disappointed desire or hope, or at least the feeling of failing in their earthly destination."

Greisinger (1), another 19th century German psychiatrist, reverted to a somatic explanation for hysteria by implicating the sexual organs almost to the exclusion of everything else. This was a digression from Pinel and Feuchtersleben.

Pierre Janet (14), an outstanding French psychiatrist of the same era, taught that sexual desires were normal and hysterical patients displayed these same desires as other people did. He claimed that hysterics are usually more frigid than sensual due to their preoccupation with themselves and their shrinking emotional radius.

Thought regarding the masturbatory etiology of mental illness and neurosis is approximately 300 years old. Dr. E. W. Hare (15) writes that "men, no doubt, have always been aware that the frequent repetition of the sexual act is often followed by a feeling of lethargy." From the time of Hippocrates, physicians have recorded their belief that overindulgence in sexual activity is harmful to health; however, there was no general notion before the 18th century that masturbation was specifically harmful to health or that it was more harmful than equivalent indulgence in sexual intercourse.

The medical dangers of masturbation became widely popularized throughout Europe as a result of the publication in London, early in the 18th century, of a book called *Onanania, or The Heinous Sin of Self-Pollution* (16). There is reason to think its anonymous author was a clergyman turned quack, since the book was more concerned with the sin than with the harm of masturbation. It went through at least eighty editions and was used by Voltaire (17) in his *Dictionnaire Philosophique*. He popularized the worn "onanism," using it as a synonym for "masturbation" and "self-abuse," despite the fact that onanism had nothing to do with masturbation.

Tissot (18), an 18th-century French physician, was the first medical authority to write on the disorders produced by masturbation. Tissot taught that sexual abuse of all types, but masturbation in particular, can cause a host of serious disorders, both mental and physical. Physical illnesses resulted from the loss of semen, which occasioned general debility and so opened the way to consumption, deterioration of eyesight, disorders of digestion, impotence, and so forth. But the most important effect was on the nervous system, since the sexual act caused an increased flow of blood to the brain. Tissot wrote that there were eight reasons why masturbation was more pernicious than excesses committed with women, the most important being "the shame and shocking remorse" which must follow masturbation "when illness had opened the criminal's eyes to his crimes and dangers." Tissot was unable to deal dispassionately with the subject, and his book abounds in moral censure. By the end of the 18th century the masturbatory hypothesis of the origins of mental illness was widely accepted throughout Europe and America. The Church had always taught the sinfulness of masturbation, and now it harmfulness was confirmed by a considerable portion of the medical profession.

Lallemand (19), Professor of Medicine at Montpellier in France in the 19th century, taught that all discharges of semen were weakening to the body and therefore dangerous to the health. However, he believed that masturbation was a relatively unimportant cause of discharge when compared to local inflammation, gonorrhea, and rectal disorders. He denied that dorsal consumption or, indeed, any other disease associated with pathological change was directly due to masturbation. He maintained that the symptoms produced by excessive voluntary pollutions were purely nervous and did not call for any of the treatments applicable to organs which are functioning pathologically. He believed that masturbation was a menace to the future of civilization although he restricted its consequences to those nervous disorders of unknown etiology.

Benjamin Rush (20), an 18th-century American physician, mentioned onanism among the causes which induce madness. "The morbid effects of intemperance in sexual intercourse with women are feeble and of a transient nature compared with the strain of physical and moral evils which this solitary vice fixes upon the body and mind." He attributed seminal weakness, impotence, dysuria, tabes dorsalis, pulmonary consumption, dyspepsia, dimness of sight, vertigo, epilepsy, hypochondriasis, loss of memory, fatuity, and death to masturbation.

The great 18th-century French psychiatrist, Esquirol (21), stated that "Masturbation is recognized in all countries as a common cause of insanity. Onanism is a grave symptom in mania; unless it stops at once it is an insurmountable obstacle to cure.

By lowering the powers of resistance it reduces the patient to a state of stupidity, to phthisis, marasmus and death. . . . Masturbation may be a forerunner of mania, of dementia, and even of senile dementia; it leads to melancholy and suicide; its consequences are more serious in men than in women." He asserted that onanism predisposes to epilepsy and may be the exciting cause, even in infancy.

Flemming (22), a German alienist of the same period, hoped he would "not be accused of having written an apologia for self-abuse; my object has simply been to question the correctness of the view that self-abuse is so very often the only or the principal cause of mental disorder." He argued that because too little was known of the etiology of insanity, the alienists of his time were apt to suspect as causal what might in fact be only a consequence or a symptom of the illness. He believed that onanism produced mental illness when it was excessive or when there were other factors such as suppressed hemorrhoidal flow. Greisinger (1), on the other hand, wrote that "onanism is an important and frequent cause of insanity as for all other physical and moral degradation." He believed that the most harmful effects of masturbation were the shame and distress caused by the inability to resist the desire; he stated that the increase in sexual excitement at the beginning of insanity was a symptom and not a cause of the disease.

P. Skae (23), an Englishman of the late 19th century, was the first physician to maintain that there was a particular and special type of insanity due to masturbation. He believed that mental illnesses should be classified according to their natural history rather than by their associated symptoms. He considered masturbation to be the third major factor in the causation of mental illness.

Maudsley (24, 25), a British psychiatrist of the same era, also believed in the malignant effects of masturbation. He wrote, "Nothing is more certain than that either of these causes will produce an enervation of nervous element which, if the exhausting vice be continued, passes by a further declension into degeneration and actual destruction thereof. The habit of self-abuse notably gives rise to a particular and disagreeable form of insanity, characterized by intense self-feeling and conceit, extreme perversion of feeling and corresponding derangement of thought, in the earlier stages, and later by failure of intelligence, nocturnal hallucination, and suicidal or homicidal propensities." Later he went on to explain that he could not differentiate between insanity due to self-abuse and that due to the processes of adolescence, "for the early symptoms of both are the same and are due to the processes of adolescence and not to the particular vice."

The physicians of the 19th century regarded anyone who was schizoid as one who practiced illicit masturbation. In 1895 Maudsley (26) abandoned his earlier views on masturbation and was of the opinion that there was another class of chronic disorders caused by it.

At the beginning of the 20th century, Charcot and his school, Gilles de la Tourette, and Binswanger denied that masturbation had a special role in the etiology of neurosis. Havelock Ellis (3), Freud (27), Krafft-Ebing (4), Erb (5), and Rohleder (6) took a middle view. They maintained that in the constitutionally disposed, masturbation may lead not only to neurasthenia but to ejaculatio praecox, impotence, and aversion to coitus—the latter helping to furnish a soil in which the perverted impulse may develop. Krafft-Ebing, Moreau, and Bloch were also among those who believed that masturbation might lead to homosexuality.

Freud's (27) contribution to the sexual origin of mental illness, and of the neuroses in particular, was the concept of infantile sexuality. Originally Freud believed that current sexual frustration. if partial, produced neurasthenia, while total sexual frustration resulted in anxiety neurosis. He also believed that conversion hysteria and obsessive-compulsive neurosis arose in childhood. If the neurotic endured a childhood seduction passively, he developed a conversion hysteria; if he participated actively in the seduction he developed an obsessive-compulsive neurosis. The obsessive-compulsive presumably had been passive in a previous seduction.

On further examination, Freud found that the seduction stories his patients told were usually fantasies. He therefore concluded that the major orifices of the infant's body, in addition to their physiological role, produced sexual gratification. Of course, other organs could become erotogenic also. Freud believed that there was a successive progression from mouth to anus to phallus or clitoris and, at adolescence, to the genitals. If the mouth, anus, etc., were either overgratified or unduly frustrated, the individual became fixated at that particular level of libidinal development. In addition, if the neurotic encountered conflicts about his phallic strivings in the oedipal situation, he would regress to an earlier level which he had already navigated successfully.

I will not discuss the validity of infantile sexuality because Dr. Irving Bieber does so in his paper. In addition, he has translated Lindner's (28) paper on thumbsucking upon which Freud based his theory of infantile sexuality.

Freud postulated that each drive was associated with libido or sexual energy. There is oral, anal, phallic, and genital libido, as well as masculine and feminine libido, narcissistic and object libido, and homosexual and heterosexual libido.

According to Freud, the psychic energy could either be bound, as in the secondary process, or free, as in the primary process. This is the opposite of the terms "free" and "bound" in physics. The energy can be instinctual or neutralized as in sublimation. Freud wrote at times as if the energy were a fluid—at other times as if it were static electricity. Freud believed that in the neuroses, libido or psychic energy was dammed up and therefore would seek other outlets—that libido always seeks discharge. Scott (29), the eminent biologist, states that nowhere but in the bladder and rectum can this occur in the human organism. He knows of no such mechanism in the central nervous system. According to Silvano Arieti (30), such phenomena as displacement, condensation, and symbolization can be explained by cognitive processes.

The psychoanalyst never uses the term libido or psychic energy with a patient. Psychic energy cannot be measured as physical energy can. Even the concept of physical energy is merely a mathematical construct which really does not exist. Contrary to what people believe, physical energy is not a thing, a fluid, or even a vortex. It is a mathematical device which physicists find useful to describe processes in a closed system. Energy only has meaning in respect to a field of forces or potential forces. Coal or petroleum has no energy. *The process of the combustion* of coal or petroleum has the energy.

Many analysts have recently discarded the concept of psychic energy. They range from Kubie (31), Colby (32), and Fairbairn (33) to Klein (34) and Holt (35). Kubie has stated: "All psychological phenomena are the result of the interplay of many conflicting intrapsychic forces. Consequently any rearrangements of these forces can release new forces of behavior without any increases or decreases of hypothetical charges of energy. Assumptions as to changes in quantities of energy are admissible only if alterations in the pattern of intrapsychic forces have been ruled out. A failure to recognize this has made all so-called economic formulations a species of *ad hoc* speculative allegory in quantitative terms."

Colby wrote (32): "Energy is controlled by structure, and structure has no function unless activated by energy . . . An organism is not a closed or isolated system. It constantly takes in and puts out energy in various forms." An organism can no longer be thought of as an equilibrium since in equilibrium the total net change is zero.

Freud, like Helmholtz, Du Bois, and Raymond, tried to reduce all mental phenomena to matter, force, and energy. I believe that Freud was right in one respect; all our symbolic operations can, in the last analysis, be traced back to a core of early childhood sensory experiences. The first ego is a body ego. The growing child constantly identifies its somatic functions with the objects of the external world. The infant constantly analogizes external processes with hearing, swallowing, refusing, taking, getting, retaining, expelling, grabbing, breaking, etc. This is why analysts of the various schools have about the same success rate.

In recent years some of Freud's basic concepts have been challenged and some new concepts have been introduced. Stoller (36) and Money (37) have introduced the concept of gender identification. By the time a child is 18 months old, its parents have assigned him or her a gender usually consistent with, but occasionally the opposite of, his or her anatomical sex. This has thrown new light on transsexualism, a psychiatric condition in which the individual believes that he or she belongs to the opposite sex.

In another area, Masters and Johnson (38) have questioned whether there is a difference between a clitoral and a vaginal orgasm. Their research has shown that physiologically there is no difference. At the same time, the concept of genital primacy is in question because some very emotionally ill people can have orgasms while some persons with no mental disorders suffer with sexual dysfunctions.

Also, the notion that sexual difficulties are deep-rooted and require a total reconstruction of the personality has been challenged, since brief, symptom-oriented techniques often cure the sexual dysfunction without extensive psychotherapy.

It is because of the above questions that we have invited workers on the frontiers of sexual research to this meeting. We hope that they will throw light on some of these problem areas and, in addition, invite psychoanalysts to explain new findings by the theory of psychoanalysis.

References

1. Greisinger, W. *Mental Pathology and Therapeutics.* Translated by C. L. Robertson and J. Rutherford. London: New Sydenham Society, 1867. P. 201.
2. Feuchtersleben, E. von. *The Principles of Medical Psychology, Being the Outline of a Course of Lectures.* Translated by H. E. Lloyd. Revised and edited by B. G. Babington. London: Sydenham Society, 1847. Originally published as *Lehrbuch der arztlichen Seelenkunde.* Vienna: Gerold, 1845. P. 225.
3. Ellis, H. *Studies in the Psychology of Sex,* Vol. I, Part I. Philadelphia: F. A. Davis, 1901.
4. Krafft-Ebing, R. von. *Psychopathia Sexualis.* New York: 1922.
5. Erb, W. H. Spinal cord. In *Cyclopedia of Medicine,* Vol. 13. Translated

by Geoghegan, Schauffler, Lincoln, and McCreery. New York: Ward, 1878.
6. Rohleder, H. *Die Masturbation.* Berlin: H. Kornfeld, 1912.
7. Galen. *De locis affectis,* Liber VI. Venice: Junta, 1541.
8. Augustinus, St. Aurelius. Writing of Saint Augustine, Vol. VII, *The City of God.* Translated by G. Walsh and D. J. Honan. New York: Fathers of the Church, 1954.
9. Maimonides, M. B. *On Sexual Intercourse. Fil-gima,* edited by M. Gorlin. Brooklyn, N.Y.: Rambash Publishing Co., 1961.
10. Kramer, H., and Sprenger, J. *Malleus Maleficarum.* Translated by the Rev. M. Summers. London: Rodker, 1921.
11. Diethelm, O. Uterine fury of sexual excitement. *Evolution Psychiatrique,* Vol. 31, p. 233, 1966.
12. Forestus, P. *Observationem et curationum medicinalium.* Libri tres. Leyden: 1590.
13. Pinel, P. *Nosographie philosophique ou la méthode de l'analyse appliquée a la médecine.* 5th edition. Paris: J. A. Brossun, 1813.
14. Janet, P. *The Mental State of Hystericals: A Study of Mental Stigmata and Mental Accidents.* Translated by C. H. Carson. New York: Putnam and Sons, 1901.
15. Hare, E. W. Masturbatory insanity: The history of an idea. *J. Ment. Sci., 108,* 1-25, January 1962.
16. *Onanania, or The Heinous Sin of Self-Pollution, and all its Frightful Consequences, in Both Sexes,* etc. Boston: S. Kneeland and T. Green, 1742.
17. Voltaire, F. A. *Oeuvres Completes.* Onan, Onanisme. In Vol. 42, *Dictionnaire Philosophique.* Geneva: Frères Cramer, 1776.
18. Tissot, S-S. A. P. *Onanism or a Treatise upon the Disorders Produced by Masturbation; or the Dangerous Effects of Secret and Excessive Venery.* Translated by A. Hume. Paris: Mark Chopius, 1767.
19. Lallemand, C. F. *Des Pertes Seminales Involontaires.* Paris: Bechel Jaune, 1838-42.
20. Rush, B. *Medical Inquiries and Observations upon the Diseases of the Mind.* Philadelphia: Dobson, 1774; John Briggs, 1912.
21. Esquirol, E. Folie. In *Dictionnaire des Sciences Medicales.* Paris: Pancoucke, 1836.
22. Flemming, G. F. Ueber das Causal-Verhaltnis der Selbstbefledrung zur Geistesuerrung. *Zeitifid. Beurtheilung u. Heilung der Krankhaften Seelenzustande, I:*1, 205, 1838.
23. Skae, P. A rational and practical classification of insanity. *J. Ment. Sci., 14,* 149, 1868.
24. Maudsley, H. *The Physiology and Pathology of the Mind.* London: 1867; New York: D. Appleton & Co., 1868.
25. Maudsley, H. Illustrations of a variety of insanity. *J. Ment. Sci.,* 1868.
26. Maudsley, H. *The Pathology of the Mind.* London: 1895.
27. Freud, S. *The Standard Edition of the Complete Psychological Works of Sigmund Freud,* Vol. 3. London: Hogarth Press, 1962.
28. Lindner, S. *Das Saugen an dem Fingern, Lippen, etc. bei den Kindern* (Ludeln). *Jahrbuch für Kinderheilkunde,* Leipzig, *14,* 68, 1878.
29. Scott, J. The emotional basis of social behavior. *Annals of the New York Academy,* Vol. 159, 1969.

30. ARIETI, S. Personal communication.
31. KUBIE. L. S. The fallacious use of quantitative concepts in dynamic psychology. *Psychoanal. Quart., 16,* 507, 1947.
32. COLBY, K. M. *Energy and Structure in Psychoanalysis.* New York: Ronald Press, 1955.
33. FAIRBAIRN, W. T. D. *An Object Relations Theory of Personality.* New York: Basic Books, 1954.
34. KLEIN, G. Peremptory ideation. In T. Holt (Ed.), *Motives and Thoughts: Psychoanalytic Essays in Honor of Dana Rapaport.* New York: International Universities Press, 1967. Pp. 78-130.
35. HOLT, R. R. A review of some of Freud's biological assumptions and their influence on his theories. In N. S. Greenfield and W. C. Lewis (Eds.), *Psychoanalysis and Current Biological Thought.* Madison: Univ. of Wisconsin Press, 1965.
36. STOLLER, R. T. *Sex and Gender.* New York: Science House, 1968.
37. MONEY, T. Sex reassignment as related to hermaphroditism and transsexualism. In R. Green and T. Money (Eds.), *Transsexualism and Sex Reassignment.* Baltimore: Johns Hopkins Univ. Press, 1969.
38. MASTERS, W. H., and JOHNSON, V. E. *Human Sexual Response.* Boston: Little, Brown, 1960.

1

Sex Hormones, Mood, and Behavior

DONALD T. LUNDE, M.D.

THERE IS A TENDENCY TODAY to view sex differences in behavior as culturally conditioned or learned behaviors. It is quite true that a great deal of previously assumed sex specific behavior in our society is simply the result of sex stereotypes. Differential child rearing gives rise to differences in expectations among the sexes later in life, and many unwarranted assumptions about the relative capabilities and incapabilities of each sex have been promulgated for generations. Many of these assumptions are being challenged. There is at the same time a growing body of knowledge which indicates that certain variations in mood and behavior in humans are associated with the effects of sex hormones on the central nervous system and other target organs.

It is a mistake to make facile extrapolations from animal studies to humans in the area of biological determinants of mood and behavior (just as it can be a mistake to apply certain results of animal experiments to human behavior in the area of learning theory). It is not known, for instance, whether or not animals experience emotional states that are in any way similar to the phenomenology of human emotions, although recent observations by ethologists, such as Jane Goodall (1), do seem to indicate that subhuman primates experience depression, anger, jealousy, irritability, and so forth. One must also be cautious in drawing comparisons across species, since the effects of sex hormones are known to vary considerably in this regard. This is particularly true among subhuman primates.

In the last ten years, however, there has been a significant increase in the quantity and quality of research involving the effects of sex hormones on humans and subhuman primates. This research has been made possible in part by dramatic advances in the development of accurate biochemical techniques that allow direct measurement of the various sex hormones in plasma or other body fluids. Previously, estimates of the amount of sex hormones present were made by bioassay techniques which were often inaccurate and nonspecific. The measurement of 17-ketosteroids in the urine as a reflection of circulating androgens also proved unsatisfactory and led to many inconclusive studies when attempts were made to correlate 17-ketosteroid levels with behavioral data. The findings were inconclusive because there are certain inherent inaccuracies in 17-ketosteroid measurement techniques and because this group of metabolites includes metabolites of cortisol and other adrenal hormones which may be present in such large amounts as to overshadow the active androgens present. For instance, many studies failed to find sex differences in 17-KS levels until well after puberty, even though it is well known that differences in androgen secretion rates between boys and girls is a crucial determinant of puberty (2, 3).

Although direct measurement of hormones in the blood allows for greater specificity in the measurement of circulating hormones, one must still keep in mind that the hormone levels in the peripheral circulation are not necessarily those in the central nervous system. It has been established, of course, that sex steroids do cross the blood-brain barrier and in some cases are selectively concentrated in certain parts of the brain (4).

Our research derived from the observations that certain clinical problems occur with increased frequency in women during periods of alterations in sex hormone secretion; namely, the postpartum period, the premenstrual period, and the menopause. There have also been observations that inherited or induced androgen deficiences (e.g., as the result of castration) cause alterations in sexual and aggressive behavior. These alterations are dramatic and well documented in various animal species. Witness, for instance, the differences in behavior between a bull and a castrated, docile ox. I shall concentrate in this paper on reporting the results of various research efforts rather than the techniques that were employed in this research. The techniques have recently been discussed in detail elsewhere (5).

FEMALE SEX HORMONES

The female sex hormones are estrogen and progesterone. Estrogen is more accurately a collective noun, referring to a group of chemically related hormones that are produced by the ovaries in women and, to a very limited extent, by the testes in men. Progesterone is produced by the corpus luteum following ovulation and by the placenta during pregnancy.

Menstrual Cycle

The menstrual cycle, with periodic shedding of the lining of the uterus, is a phenomenon unique to humans and some subhuman primates. Menstruation occurs in non-pregnant human females as the result of a cyclic withdrawal of the ovarian steroid hormones as shown in Figure 1. Plasma progesterone levels prior to ovulation are extremely low, less than one microgram per one hundred ml. Following ovulation, secretion of progesterone by the corpus luteum increases rapidly and then falls off rapidly several days before the onset of menstruation if conception has not occurred. There is also a concomitant elevation and drop-off in the estrogen levels during the postovulatory phase of the menstrual cycle.

During the four to seven days preceding the onset of menstruation, many women experience symptoms which include irritability, fatigue, headache, pain in the lower back, depression, and insomnia. When these symptoms are severe, they constitute a syndrome known as premenstrual tension. In addition to these symptoms of premenstrual tension, a number of other disturb-

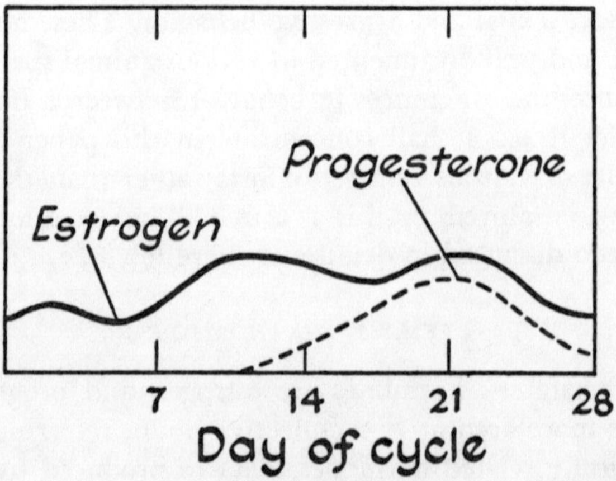

FIGURE 1
Normal Secretion of Female Sex Hormones During the Menstrual Cycle

ances have been noted to occur disproportionately in the premenstrual phase, including emergency psychiatric hospital admissions, suicide attempts, neurotic and psychotic depressions, assaultive behavior in hospitalized psychiatric patients, accidents, crimes of violence, and a decline in school or work productivity (4). Our studies of fluctuations in symptoms and mood over successive menstrual cycles have shown certain correlations with the hormonal fluctuations (6).

Figure 2 indicates that water retention and pain symptoms are high in the menstrual phase but decrease rapidly thereafter and subsequently show a slow but steady increase in the postovulatory phase. Figure 3 indicates that feelings of anxiety and aggression are high during the menstrual phase, but then diminish. Anxiety gradually increases in the postovulatory phase, reaching a peak in the premenstrual period. Aggressive feelings show a peak on day 18 of a 28-day cycle, and then gradually diminish until the onset of menstruation.

Moods of a more positive sort show a quite different pattern, as indicated in Figure 4. Pleasantness is highest during the middle of the cycle, but low during the premenstrual and menstrual

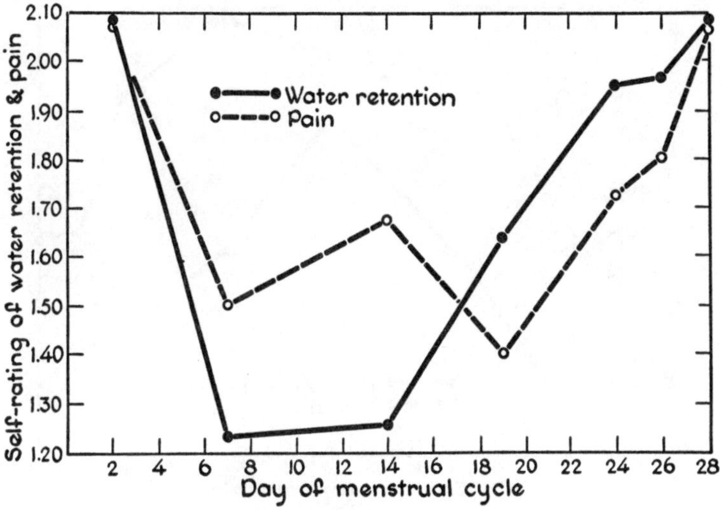

FIGURE 2

Average Self-rated Water Retention and Pain of 15 Women in Two Consecutive Menstrual Cycles

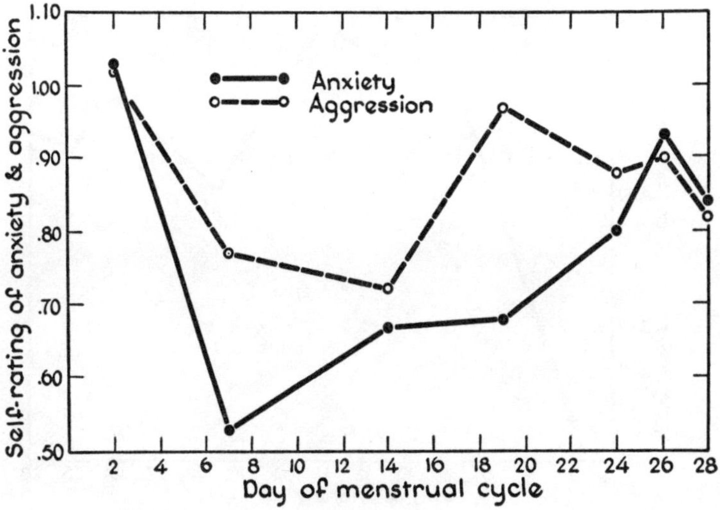

FIGURE 3

Average Self-rated Anxiety and Aggression of 15 Women in Two Consecutive Menstrual Cycles

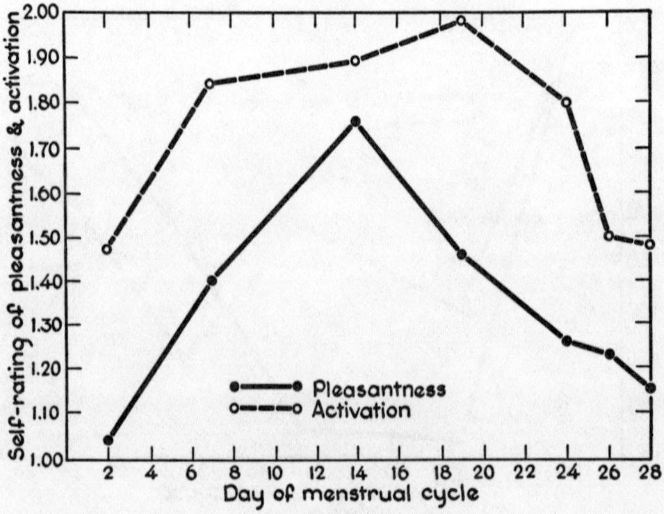

FIGURE 4
Average Self-rated Pleasantness and Activation of 15 Women in Two Consecutive Menstrual Cycles

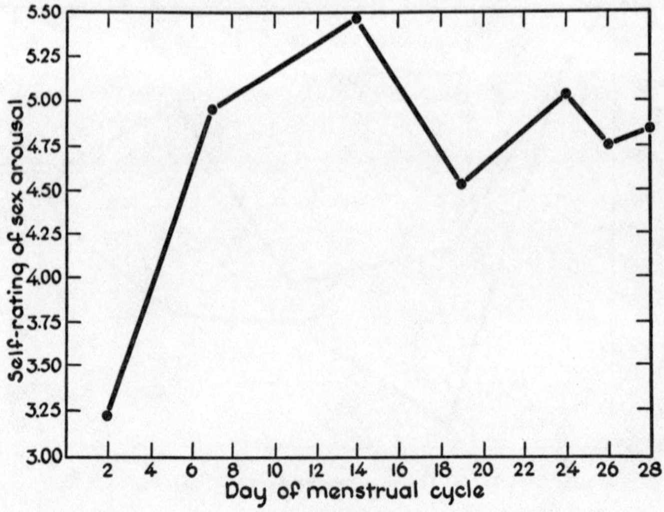

FIGURE 5
Average Self-rated Sexual Arousal of 15 Women in Two Consecutive Menstrual Cycles

phases. Activation (including feelings of extroversion and a desire to be active and outgoing) shows a similar pattern with an even more dramatic peak at the time of ovulation. Sexual arousal, as illustrated in Figure 5, is found to be relatively low during the menstrual phase, but shows a sharp and continuing rise until the ovulatory phase. Following ovulation, there is a decrease followed by a slight increase in the premenstrual phase. Other studies on the incidence of sexual intercourse have shown similar fluctuations during the menstrual cycle (7). From an evolutionary standpoint, it might seem quite logical for sexual arousal and sexual activity to peak at the time of fertility. On the other hand, one can also argue that there is adaptive value in fostering the stability of the human parent pair-bond by the relative state of receptivity which occurs in humans at times when there is no possibility of reproduction. This is in marked contrast to the situation in subprimates. The only time that many human females appear to be unreceptive is during the menstrual period, and this is most likely the result of cultural conditioning. The Old Testament, the Koran, and Hindu law books all specifically prohibit intercourse during menstruation on the grounds that women are polluted at this time and that the man who has contact with the menstrual discharge may be defiled. Many primitive tribes believe that a man will become ill or will lose his virility if he has intercourse with a woman who is menstruating.

It seems likely that cultural attitudes about menstruation account for a certain amount of the change in mood which occurs before and during menstruation. One way of eliminating the variable of attitudes about menstruation would be to study fluctuations in mood of women who have had hysterectomies, but still have functional ovaries. Such studies have not been done thus far. Another way of studying the hormonal effects of mood during the menstrual cycle is to compare women who are on the birth control pill to women who are not. In women taking the pill, the estrogen and progesterone levels are relatively constant from day to day during the twenty days of the cycle on which pills are taken. The rise and fall of estrogen and progesterone in the

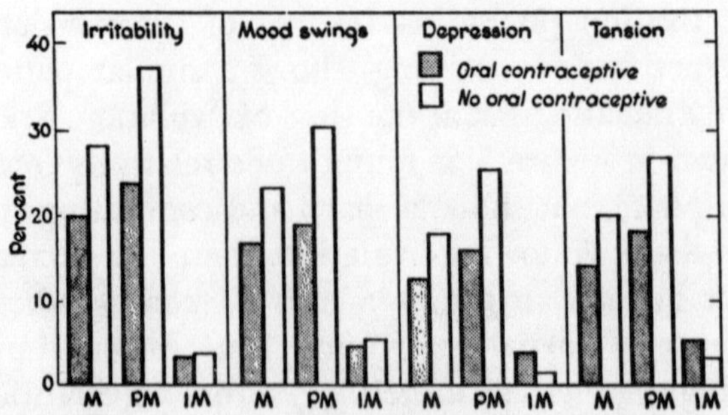

FIGURE 6

Percent of Women Reporting Moderate, Strong, or Acute Symptoms in the Menstrual (M), Premenstrual (PM), and Intermenstrual (IM) Phases of Most Recent Menstrual Cycle. (n = 718)

Pain		
Cramps	M	
Backache	M	
General aches and pains	M	PM
Concentration		
Confusion		PM
Lowered judgment		PM
Difficulty concentrating	M	PM
Distractible		PM
Lowered motor coordination	M	PM
Behavioral Change		
Lowered school or work performance	M	PM
Decreased efficiency	M	PM
Autonomic Reactions		
No differences		
Water Retention		
Weight gain		PM
Skin disorders	M	PM
Negative Affect		
Restlessness		PM
Irritability		PM
Mood swings	M	PM
Depression		PM
Tension	M	PM
Arousal		
No differences		
Control		
No differences		

TABLE 1

Symptoms Significantly Differentiating Between Women in Oral and Non-oral Contraceptive Groups During Menstrual and Premenstrual Phases

(p. 0.01; women on oral contraceptives lower on all symptoms)

postovulatory phase is eliminated by suppression of the pituitary gonadotropins. In general, there is a lower incidence of irritability, mood swings, depression, and feelings of tension in women who are on oral contraceptives (Figure 6). The differences in self-reported symptomatology during the premenstrual and menstrual phases are quite different, according to a study of 718 women which was done at Stanford (8). Table 1 shows those symptoms which were significantly lower in the women on oral contraceptives. Although the general incidence of unpleasant emotional states is less in women on the pill, it should be noted that a certain subgroup of women are prone to increased depression while on oral contraceptives.

Pregnancy and the Postpartum Period

Benedek, in her observations of pregnant women (9), noted, "The pregnant woman in her vegetative calmness enjoys her body. Many neurotic women who at other times suffer from anxiety, become free of it during pregnancy; others become free from depressions and from desperate mood changes. Many women, despite physical discomfort and nausea, feel emotionally stable, and have a 'good time' during pregnancy." There is evidence that the synthesis of progesterone increases from about 30 milligrams per day in the luteal phase of the menstrual cycle to 200-300 milligrams per day during pregnancy (10). This tremendous increase in the output of progesterone is primarily due to the significant secretion of progesterone by the placenta during pregnancy. Beginning one to five days before delivery, there is a drop in progesterone level which in fact may be one of the important determinants for the onset of labor. With the expulsion of the placenta, the progesterone output and circulating blood levels of progesterone fall precipitously. Indeed, the changes in levels of the sex hormones, particularly progesterone, in the immediate postpartum period are the most dramatic hormonal changes that the normal woman undergoes in her entire life. It has long been known that about one in 1000 women who give birth experiences a serious psychiatric illness known as postpartum psychosis. Menzies, as long ago as 1893, made the following observations in his analysis of 140 cases of "puerperal insanity": "The prodromal disturbance may be all there is of the illness. Delirious excitement may follow, however, and if it lasts more than one week, it may develop into melancholia or mania. Stupor may precede or follow delirium or melancholia. Dementia is rare but may arise out of prolonged stupor. Mania may develop into a fixed delusional state" (11). It is of interest to note that the onset of postpartum psychosis usually coincides with a time period in which the large amounts of progesterone of placental origin have been significantly metabolized, i.e., removed from the blood stream. In one study, it was noted that 229 out of 231 cases showed no symptoms of psychosis until the third day postpartum (12). A number of studies have reported positive results in the treatment of postpartum psychosis with supplemental progesterone (13, 14, 15).

Mild transient depressions occurring postpartum are much more common than postpartum psychosis and have been a subject of casual clinical observations for many years. In 1875, Savage used the term "milk fever" to refer to the mild dysphoria that appeared to coincide with the onset of lactation (16). More recently, we have done studies of the incidence and symptomatology of this disorder in normal women who gave birth on a university obstetrics service. The incidence and degree of postpartum symptomatology were studied utilizing structured interviews, behavioral observations, and psychological tests (17). Comparative data for the same group of women were drawn from observations made during the ninth month of pregnancy and eight months after delivery. A summary of the findings from the structured prenatal interview is given in Table 2. Note that 73 percent of our multiparous subjects had experienced postpartum depression with at least one previous childbirth, although none of the women had had psychiatric treatment for these reactions.

Each of the women was studied intensively for the first ten days postpartum. They were interviewed at regular intervals and rated by the interviewers on a number of variables related to mood,

	Absent, %	Mild, %	Moderate, %	Severe %
Nausea	48.7	38.5	12.8	–
Fatigue	35.0	37.5	20.0	7.5
Overall discomfort	40.5	43.2	13.5	2.7
Fear of labor	43.2	37.8	13.5	5.4
Previous postpartum depression	26.7	30.0	20.0	23.3
Dysmenorrhea	62.9	34.3	–	2.8
Premenstrual tension	54.1	10.8	24.3	10.8
Menstrual irregularity	71.4	8.6	8.6	11.4
Rejection of pregnancy	26.3	29.0	21.1	23.7

Previous Mental Health	
1. Good adjustment	15.4%
2. Mild maladjustment	56.4%
3. Moderate maladjustment	15.4%
4. Moderate emotional disturbance	12.8%
5. Severe emotional disturbance	0

TABLE 2
Summary of Prenatal Interviews

including depression, anxiety, irritability, and distractibility. The subjects rated themselves on these same variables and also completed the Nowlis Mood Adjective Check List daily. All episodes of crying were noted and described. The duration and frequency of these crying episodes are shown in Table 3. The distribution of the crying episodes over a ten-day postpartum period of observation is shown in Table 4. Note that two thirds of the women had episodes of crying which lasted five minutes or more. The distribution of crying spells was fairly even over the ten days but with a slight tendency toward greater severity in the fifth through tenth days.

By intercorrelating the observed ratings, self ratings, Nowlis MACL scores, and the daily crying scores, a principal-component factor analysis could be performed yielding a daily depression score for each woman. The mean depression scores for this group

	Over 2 Hr	1 to 2 Hr	Few Min to 1 Hr	Zero to Few Min
No. women having at least 1 episode	5	6	15	13

TABLE 3
Crying Episodes—Duration and Frequency

	Days									
	1	2	3	4	5	6	7	8	9	10
Over 2 hr	1	0	0	1	0	1	2	1	1	1
1 to 2 hr	0	0	2	1	0	1	0	1	2	1
Few min to 1 hr	3	6	4	4	3	6	4	4	0	0

TABLE 4
Time Distribution of Crying Episodes (N = 48 Total Episodes)

Days	
1	187.25
2	235.58
3	100.05
4 in hospital	115.00
4 out of hospital	148.44
5	121.90
6	103.40
7	176.89
8	165.53
9	202.43
10	161.85

TABLE 5
Mean Depression Scores

of women are shown in Table 5. The data indicate that the terms "third day blues" or "milk blues" sometimes used to describe these mild postpartum depressions are somewhat inaccurate. Many of the women were most depressed prior to the third day postpartum and prior to the onset of lactation. It should also be noted that crying was not necessarily synonymous with depression. Many women cried because of an affect other than sadness. For instance, in some women, crying was associated with low scores on sadness but high irritability scores. Furthermore, several women cried briefly with no associated unpleasant affect. On the other hand, some women were feeling quite depressed but did not cry at all. The increased irritability may well be associated with the low progesterone levels and indeed it may well be that the relative state of calmness associated with pregnancy is due to an inhibiting effect of progesterone on the central nervous system. In this regard, it is noteworthy that women with epilepsy who are prone to seizures in the premenstrual period have been treated successfully with progesterone supplementation.

At the time of the eight-month follow-up, we learned that, with one exception, none of the women in our study had required psychiatric treatment, and that the "postpartum blues" was apparently self limited. With the return of regular menstruation, however, a number of subjects reported a recurrence of premenstrual tension.

Menopause

Menstruation most commonly ceases between the ages of 46 and 50. The ovaries at menopause become unresponsive to the pituitary gonadotropins, with the result that ovulation ceases and sex hormone production diminishes drastically. It is interesting to note that this cessation of fertility relatively early in the life cycle appears to be unique to humans, as are a number of the phenomena associated with sex hormones. Although the incidence and phenomenology of symptoms occuring during menopause have not been studied as systematically as one would like, it is known that about 10 percent of women are incapacitated to some extent by the occurrence of such symptoms as hot flashes, headaches, dizziness, heart palpitations, and pains in the joints. These symptoms are sometimes relieved by treatment with estrogens. Psychiatrists have been most interested in the form of depression known as involutional melancholia, which may occur at this time in women with no previous history of mental illness. While it is tempting to attribute these various disturbances to the state of hormonal imbalance or "deficiency" of female sex hormones which exists at menopause, there are not sufficient data at this time on which to base such conclusions. Obviously, many other factors are involved, including the woman's realization that she has lost her reproductive capacity and the fact that her children are leaving home. Because so many women are routinely treated with supplemental sex hormones nowadays, it would be of interest to compare the incidence of alterations of mood such as depression in two large samples of women who do and do not take sex hormones during and after menopause. To my knowledge, such a study has not been done to date.

MALE SEX HORMONES

The primary male sex hormone in humans is testosterone, which is secreted by the testes. The term "androgen" is a generic term for a group of chemically and physiologically related hormones including testoterone and other "male" sex hormones of testicular and adrenal origin. In females, some androgens are produced by the adrenal glands.

Developmental Influences of Androgens

Since Professor Money will be dealing with this subject in great detail elsewhere in this conference, I will only briefly mention some of the most striking effects of androgens on brain and behavior during early development. During fetal or neonatal life, the sex hormones act in an inductive way on the undifferentiated brain much as they do on the undifferentiated genital tract to organize certain circuits in male or female patterns. It is important to note that in the absence of any sex hormones, the brain as well as the genitalia tend to develop along female lines. Some ten years ago it was noted that male rats who were castrated during the first 24 hours of life retained the basic female hypothalamic mechanism for the secretion of gonadotropic hormones in later life, that is, a cyclic secretion of follicle stimulating hormone and luteinizing hormone (18). By the third day of life, however, all male rats have developed a male-type hypothalamic mechanism.

It has also been demonstrated that administration of a single dose of androgen to a newborn female rat results in a permanent alteration of the sexual behavior of the animal. Female rats exposed to androgen early in development may show acyclic sexual receptivity as adults, as well as various forms of aberrant sexual behavior when mature (19). Goy, Phoenix, and others at the Oregon Regional Primate Research Center have done related studies on rhesus monkeys that involved exposing the pregnant females to daily injections of testosterone during the presumed period of sexual differentiation in utero. The pseudohermaphroditic female offspring which have resulted from these pregnancies have been studied closely over a period of years through various stages of development. Sexual behavior has been found to be masculinized in those females whose mothers were exposed to androgen. There is an increase in mounting behavior, which among these monkeys is normally typical of the male rather than the female. On the other hand, hormonal puberty is female in these animals and they have estrus cycles. In addition to the effects on sexual behavior, several social behavior patterns which are known to be sexually dimorphic and irrelevant to mating behavior are also influenced in the masculine direction by prenatal administration of androgen. For instance, these females exhibit masculinized aggressive behavior which involves initiating play, threats, rough and tumble play, and chasing, which is much more typical of the young male rhesus. Furthermore, these masculinized females also withdraw less often from the initiations, threats, and approaches of other monkeys as compared with controls (20, 21).

The possibility that early exposure to androgens might have far-reaching effects in human females is an intriguing one and there is a certain amount of data largely gathered by Money, Ehrhardt, and others at Johns Hopkins which, as has been noted, will be presented later.

Effects on Adult Sexual Behavior

It now seems quite clear that androgens enhance sexuality in both male and female humans. The evidence for this conclusion comes from many sources. It has been known for many centuries that castration, particularly if performed early in life, greatly diminishes the sex drive in human males. More recently, "hormonal castration" has been performed by a number of investigators who have been treating hypersexual and sexually deviant men and women with antiandrogen compounds such as cyproterone acetate (22, 23). These drugs diminish sex drive and sexual activity by chemically blocking the effect of testicular and adrenal androgens. The effects are reversible with cessation of treatment. Androgen administration to hypogonadal men leads to increased sex drive and sexual activity, which appears to be hormone dependent since there is a notable decline in libido when treatment is stopped (24).

The effects of androgen on libido in women can be quite striking and are perhaps more surprising. When adrenal androgens are blocked by administration of an antiandrogen compound or when adrenal androgens are eliminated as a result of adrenalectomy, there is a rather consistent decrease in desire for sexual experience and actual sexual activity. On the other hand, when androgens are administered, for instance as part of a therapeutic regimen for carcinoma of the breast, one often sees a striking increase in sexual desire and activity even in seriously ill and debilitated women (25, 26).

The site of action of androgen in this respect is probably multiple. It appears to have an effect on the central nervous system such that the individual has a lower threshold of arousal for sexual stimuli. There also appears to be a local effect on the genitalia which involves increased sensitivity to tactile stimulation. Finally, there seems to be an effect of enhancing the intensity of orgasm.

While it seems fairly clear that androgens play a role in determining the general level of sex drive and sexual arousal, it is

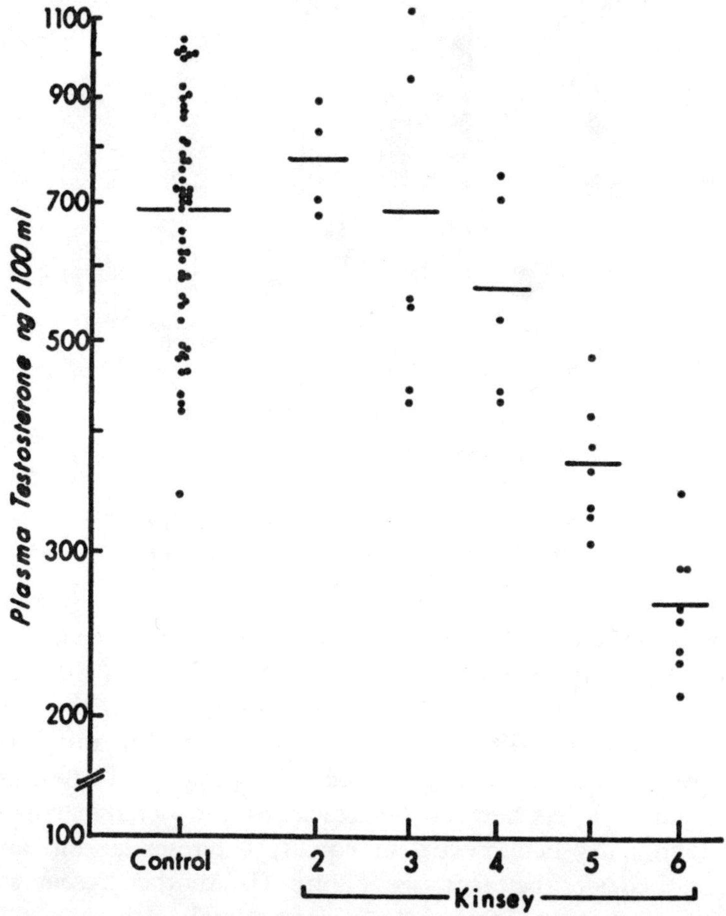

FIGURE 7
Plasma Testosterone Levels in Heterosexual and Homosexual Men (the horizontal bars denote group means)

not clear as yet what role, if any, sex hormones play in the choice of sexual object. Nevertheless, there have been recent reports to the effect that abnormal levels of sex hormones had been found among homosexuals. In one recent study, the plasma testosterone levels of 30 young male homosexuals were compared to those of

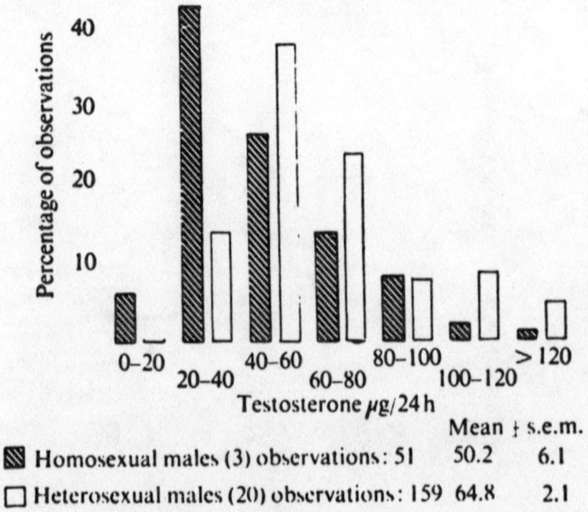

FIGURE 8

Distribution of Urinary Testosterone Values in Normal Heterosexual and Homosexual Males

a control group of 50 heterosexual males of the same age and were found to be significantly lower (27). The differences were noted only in those homosexuals who rated five or six on the Kinsey scale of homosexuality, that is, they were predominantly or exclusively homosexual. There were no significant differences in testosterone levels between heterosexuals and homosexuals with predominantly heterosexual or equally heterosexual and homosexual behavior patterns (see Figure 7). Another recent study of three male and four female homosexuals also showed low testosterone levels in the male homosexuals (Figure 8). Furthermore, abnormally high testosterone levels and relatively low estrogen levels were found in the female homosexuals as compared to heterosexual controls (28).

It is not known whether these hormonal abnormalities observed in male and female homosexuals are a secondary or primary factor in homosexuality. It could be, for instance, that different patterns of sexual activity and accompanying psychological states exert an influence on the hypothalamus, which in turn alters the secretion of gonadotropins by the pituitary. On the other hand, it is possible that a hormonal imbalance, if present during critical periods of development, may in some way influence the direction of future sexual behavior. Whereas the latter hypothesis has some support from the results of animal studies, it is too early to say whether or not this is the case in humans. If hormonal factors do play a role in human homosexuality, my own opinion is that hormonal factors are probably of importance only for a certain small subgroup of homosexuals. Furthermore, homosexual behavior, like other forms of sexual behavior, is influenced by a multiplicity of factors which may be psychological, social, biological, economic, and so forth. Obvious factors such as availability only of sexual partners of the same sex play a role in the increased incidence of homosexual behavior that is seen in prisons, for instance. Furthermore, apparent homosexual behavior is not always sexual in nature. Among various animal species including primates, it may be a means of expressing dominance over other members of the social group. The same may apply to some of the homosexual behavior that is seen in a prison population.

Influences on Aggressive Behavior

There is a long-standing theory that aggressive behavior is in some way associated with a chemical substance in the blood. Hippocrates suggested that an excess of yellow bile was responsible for the aggressiveness and irritability of the choleric individual. I have already noted that castration has long been practiced as a means of pacifying various aggressive male animals. Less successful results have been obtained by castrating humans, particularly sex offenders, but the laws of many states still provide for castration of rapists and other sex offenders as a means of "rehabilitation."

Aggressive behavior, particularly in humans, is not easily defined. Although behavioral observers generally mean intraspecies fighting or attack behavior when they speak of aggression, it is quite obvious that this definition cannot be easily applied. If a person swings his arms behind him intending to stretch and relax and inadvertently strikes another person standing behind him, he has not committed an aggressive act. Yet, to a behavioral rater unaware of the individual's intentions, such an act might be rated as an attack. On the other hand, if a person heaps verbal abuse on another individual in an aggressive fashion or destroys the property of another person perhaps as a substitute for a direct attack, one might define such behavior as aggressive even though no fighting behavior per se has taken place. What is obvious is that the intent of the individual is crucial in defining aggressive behavior. If one also includes displaced aggression, the definition becomes even more complicated. Finally, predation or interspecies fighting and killing has been considered exempt as a form of aggressive behavior by some ethologists. Their reasoning is that for a carnivore, predatory behavior is simply food-gathering activity, but if one looks at the predatory activity of humans such as big game hunting, or other interspecies forms of fighting like bull fights, it is clear that there is much more involved than the food-gathering needs of the persons participating in or viewing these activities. The most horrendous form of human aggressive behavior, namely modern warfare, is most difficult to analyze because of the various political and technological factors involved. Who is more aggressive, the prizefighter who knocks out his opponent in hand to hand combat as a means of making a living, or the B-52 pilot who flicks a switch and drops tons of bombs on unseen targets 30,000 feet beneath him?

If, indeed, androgens are one of the variables involved in human aggressive behavior, this influence is probably exerted on the central nervous system and on other organ systems in such a way as to provide or facilitate the capacity and the impulse to react in certain ways given certain stimuli. In subhuman primates, androgens have been noted to influence dominance, rank, and aggressive behavior (29). Rose and his colleagues (30, 31) have also demonstrated that testosterone levels in subhuman primates as well as in humans may be altered as a secondary effect of various environmental and intrapsychic factors. For instance, male rhesus monkeys who were provided access to receptive females showed dominant behavior and increased sexual behavior which was accompanied by a two- to three-fold increase in plasma testosterone. However, when each male monkey was subjected to aggressive attack by placing him with a well-established group of 30 adult males, plasma testosterone levels dropped. Similar results were noted in a study of American soldiers in Vietnam under conditions of combat stress. The point here is that although there are well-documented correlations between variations in androgen levels and various behavior patterns, these fluctuations in at least some situations are an effect rather than a cause of the behavior.

In addition to the cause versus effect phenomenon, there is of course also the nature versus nurture aspect to be considered in this discussion. Clearly, at all ages human males are more aggressive, at least in terms of overt fighting and assaultive behavior, than are human females. It also seems obvious that a good deal of this sex difference can be accounted for by differential child rearing practices in our society which reward aggressiveness in the growing boy but tend to punish its overt expression in girls. However, on the hereditary side of this discussion, there has been considerable interest in recent years in the possible association of aggressive behavior and the XYY genotype. A number of studies have shown that there is a greater incidence of XYY individuals in mental-penal institutions (sometimes called "hospitals for the criminally insane") than in the population at large or in other kinds of institutions (32). Certain physical characteristics are associated with the XYY syndrome, such as tallness (usually over six feet) and severe acne. Neurological studies of these individuals have been inconclusive to date. Some investigators report an increased incidence of "soft" signs such as intention tremors or uncoordination and occasional EEG abnormalities, usually nonspecific. Hormonal studies have shown elevated plasma or urinary testosterone levels in some XYY individuals, but again these findings are inconclusive. One of the reasons for this may be the fact that some of the XYY males are hypogonadal and have undescended inactive testes so that mean values for a group of XYY individuals are difficult to interpret. In any event, the finding of a higher percentage of XYY individuals in prisons and maximum security hospitals has led some courts, notably in France and Australia, to allow the finding of an XYY karotype to be admitted as evidence for mitigation in criminal trials. Although such a step does not seem justified by the state of our present knowledge, further investigation of this genetic defect might yield some important knowledge about the effects of androgens on aggressive behavior. One can postulate that the extra Y chromosome may cause excessive production of androgens by fetal and neonatal testes in such a way as to alter the early differentiation of the central nervous system. Thus, the CNS might become sensitized to certain types of stimuli that might not otherwise provoke aggressive behavior. Depending on the individual's life experiences, along with a greater endowment in terms of size and physical strength (also mediated by androgens), this genetic defect might predispose a person toward violent assaults or other behaviors otherwise not readily explained.

CONCLUSION

I have reviewed here several lines of recent inquiry into the effects of sex hormones on mood and behavior. In general, the fluctuations of female sex hormones during the menstrual cycle, in the postpartum period, and during menopause seem to correlate with alterations of mood, particularly in the depressive sphere. There is increasing evidence to suggest that the male sex hormones exert some influence on human sexual and aggressive behavior. Freud, of course, was well aware of the common psychological substrate for sex and aggression. There is now reason to believe that there may also be a common biological, that is hormonal, substrate as well. For this reason, manipulation of the sex hormones by administering additional hormones, treating a patient with drugs which block the effects of sex hormones, or surgically removing the sources of the sex hormones, is fraught with far-reaching ramifications. Exposure of the developing fetus to sex hormones via the pregnant woman, which has already occurred on a fairly wide scale in this country, may lead to alterations in the psychosexual development of the offspring which are not readily reversible.

In conclusion, one can see that the complex interactions between genetic, hormonal, and environmental variables are a fertile area for further research which must of necessity involve the integration of concepts and techniques from both the biological and behavioral sciences.

References

1. Lawick-Goodall, J. van. *In the Shadow of Man.* Boston: Houghton Mifflin, 1971.
2. Miller, S., and Mason, H. L. The excretion of 17-ketosteroids by diabetics. *J. Clin. Endocrin., 5,* 220, 1945.
3. Talbot, N., et al. *Amer. J. Dis. Child, 65,* 364, 1943.
4. Hamburg, D. A. Effects of progesterone on behavior. Association for Research in Nervous and Mental Diseases, *Endocrines and the Central Nervous System* (its research publication), *43,* 251, 1966.
5. Lunde, D. T., and Hamburg, D. A. Techniques for assessing the effects of sex hormones on affect, arousal, and aggression in humans. *Recent Progress in Hormone Research, 28,* 627, 1972.
6. Moos, R., et al. Fluctuations in symptoms and moods during the menstrual cycle. *J. Psychosom. Res., 13,* 37, 1969.
7. Udry, J. R., and Morris, N. M. Distribution of coitus in the menstrual cycle. *Nature, 220,* 593, 1968.
8. Moos, R. Psychological aspects of oral contraceptives. *Arch. Gen. Psychiat., 19,* 87, 1968.
9. Benedek, T. In F. Alexander (Ed.), *Psychosomatic Medicine.* New York: W. W. Norton, 1950. Pp. 216-262.
10. Zander, J. In A. C. Barnes (Ed.), *Progesterone.* Augusta, Mich.: Brook Lodge Press, 1961. Pp. 77-90.
11. Hamilton, J. A. *Postpartum Psychiatric Problems.* St. Louis: Mosby, 1962.
12. Karnosh, L. J., and Hope, J. M. *Arch. Gen. Psychiat., 94,* 537, 1937.
13. Bomer, W. H., and Altschule, M. D. Use of progesterone in the treatment of post-partum psychosis. *N. Eng. J. Med., 254,* 157, 1950.
14. Blumberg, A., and Billig, O. Hormonal influence upon puerperal psychosis and neurotic condition. *Psychiat. Quart., 16,* 454, 1942.
15. Schmidt, H. J. The use of progesterone in the treatment of postpartum psychosis. *JAMA, 121,* 190, 1943.
16. Savage, G. Insanity of pregnancy and childbirth. *Guy's Hospital Report, 20,* 83, 1875.
17. Yalom, I. D., Lunde, D. T., et al. Postpartum blues syndrome. *Arch. Gen. Psychiat., 18,* 16, 1968.

18. HARRIS, G., and LEVINE, S. Sexual differentiation of the brain and its experimental control. *J. Physiol., 163,* 42, 1962.
19. LEVINE, S., and MULLINS, R. Hormonal influences on brain organization in infant rats. *Science, 152,* 1585, 1966.
20. GOY, R., BRIDSON, W., and YOUNG, W. Period of maximal susceptibility of the prenatal female guinea pig to masculinizing actions of testosterone propionate. *J. Comp. and Physiol. Psych., 57,* 166, 1964.
21. GOY, R. In R. P. Michael (Ed.), *Endocrinology and Human Behavior.* London: Oxford Univ. Press, 1968. P. 12.
22. LASCHET, U., et al. Results in the treatment of hyper- or abnormal sexuality of men without antiandrogens. *Acta Endocrin.* (Copenhagen), Supplementum 119, *56,* 54, 1967.
23. SERVAIS, J., and HUBIN, P. Synthese des connaissances actuelles concernant en inhibiteaur de la libido chez le male, la methyloestrenolone. *Encephale, 57,* 333, 1968.
24. MONEY, J. In W. C. Young (Ed.), *Sex and Internal Secretions,* Vol. 11. Baltimore: Williams and Wilkins, 1961.
25. FOSS, G. L. The influence of androgens on sexuality in women. *Lancet, 1,* 667, 1951.
26. WAXENBERG, S. E., et al. *J. Clin. Endocrin., 19,* 193, 1959.
27. KOLODNY, R. C., MASTERS, W. H., HENDRYZ, J., and TORO, G. Plasma testosterone and semen analysis in male homosexuals. *N. Eng. J. Med., 21,* 1170, 1971.
28. LORAINE, J. A., et al. Patterns of hormone excretion in male and female homosexuals. *Nature, 234,* 552, 1971.
29. ROSE, R., HOLADAY, J., and BERNSTEIN, J. Plasma testosterone, dominance rank and aggressive behavior in male rhesus monkeys. *Nature, 231,* 366, 1971.
30. ROSE, R., et al. Plasma testosterone levels in the male rhesus: Influences of sexual and social stimuli. *Science, 178,* 643, 1972.
31. ROSE, R. In P. Bourne (Ed.), *The Psychology and Physiology of Stress.* New York: Academic Press, 1969. Pp. 117-148.
32. HOOK, E. B. Behavioral implications of the human XYY genotype. *Science, 179,* 139, 1973.

Discussion

ALFRED H. RIFKIN, M.D.

Unless one conceives of a non-material mind, it seems plausible to suppose that the operations of the body are in some way related to the operations of the mind. This age-old problem has roots in philosophy, theology, and mythology, but is a subject for scientific investigation in the modern era. Mind as an abstraction has been replaced by psychological functions or states, the body is studied in terms of its organs or systems, and the relationship is usually formulated in an interactional framework. As Dr. Lunde points out in connection with sex differences, there have been major shifts of opinion. A little less than a century ago, no doubt because of the then recent discovery of localization of cerebral function and progress in identifying tracts and nuclei, the theory of "centers" engaged much attention. Degeneration and weakness of specific centers were widely accepted concepts. Krafft-Ebing, for example, held that there were specific centers for masculinity and femininity and that homosexuality and the so-called perversions resulted from degenerations or imbalances in these centers. Freud, after a careful study of the then current views on aphasia, concluded that speech was too complex a function to be attributed to a particular location as a "center". Later, in abandoning the *Project for a Scientific Psychology,* he also gave up the concept of specific neurological localization for any of the psychological processes with which he was concerned. In the "Three Essays on the Theory of Sexuality" he discarded all notions of center weakness or degeneracy, but retained the expectation that a "sexual chemism" would one day be discovered. About masculinity and femininity he concluded that only activity and passivity could be considered characteristic of the male and female respectively.

In one of the cyclic movements of scientific progress, we seem now to be returning to many of the older ideas, hopefully on a higher dialectical level. The chemistry of the "sexual substances" is well advanced, and we now hear of "pathways and structures that mediate masculine or feminine behavior" and the "organizing functions of the steroid hormones on the brain" and "male brain" or "female brain." These ideas derive from new investigations made possible by the new techniques mentioned by Dr. Lunde, and represent important extensions of previous views.

These technical advances exemplify another significant aspect of scientific progress. Much has been written about the resistance to new ideas in the sciences. Established views and ways of thinking tend to persist until incompatible evidence becomes overwhelming. A scientific "revolution" ensues and a new paradigm is established. This persists until it in turn is replaced in a subsequent revolution. While these formulations are quite persuasive, they overlook the role of technical advances. Many problems have remained unexplored and valuable ideas have lain fallow not so much because of resistance but because there were no suitable methods by which they could be approached. Major new techniques often trigger a burst of new investigations and produce new ideas. Later it may come to light that the same ideas were advanced previously but they remained only speculations for want of any way to confirm or deny them.

Still another aspect of this matter deserves attention. Although the resistance to some new ideas is well documented, there is also an opposite phenomenon that might be called the bandwagon effect. Some new ideas are accepted with enthusiasm because they seem to clarify hitherto unresolved problems.* Sometimes the new ideas are carried over into fields where they are inappropriate. A familiar example is Herbert Spencer's adaptation of Darwin's evolutionary theory and the "survival of the fittest" doctrine to social theory and laissez faire economics. Psychoanalysis went through a similar phase. Though opposed by many, psychoanalysis was also uncritically accepted by some and applied without due caution, so that Freud felt impelled to write a paper on the dangers of "wild Psychoanalysis."

The lines of investigation described by Dr. Lunde offer great promise. At the same time, he has been properly cautious in

---

* Though published after this discussion was written, the following editorial in *Nature* is worthy of quotation: "An unseemly phenomenon familiar to all scientists is the rolling bandwagon, on which our logical fallacy frequently rides. A first-rate new idea is introduced into a subject. It is instantly attractive since it explains a variety of previously mystifying observations. Whole laboratories swing into action and, within months, papers are emerging which run thus—the new ideas imply the following predictable observations; we have made these observations and therefore we have helped verify the idea. A frequent phrase is 'we consider that our observations strongly support the notion that. . . .'" What to Say About Scientific Evidence. *Nature, 245,* 227, October 5, 1973.

warning against hasty conclusions and too facile transposition from animals to humans. The relevance of animal findings for human behavior is always a difficult question. The broad principle of evolutionary continuity of behavior, analagous to the evolutionary continuity of structure, is well established. On the other hand, it is also well established that there is progressive encephalization of function in the evolutionary ladder. Actions and responses are found to be less automatic and more readily adapted to situations. Transposition to humans appears uncertain in many situations. There appears to be no simple, general rule governing the issue; each case must be evaluated on its own terms and merits. Animal experiments have mainly heuristic value, making some findings more plausible, others less so. Plausibility is too subjective, and too time- and culture-bound.

With Dr. Lunde's cautions in mind, and with the additional strictures just mentioned, I return to the lines of inquiry he summarized so concisely. Because the issues raised are of major importance they deserve careful critical scrutiny.

Variations in mood during the menstrual cycle in the human female are so much a matter of ordinary observation as to hardly require further documentation. The studies cited by Dr. Lunde provide details as to the nature and content of the variations. Research here requires precise specification of the relationship between hormonal and mood changes. Benedek's classical investigations were based on very rough measures of hormonal levels. These studies should now be repeated, taking advantage of the new technology. Psychoanalysts would be interested in more detailed reporting of mood, and would want to know about the more subtle expressions of changes, including dreams, fantasies, and sexual preferences.

This is perhaps the appropriate place to point out that although current methods for determining levels of circulating hormones are great steps forward, they are still cumbersome, slow, and expensive. The drawing of blood samples daily or several times a day is an obvious handicap in conducting the kinds of long-term studies that would be most likely to yield significant results. Non-invasive methods are needed, but to develop such methods would require major investments of time, money, and scientific man- and brain-power. Perhaps hormones could be measured by some spectrophotometric device analogous to the earlobe oximeters now used routinely in space experiments.

It is disappointing that the therapeutic yield from the vast number of hormonal and other studies of menstrual tension has been so meager. Postpartum dysphoria and the menopausal syndrome remain major clinical problems. It may turn out that the sexual steroids are but a small part of the complex systems involved in the menstrual cycle. Water and salt balance have long been recognized as part of the problem. Recent reports indicate that renin, angiotensin, and aldosterone may be implicated through their effects on potassium/sodium ratios, which in turn may affect central neurotransmitters (1). The relation of these substances to the sexual steroids will require much further study.

The investigations of the effects of intrauterine and neonatal androgens are of surpassing interest. Here the cautions expressed by Dr. Lunde take on added weight. It would be very comforting to believe that we are on the verge of demonstrating that levels of testosterone determine not only sexual drive but aggression in general, homosexuality, and the so-called perversions. Management of these "undesirable" human behaviors would be much simpler, and we could be confident that the chemists would soon create substances that would raise, lower, or replace undesirable hormones as needed. The concept of sexual centers, expressed now as the "structures that mediate sexual behavior," has even more far-reaching implications. The most revolutionary suggestion is that not only are the central brain structures controlling hormonal secretion masculinized, but adult behavior is permanently altered by fetal exposure. Dr. Lunde mentioned only some highlights of these investigations. I will confine my discussion to some general issues and take up only a few items in any detail.

Dr. Lunde has already pointed to the difficulties in defining aggression in humans and in measuring whatever is defined. One of the most important sources of difficulty is the necessity to distinguish between aggression and dominance. In rats, hamsters, rabbits, and similar animals, aggression consists of direct attack, and dominance in cage situations directly reflects aggression. In monkeys the situation is less clear. In the cited studies by Rose (2) there was an overall correlation among plasma testosterone, dominance rank, and aggression. However, the most aggressive monkeys were not always the most dominant, and the least aggressive was not the lowest in the dominance hierarchy. In fact, the alpha male was 12th in order of frequency of aggression while the monkey showing the highest frequency was tenth in rank. Rose's paper gives no indication of what other factors may have influenced the dominance ranking. In bands of free-ranging macaque monkeys, adolescent sons of high ranking females rise to high rank in circumstances where one would expect age, size, and aggression to be most influential (3). Goodall (4) reports that the dominant chimpanzee during one period of her study was not the most aggressive, but rather the one who learned to make a great deal of noise hitting and kicking empty kerosene cans. Goodall comments, "Mike rose to be the alpha male of his community in about four months without engaging in any actual attacks on other males." Mike displaced a powerful and aggressive male "apparently . . . by means of bluff and, without doubt, superior intelligence." Schaller (5) found that among gorillas the dominant rank is held by a "silverback male," a mature, vigorous animal. The source of his authority is not clear from the descriptions. Schaller observed very little direct aggression in these supposedly ferocious creatures and found them generally very peaceful. Money comments that direct aggression is probably not the appropriate measure of androgenic influence in humans and proposes dominance assertion instead (6). This criterion would appear to be most applicable in Western competetive societies, and dominance assertion does not seem to be an exclusively male trait even in these societies.

The XYY syndrome further illustrates the complexity of the issues in relating agression and testosterone. The implicit expectation appears to be that the extra Y-chromosome produces a "supermale." The actual findings to date seem limited to only a few specific items. XYY males are likely to be taller than average, are more likely to have severe acne, and are found more often (in proportion) in mental-penal institutions than outside. Extensive surveys of the general population have not yet been done. However, there have been surveys of newborns, and in at least one study it was found that in penal institutions the incidence of XYY men was not greater than would be expected from the newborn surveys. "The increased risk of criminal behavior . . . is confined to those that are mentally disordered and liable to be admitted as patient offenders" (7). "But in those mental-penal settings where XYY's have been found, they do not appear to be concentrated among the most dangerous, violent, and physically aggressive inmates. And, in general, their offenses are similar to or less serious than those of XY's there" (8). Elevated plasma testosterone levels have not been demonstrated (9). There have been relatively few studies of XYY's outside of institutions, but some apparently normal XYY's have been reported. A few are described as "notably mild mannered" (10). On the other hand, low intelligence, impulsiveness, and poor tolerance for frustration are frequently mentioned. It is possible that the higher risk for institutionalization reflects the XYY's social ineptitude more than any aggressive tendencies. It is of some interest that aggression and violence have also been associated with 47 XXY males (Klinefelter's syndrome) (11). In one of the few prospective studies of XYY boys, three were "found to be functioning and developing normally but the fourth child was described as hard to manage, hostile . . . He was the one child of the four who had been placed in a foster home, and by the time he was four years old, had already been in multiple foster homes" (12).

Similar difficulties are to be found in studies of hormone levels among homosexuals. The correlation between testosterone levels and degree of homosexuality as measured by the Kinsey scale raises many questions. The implicit assumption appears to be that predominantly or exclusively homosexual males are less "masculine" or more "feminine." There are, however, many exclusively homosexual males who are extremely "masculine" in appearance and manner. Some of these are "passive," or "receptors" insofar as their sexual practices are concerned. Hostility is not confined to nor greater among the more masculine ones, and many overtly effeminate male homosexuals are extremely hostile. Clinical experience with Lesbians appears to be similar, mutatis mutandis. It is therefore difficult to know what weight to give to the studies by Kolodny and Loraine cited by Dr. Lunde. Psychoanalysts would want to know more about the appearance and sexual practices of the homosexuals studied, not merely their Kinsey rating. They would also want information about dreams and fantasies, and about manifestations of hostility in daily life of these individuals. Only then would it be possible to evaluate the correlations found. In any event, a much larger sample would be required.

The problem of distinctively masculine or feminine traits or behavior arises also in connection with the newly popular concepts of male and female brain. As Dr. Lunde points out, the recent experiments suggest that "the sex hormones act in an inductive way on the undifferentiated brain much as they do on the undifferentiated genital tract to organize certain circuits in male or female patterns." Similar statements are made by many authors and investigators. The analogy between anatomical and behavioral differentiation is an example of the kind of "first rate idea" that has stimulated a great burst of research and theorizing. Its importance can be seen in such conclusions as those drawn by Money and Ehrhardt, that fetal exposure to androgens will alter a girl's later interest in doll play, predispose her to be a tomboy, and alter her outlook toward many aspects of her "feminine" role in adult life. I will not attempt to comment on the very extensive and rapidly growing literature. Money has presented summaries of his views in numerous papers and his recent book (6). Dr. Lunde's earlier paper provides a comprehensive review. A detailed compilation of experimental work is given by Davidson and Levine (13). Mindful of the bandwagon effect, I will attempt only to raise some cautionary questions.

A fundamental question has to do with the specificity of male and female behaviors and also with the specificity of the effects of androgens and estrogens in influencing the behaviors taken to be characteristic of the sexes. Much of the experimental work has been done in rodents (rats, guinea pigs, and hamsters). Beach (14), in a witty and incisive critique of the "organizer" concept, points out that the relevant behavior patterns are far from specific even in these species. The effects of hormones are likewise not as specific or characteristic as the theoretical constructs would seem to require. Beach comments on " . . . certain unwarranted generalizations about behavior which depend on highly questionable extrapolations from perfectly sound evidence relating to hypothalamic control of hypophyseal function. There seems to be no reason to question that the gonadotropic function of the pituitary is cyclic in female rats and acyclic in males . . . this sex difference is related to functional differences in the hypothalamus . . . what can be most seriously challenged is the derived assumption that during the same period of development androgen stimulates differentiation and functional organization of imaginary brain centers that eventually will control masculine mating behavior."

Davidson and Levine write: "By appropriate manipulation of experimental conditions it can be shown that heterotypical (pertaining to the opposite sex) and homotypical hormones can produce both homotypical and heterotypical behavior in males and females." Perhaps because of the bandwagon effect, heterotypical phenomena receive less attention and fewer experiments are designed to elicit them. Yet heterotypical effects are important as negative controls with respect to theories of organizers, centers, or circuits. Thus the effects of androgen on females have been most studied, while the effects of estrogen on males are less often investigated. There appears to be only one study comparing neonatal androgen and estrogen. In female mice neonatal androgen facilitates later androgen-induced aggressive behavior, but neonatal estrogen has an almost equal effect (15). Female rats manifest maternal behavior (nest building, retrieval of pups, assumption of a nursing posture) promptly upon delivery of the litter. Virgin females will manifest maternal behavior after constant exposure to pups for five or six days. Male rats will also exhibit typical maternal behavior if exposed for five or six days. If the females are ovariectomized and males castrated and exposure to pups is delayed for eight weeks, the latency time to elicit maternal responses from both female and male is sharply reduced. Injection of estrogen or androgen in female and male respectively produces a latency time of five or six days again. This experiment yields results quite contrary to expectations, for here it appears that the homotypical steroid is inhibitory rather than facilitatory (16). It is well established that neonatal androgen given to females disrupts later mating patterns while estrogen disrupts later mating patterns in males. One study investigated the effects of neonatal estrogen in females. The authors conclude: "Thus, estrogen treatment at the appropriate dose level during the neonatal period acts, as does testosterone, to reduce the sexual responsiveness in females which is normally induced by estrogen and progesterone" (17).

For the obvious reasons of convenience and expense, studies of rodents are the most numerous. The repertory of behaviors is more limited, the patterns are less variable, and the effects of the experimental conditions are more easily identified. Most investigations have concentrated on behaviors directly related to the reproductive process, mainly copulatory and maternal sequences. Among primates the experimental problems are more complex. The total behavioral repertory is far wider, and there may be significant differences between laboratory and natural sequences. For the most part, among rodents, copulatory and maternal sequences appear "full-blown" under the appropriate conditions, apparently without trial and error or other learning. There is thus a reasonable basis for assuming programming within the central nervous system, perhaps in the form of predetermined circuits or centers. Learning through trial and error, play rehearsal during development, and direct observation play a significant role in primates. In addition, various antecedent conditions must be satisfied, as elucidated, for example, in Harlow's studies of isolated monkeys. Copulatory patterns are fairly characteristic and fixed for various monkeys; among the apes they are conspicuously variable. Maternal behavior varies widely among different monkey species, for example macaques as compared with lemurs. It is exceedingly difficult to identify human behaviors as characteristically male or female across cultural lines.

Money's findings in girls exposed to androgenic influence in utero deserve more extensive consideration than can be given here. The rough and tumble play of male juvenile monkeys, which seems to be sexually dimorphic, is an appealing analogue to the tomboyishness observed in these girls. On the other hand, clinical experience indicates that many factors affect tomboyishness, doll play, fantasy rehearsals, and role expectations. Psychoanalysts would want to know much more about family relationships and structure in the cases studied. Were there siblings, and what was the age and sex sequence? What were the parents like? Were there favored or unfavored children, and by which parent? What were the circumstances of life at crucial stages in development?

It is a significant loss that such data were not collected, for the experiments of nature investigated by Money cannot be repeated. I believe that psychoanalysts must share the responsibility for the loss. Psychoanalysts and other clinicians should seek out the places where such investigations are in progress and should add their experience to the plans of study. The investigators, for their part, should make it their business to seek out the clinicians, and should find ways to incorporate their viewpoints into their approach. The result can only be mutual enrichment and more thorough research.

Having pointed in this discussion mainly to the necessity for caution in interpretation and application of the new findings, I must close by emphasizing that I regard the areas of investigation reported by Dr. Lunde as of the utmost importance. These investigations should be extended and intensified. What has been achieved thus far is the result of the combined efforts of scientists from many disciplines, wisely and generously supported by private and public funds. Unhappily, at the time of this writing, this support is being withdrawn in the interest of shortsighted fiscal retrenchment. All scientists should make known their views and urge upon the appropriate officials the importance of the work and the need to continue and to broaden it.

References

1. Janowsky, D. S., Berens, S. C., and Davis, J. M. Correlations between mood, weight, and electrolytes during the menstrual cycle: A renin-angiotensin hypothesis of premenstrual tension. *Psychosom. Med., 35,* 143, 1973.
2. Rose, R. M., Holaday, J. W., and Bernstein, I. S. Plasma testosterone, dominance rank and aggressive behavior in male rhesus monkeys. *Nature, 231,* 366, 1971.
3. Koford, C. B. Rank of mothers and sons in bands of rhesus monkeys. *Science, 141,* 356, 1963.
4. Lawick-Goodall, J. van. The behavior of chimpanzees in their natural habitat. *Amer. J. Psychiat., 130,* 1, 1973.
5. Schaller, G. B. *The Mountain Gorilla.* Chicago: Univ. of Chicago Press, 1963.
6. Money, J., and Ehrhardt, A. A. *Man and Woman, Boy and Girl.* Baltimore: Johns Hopkins Univ. Press, 1972.
7. Jacobs, P. A., et al. Chromosome surveys in penal institutions and approved schools. *J. Med. Genet., 8,* 49, 1971.
8. Hook, E. B. Behavioral implications of the human XYY genotype. *Science, 179,* 139, 1973.
9. Griffiths, A. W., et al. Prisoners of XYY constitution. *Brit. J. Psychiat., 121,* 365, 1972.
10. Baughman, F. A., and Mann, J. D. Ascertainment of seven XYY males in a private neurology practice. *JAMA, 222,* 446, 1972.
11. Kerr, C. B. Cytogenetics and genetic mechanisms. In R. P. Shearman (Ed.), *Human Reproductive Biology.* Oxford: Blackwell, 1972.
12. Kessler, S., and Moos, R. H. Behavioral manifestations of chromosomal abnormalities. *Hospital Practice, 8,* 131, 1973.
13. Davidson, J. M., and Levine, S. Endocrine regulation of behavior. *Ann. Rev. Physiol., 34,* 375, 1972.
14. Beach, F. A. Hormonal factors controlling the differentiation, development, and display of copulatory behavior in the ramstergig and related species. In E. Tobach, L. R. Aronson, and E. Shaw (Eds.), *The Biopsychology of Development.* New York: Academic Press, 1971.
15. Edwards, D. A., and Herndon, J. Neonatal androgenization and estrogenization and the hormonal induction of sexual receptivity in rats. *Physiol. Behav., 5,* 115, 1970.
16. Leon, M., Numan, M., and Moltz, H. Maternal behavior in the rat: Facilitation through gonadectomy. *Science, 179,* 1018, 1973.
17. Whalen, R. E., and Nadler, R. D. Suppression of the development of female mating behavior by estrogen administered in infancy. *Science, 141,* 273, 1963.

2

Nativism versus Culturalism in Gender-Identity Differentiation

JOHN MONEY, M.D.

Introduction

From our Platonic and Biblical forebears, you and I have the heritage of dichotomizing. Dichotomies are dangerous, for they may be wrong. It is wrong to dichotomize the learned and the biological—learning is a biological function, for all acts of learning are also activities of the central nervous system.

In order not to separate learning from biology, I have set up a $2 \times 2 \times 2$ scheme (Table 1) in which nativism versus culturalism is cross classified with that which is species shared (phyletic) versus that which is individually unique (biographic), and subclassified as imperative versus optional. Imperatives, which may be decreed phyletically or may be unique to a single biography, represent inevitable sequelae or conditions that follow given prior events or conditions. Options, which also may be decreed either phyletically or individually, represent sequelae or conditions for which there is at least one degree of freedom that there may have been an alternative or substitute event or condition.

The entries in Table 1 are illustrative examples only, with no pretense at enumerative completeness.

Supported by grant USPHS HD-00325, and by funds from the Grant Foundation and the Erickson Educational Foundation.

Sequential Variables

There are imperative and optional, nativistic and cultural, and phyletic and individual components of the differentiation of sex role, variously represented in chronological sequence in Figure 1.

Instead of sex role, I prefer the term gender role. It is more comprehensive than sex role, which is too readily confounded with copulatory role. Moreover, the reciprocal of gender role is gender identity, which is one's own experience of one's gender role, which itself is the public manifestation of one's gender identity.

TABLE 1

EXAMPLES OF GENDER ROLE DETERMINANTS
CLASSIFIED ACCORDING TO A 2 × 2 × 2 SCHEME

		Nativistic	*Cultural*
Species-shared or PHYLETIC	Imperative	Menstruation, gestation, lactation (women) *vs.* impregnation (men).	Social models for identification and complementation in gender-identity differentiation.
	Optional	Population size, fertility rate and sex rates.	Population birth/death ratio. Diminishing age of puberty.
Individually unique or BIOGRAPHIC	Imperative	Chromosome anomalies, e.g., 45,XO; 47,XXY; 47,XYY. Vestigial penis. Vestigial uterus. Vaginal atresia.	Sex announcement and rearing as male, female, or ambiguous.
	Optional	Getting pregnant. Breast feeding. Anorexic amenorrhea. Castration.	Gender-divergent work. Gender-divergent cosmetics and grooming. Gender-divergent child care.

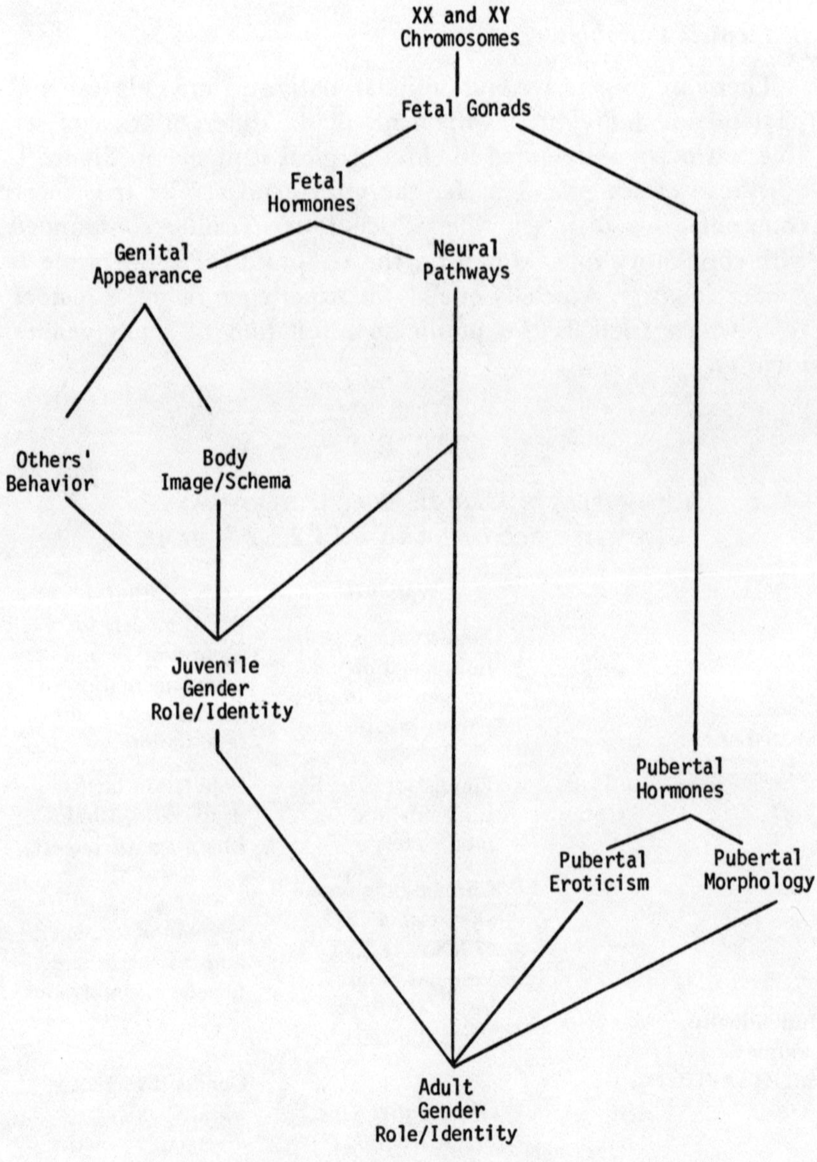

FIGURE 1
Variables in the Differentiation of Gender Role/Identity

You can see in Figure 1 that the early variables of gender-identity differentiation variously lend themselves to being identified as biological or innate. The more comprehensive term is nativistic. It encompasses everything which is native to the organism, regardless of its etiology, including those factors which will subsequently facilitate or impede postnatal learning, or selective aspects thereof.

Nativistic determinants of gender-identity differentiation may be phyletically shared by other members of the species, or they may be biographically unique to a particular individual. Likewise, though contrary to the way most people take for granted, cultural determinants, transmitted to the individual by other members of the species—or even by members of other species—also may be either phyletically shared or biographically unique. Cultural determinants are heavily weighted in favor of information and learning, though not exclusively so. Among the Aboriginal Australians of Arnhem Land, the anatomical circumcision ceremony at age nine or ten is a cultural determinant of a boy's masculine anatomy as well as of his gender-identity.

Matched Pair of Cases, Concordant for Diagnosis, Discordant for Rearing

Let me now bring Figure 1 to life by reference to the development of two children. They constitute a matched pair, concordant for diagnosis, as genetic and gonadal females with the adrenogenital syndrome of female hermaphroditism, but discordant for sex of rearing—that is, one was reared as a girl, and one as a boy. There are other similar matched pairs I have studied, though extra cases of boys by rearing are hard to find in the modern era of early, accurate diagnosis. By contrast there are many parallel cases of girls by rearing.

At the moment of conception, each possessed the pair of X chromosomes (46,XX) characteristic of the female. The genetic code of these chromosomes soon instructed the indifferent tissue that would become the sex glands to differentiate as ovaries, not testes. With no testes present, the mullerian ducts, precursors of

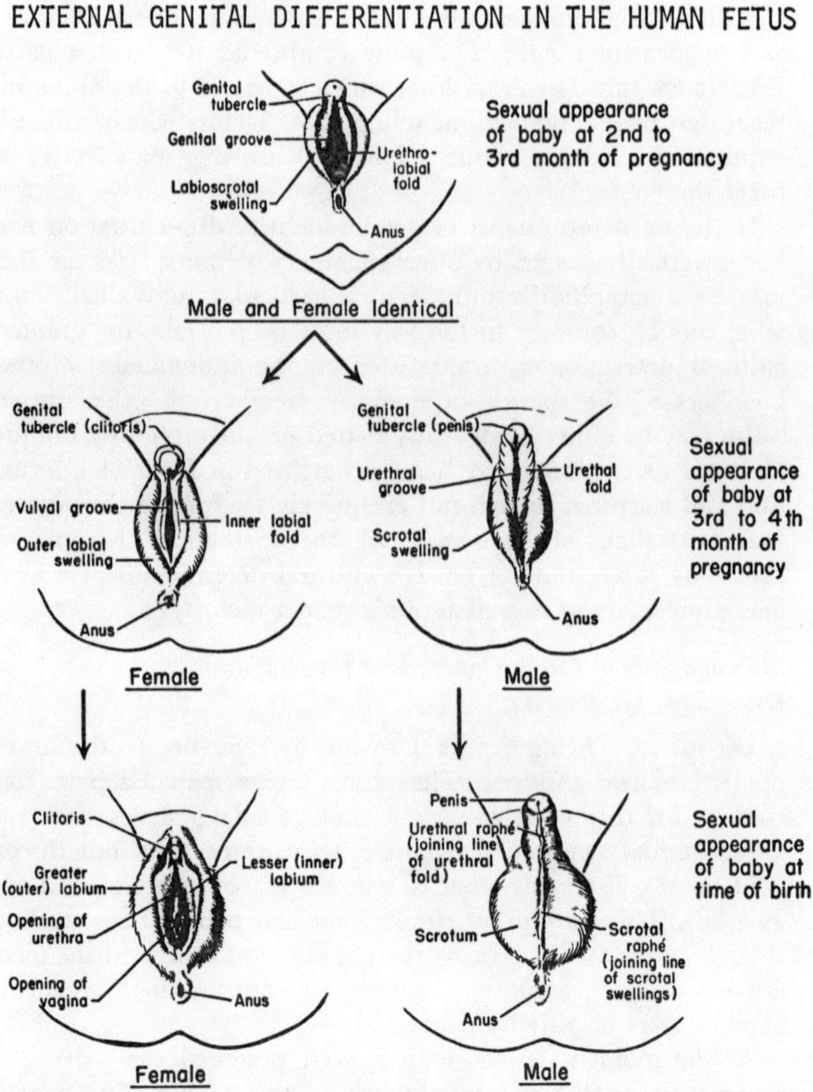

FIGURE 2
Male and Female Progression of Sex-Organ Differentiation

the internal female organs, were instructed to differentiate into a uterus and its two fallopian tubes. In the absence of androgen from testes, the undifferentiated anlagen of the external genitalia should have differentiated as female. But they did not. Instead, they were instructed by an excess of fetal androgen produced by abnormally functioning cortices of the two adrenal glands (their abnormality itself the product of a genetically dictated error) to differentiate as male. The genital tubercle (Figure 2) became a penis with a foreskin plus, on the underside, a midline fusion of skin to form the urethal tube, instead of a clitoris with a hood and two unfused labia minora. The labioscrotal swellings fused to become an empty scrotum, instead of two unfused labia majora.

At around the same time in fetal life when the external genital tissues were responding to the excess of adrenocortical androgens, certain pathways in the central nervous system of this pair of patients also were making their own response. At least one infers this to have been so on the basis of direct brain-hormone experiments in laboratory animals, and on the basis of behavioral parallels in genetic female rhesus monkeys, experimentally androgenized in utero, and in human genetic females affected by prenatal androgenization. The one word that succinctly describes the behavioral effect of this prenatal androgenization is tomboyism.

Before the central nervous system has sufficient time, developmentally, in which to instruct behavior to be tomboyish, however, the external genitalia, on the day of birth, instruct other people how to behave toward the new child, then and subsequently. In each of the pair presently under consideration, the external genitalia informed the world, "It's a boy." In one case the announcement remained unchanged, and the child was, thenceforth, reared consistently as a boy, with presumedly undescended testes. In the other case, the complicating symptoms of neonatal dehydration and salt loss led to further diagnostic workup. In consequence, the child's sex was soon reannounced as female, to agree with the genetic sex, the ovaries and the internal reproductive organs. Shortly thereafter the first stage of surgical feminization of the external organs was carried out, so that their appearance thenceforth instructed others to treat her as a girl. As her comprehension grew, the child absorbed the same instruction from her genital appearance.

Both children, as they advanced through the stage of understanding language and, in particular, the gender differences embodied in language, had antithetical experiences. These experiences signified to one that he was a boy, and to the other that she was a girl. The language of the vocal cords was paralleled by body language—the language of gesture, haircut, and clothing, assisted by toys and other artifacts. For each child, vocal language and body language both were subject to positive and negative reinforcement, that is to reward and punishment training. Day by day, this dimorphism of exogenous training and expectancy was reiterated and expanded. At the same time the endogenous or self-perceived image or schema of the body directly reinforced the exogenous or socially prescribed schema of sexual dimorphism. The morphologic, visual and haptic instructions of body image coalesced with the historical and cultural instructions of how to behave as a boy versus how to behave as a girl. Between the ages of approximately eighteen months and four years, this coalition of instructions completed its function of establishing in each individual an irrefutable conviction of gender identity—the juvenile gender identity of Figure 1.

What about the prenatal, androgenic instruction of the central nervous system to program postnatal tomboyish behavior? The effect of this instruction was, analogically speaking, to add a special tint or flavor to the differentiation of the girl's feminine gender identity, though not to defeminize it. The same addition, in the case of the boy, was perfectly compatible with the differentiation of a masculine gender identity.

The girl's tomboyism was marked especially by outdoor vigor of energy expenditure, competitiveness, and dominance assertion. She liked to join boys in their competitive group games. The boy did likewise. Other boys permitted him the license of assertive dominance, though he seldom bothered with jockeying for position in the boyhood power hierarchy. By contrast, the girl was more or less kept in her place from becoming too dominantly assertive among the boys whose acceptance of her in their play activities was provisional. Belligerent aggressiveness and fighting were not noteworthy manifestations in either child.

The counterpart of energetic competitiveness and dominance assertion in tomboyism might well be a high barrier or threshold for the rehearsal of maternal caretaking in childhood play and other mothering opportunities. When the girl played house with her girlfriend and their dolls, she played the role of father. In preference to stereotypic girls' toys, she preferred boys' toys and the activity generated in using them.

Both children preferred utility styles in clothing and personal grooming. For the boy, this preference was in accordance with cultural dictates in boyhood. For the girl it meant indifference toward the idealized feminine stereotypes of ruffles and lace, embroidery and jewelry, though not a phobic avoidance of them such as one might see in a child with a diagnosis of transvestism. She preferred overalls for school and play, but did not balk at wearing a dress for Sunday school and other dressy occasions.

In the childhood years, boys and girls both are able to evaluate the relative merits of membership in either sex. The boy of the present pair had no second thoughts about having been born a boy. The girl, like other tomboy girls with her diagnosis, saw many merits to being a boy, could she have chosen the sex in which to have been born. Yet there was no overt or expressed inclination toward a reassignment of sex.

She anticipated the eventual probability of reaching the boyfriend stage, marriage, and motherhood. Like many girls in childhood, she already had a companionship with a boy whom she considered her special boyfriend. Nonetheless, she shared with other, older girls of the same diagnosis the ideal of priority for a nondomestic career in addition to marriage and domesticism.

The boy, who was already adolescent in development, had a special companionship, elaborated into true romance in his imagery, the companion being a girlfriend. He fitted easily into the stereotype of the male role in marriage, irrespective of the fact that he and his partner would both have 46,XX chromosomes.

Prenatally androgenized tomboyish girls, like those among their genetically male brothers who also were exposed to an excess of prenatal androgen, tend as a group to be elevated in IQ. The girls tend also to be high achievers scholastically and vocationally—the brothers perhaps somewhat less so. The girl, in the pair under consideration, was a good scholar. The boy's scholastic achievement was adequate, but secondary to his outdoor, athletic, and sporting interests.

The girl in this matched pair was too young to manifest evidence of adolescent lesbian eroticism. Twenty-odd older girls of the same diagnosis and similar medical history, however, but born with less masculinized genitalia, have, when mature, shown no lesbian erotic traits. Thus, one may infer that prenatal androgenism does not predestine the differentiation of a lesbian gender identity. The latter requires additional social input during the postnatal, primarily social stage of gender-identity differentiation.

The child reared as a boy did, in fact, encounter a full complement of this additional, masculinizing social input. His case, therefore, raises the tendentious question of whether or not it is one of contrived or iatrogenic lesbianism. In physique and appearance, and by rearing, he is a boy with a penis whose romantic attraction is toward a girl. According to the record of his chromosome count and gonadal sex, he is, by birth, female. Common sense dictates that the chromosomal and gonadal sex are here subordinate to the sex of physique, external genital anatomy, behavior, and to the gender identity, all of which declare the boy to be a heterosexual male. In coitus he can function as a man, not as a woman.

Differentiation of the juvenile gender identity in these two cases, as in the case of all normal children, included erotic functioning, if at all, only as play. Erotic and sexual play in childhood is a rehearsal, so to speak, in anticipation of instructions that will be added by the hormones of puberty. The pubertal hormones instruct the body in somatic dimorphism of maturation. They also lower the threshold for the arousal of erotic response and the release of erotic behavior, androgen being requisite to this effect in both sexes. In the girl of the present pair, masculinizing early puberty would have occurred as a sequel to adrenocortical malfunction had it not been therapeutically regulated by treatment with cortisone. Early adrenal masculinizing puberty had appeared in the boy and then, by reason of therapeutic confusion and poor management, had been changed to ovarian feminization under the influence of late-instituted cortisone therapy. This turn of events is especially noteworthy, for the growth of breasts and approaching onset of menstrual bleeding (through the penile urethra) did not change or negate the boy's masculine gender identity. He viewed feminization as a disease or deformity and urgently wanted to be relieved of it. His treatment, surgical and hormonal, thenceforth was masculinizing.

The discrepancy between the discordant gender identity and the concordant genetic and gonadal sex of this boy and his matched partner, the girl, is indeed remarkable. This pair is not unique. I have already indicated that I have studied several other pairs and there are more, in other clinics around the country, who exhibit the same discrepancy. There are also parallel pairs of individuals who are genetic males. In two instances, one of the pair began life as a normal male, and was reassigned as a female after total loss of the penis in an accident of circumcision by cautery. One child, now aged seven, clearly shows female gender-identity differentiation. The other child is still a baby.

Postnatal Differentiation: Complementation and Identification

All of these matched pairs demonstrate the extensive proportion of gender-identity differentiation that, by nature's decree, is destined to take place after birth. One finds here an analogy with native language: whereas full linguistic communication is exclusively dependent on a human central nervous system prenatally differentiated in preparation for language use, without linguistic stimulation from others the human central nervous system does not differentiate the function of linguistic communication. Gender-identity differentiation also needs a central nervous system prenatally differentiated in preparation for the postnatal establishment of full gender identity under the influence of social stimulation and response.

The social stimuli of gender-identity differentiation fall into two great classes, those for identification and those for complementation. The principle of identification has long been recognized in sex-role learning, but the principle of complementation is newly recognized. Identification means that a girl copies her mother, or other female models, whereas a boy copies his father, or other male models. Ideally, both parents and all other subsidiary models agree in reinforcing and approving of a child's behavioral manifestations of gender-identification.

Complementation means that a girl reciprocates her behavior as a complement to that of her father or other males. A boy reciprocates his behavior as a complement to that of his mother or other females. Ideally, as in the case of identification, each parent and other members of each sex agree in reinforcing and approving of a child's behavioral manifestations of gender-complementation. Inconsistency and contradiction on the part of parents and/or other leading identification and complementation models in a child's life induce inconsistency and contradiction into the child's own gender identity as it differentiates.

Identification and complementation learning entail that every child, girl or boy, establishes and stores in the brain two gender schemata. One is masculine, the other feminine. One is coded as positive and as belonging personally to oneself. The other is coded as negative and not belonging personally, except as a schema of what to expect to have to respond to, or complement, in relations with the other sex. In most children, these two schemata differentiate with clear boundaries. When they do not, the result is an error of gender-identity differentiation, of which there are many variants.

Errors of Gender-Identity Differentiation

The errors of gender-identity differentiation may be classified on two dimensions: total versus partial transposition and episodic versus chronic transposition. To illustrate: a total episodic transposition appears clinically as transvestism with dual personality, each personality having its own name and wardrobe. By contrast, a total chronic transposition appears clinically as transsexualism, the condition in which the individual has the chronic and pervasive conviction of belonging to the sex opposite to that of the genital anatomy, and becomes rehabilitated as a member of that sex or yearns to do so, with appropriate hormonal and surgical sex reassignment. Partial transposition on an episodic basis appears clinically as bisexualism (or facultative homosexualism); and on a chronic basis as essential or obligative homosexualism. Obligative homosexualism may manifest itself as effeminate or virile, dependent on the extent or degree of partial gender-identity transposition.

By nosological convention, the diagnoses of transvestism, transsexualism, bisexualism, and homosexualism (and of transitions between them) imply a variable degree of gender-identity transposition, which itself implies involvement of the sex organs and their erotic functioning. In the majority of instances, these diagnoses also imply transposition of gender role in the affected person's imagery, if not in his actual erotic practice, vis-à-vis the sex of the erotic partner as man or woman.

These four diagnoses also involve, in varying degrees, transposition of nonerotic aspects of gender role, for example, work and avocational activities conventionally dichotomized as masculine or feminine. Transposition of these nonerotic aspects or attributes of gender role also may be manifested, either episodically or chronically, in the absence of erotic transposition—that is, in people who are not bisexual, homosexual, transvestic, or transsexual. The relationship of the six types of transposition to one another are shown in the 3 × 2 arrangement of Table 2. In the table it can be seen that, apart from tomboyism, there are no nouns in our language with which to identify gender-role transpositions that apply to nonerotic sex-stereotypes in avocations and careers. For example, there is no antonym for tomboy. The nearest approximations are dandy or dude, which carry too strong a connotation of ridicule; and sissy or effeminate, which carry too strong a connotation of homosexuality. There is no name for men and women whose avocations depart from sex-stereotypic conventions. The deficiency of our language in not providing names for optional, nonerotic types of sex-stereotypic nonconformity undoubtedly indicates how strong is the taboo in our society against nonconformity to the stereotypes. Especially in the case of males, nonconformity to the stereotype is likely to be construed as carrying homosexual overtones. There is an important implication here for liberated women of the Women's Lib generation: until their number is matched by a new generation of men liberated from the masculine sex stereotype, there will be a shortage of liberated males to be the partners of liberated females.

TABLE 2

GENDER-ROLE TRANSPOSITIONS

	Total	*Partial*	*Optional*
Episodic	Transvestism	Bisexualism	Recreational Role Transposition
Chronic	Transsexualism	Homosexualism	Occupational Role Transposition (e.g., Tomboyism)

Optional versus Imperative Sex Differences

As compared with the multiplicity and range of conventional, stereotypic and optional gender-role differences, the imperatives of sex difference can be reduced to four: women menstruate, gestate, and lactate whereas men impregnate. These four are the basic nativistic and phyletically decreed sex differences. Other, secondary differences derive from these four, notably the hormonal and somatic secondary sexual characteristics of puberty. However, none of these derivative sex differences, nor of associated sexually dimorphic behavior, is absolute or imperative. Variations in the quality, intensity, or frequency of their manifestations among the members of one sex cover so wide a range that, at the extremes, individuals of one sex may be more disparate from one another than from representatives of the other sex. In statistical parlance, male and female within-group differences are as extensive as between-group differences.

The range of male or female within-group variation in morphologic and behavioral sex has its basis in variable thresholds of response. Among genetic males, to give but one example, there are different thresholds of growth response in breast tissue, so that the range of breast development in adolescent males is from zero to female size (adolescent gynecomastia). The same range applies to genetic females, but in reverse order, and with an extension at the positive extreme of excessive, ever-expanding breast growth (virginal hyperplasia of the breasts).

Variable response thresholds in the differentiation of sexual dimorphism of both bodily and behavioral traits constitute the basis on which cultural definitions of idealized masculinity and idealized femininity have differentiated, historically, and become fixed in social custom, religion, and law. Parentalism, or caretaking of the young, is a good example. Whereas care of the young is not a sexually dimorphic but an ambisexual trait among mammals, the threshold of its elicitation is distinctly sexually dimorphic. The threshold is typically lower in females than males, and is especially low in lactating females. In the human species, the ideal of paternal caretaking, once defined in our culture as clearly unmasculine, is now, as everyone knows, undergoing a redefinition as ambisexual.

Parentalism in child care constitutes an example of behavior that can be either gender-shared or gender-divergent. It represents a cultural and personal biographic option, the opposite of a nativistic and phyletic imperative (Table 1).

The majority of gender-divergent roles belong in the optional category. Historically, however, there has been extensive stereotyping of roles as masculine or feminine. In consequence, they are transmitted to each new generation of children as male-female absolutes, and not as optional and ambisexual or gender-shared. Masculine-feminine divergency tends to have prevailed over gender-sharing, much to the disadvantage of those individuals, not only women, but men also, who do not neatly fit the dichotomies dictated by cultural custom.

Those men and women who did obey the cultural dictates of gender divergency as they grew up do not, and cannot, automatically change themselves by edict. Therefore, they tend to perpetuate their own conventional, gender-divergent roles by transmitting them to their children. The children of parents with less divergent roles, by contrast, more easily learn gender roles that are more sex-shared. The disparity between the sharing and the divergent types is now strong enough itself to be a cultural force in our midst.

Discussion

CHARLES L. IHLENFELD, M.D.

The paper Dr. Money has given represents a landmark in our efforts better to understand behavior in general and sexuality in particular. He has presented a thesis based on enormously careful clinical and laboratory research. His ideas, outlined in this paper and detailed in his new book with Dr. Ehrhardt, bridge the gap between biology and psychology. As he says in his opening paragraph, "It is wrong to dichotomize the learned and the biological —learning is a biological function, for all acts of learning are also activities of the central nervous system." Beyond this, he shows how biology affects psychology, both prenatally, in the form of early neuroendocrine coloring of the hypothalamus, and postnatally in the way that biology, particularly genital biology, influences the attitudes and actions of those who in turn influence us as we grow and develop. The net result of all of this, it would seem to me, should be the lessening of day-and-night contrasting of stereotypic male and female roles and an increase in our understanding of and tolerance for those whose behavior, and sexual behavior especially, falls in the areas at the extreme ends of the bell-shaped curve. Thus, in addition to being a scientific document of great moment, Dr. Money's paper is also a most significant and timely social document.

The case of the children with the congenital adrenogenital syndrome illustrates beautifully the manner in which prenatal hormonal influences can color later development. Both children had the female 46,XX chromosome complement. Both were exposed to excessive adrenal androgens from very early in fetal life. In both cases, also, there is indirect evidence to indicate that certain pathways in the central nervous system were affected in such a way that the effects of the androgenic influence were quite discernible in later life. Because of clinical evidence of the salt-losing syndrome in the neonatal period, one of the twins had diagnostic tests which indicated the presence of the adrenogenital syndrome in a genetic female. Consequently, this child's gender was reannounced as female, and appropriate plastic surgery was performed to correct the appearance of the external genitalia. It seems remarkable to me that the correct diagnosis of the other twin was not sought at that same time, especially since no testes were palpable in the scrotal sacs. A high degree of suspicion certainly seems both justified and wise when cases such as this are seen. At any rate, the parents arrived home with a boy baby and a girl baby and reared them as such. As they grew, vocal language and body language taught one to be a boy and the other to be a girl. The paper describes in some detail how between the ages of one-and-a-half and four years these instructions worked to establish in each child "an irrefutable conviction of gender identity." It is important to realize that this gender identity was totally in concordance with the gender of rearing in each case. But the prenatal influence was not lost.

In the case of the girl, her behavior had "a special tint or flavor" which represented a variation of feminine gender identity. This girl was described as "tomboyish." Certainly when we use the word "tomboy" in our culture we have no reason to doubt that we are describing a girl—and undoubtedly a heterosexual girl at that. In this paper as well as elsewhere Dr. Money has enumerated those qualities or traits which are characteristic of individuals who have had prenatal androgenization. A careful reading of these traits clearly shows that a prenatally androgenized genetic female is not a male but rather is simply a special type of female. In contrast to the female transsexuals I have known, this girl was quite willing to accept being a girl and to anticipate that eventually she would become a mother. While she could see many good things about being a boy could she have had a choice, she still had "no overt or expressed inclination toward a reassignment of sex." Dr. Money tells us that this girl was more inclined, however, to give her higher priority to a nondomestic career, with marriage and domesticism ranking somewhat lower in importance to her. He also tells us that as a group prenatally androgenized tomboyish girls tend to be elevated in IQ. Just as a personal note, I have at times been confused when I have seen women who have been highly successful in traditionally masculine career roles and who at the same time have had totally and appropriately feminine responses to social and family situations. As Dr. Money points out later in his paper, "male and female within-group differences are as extensive as between-group differences."

This girl's "brother" shows us the other side of the coin. Here we see a genetic XX female with a full complement of female internal reproductive organs but with highly masculinized external genitalia. In addition, we presume that the central nervous system was affected in this child in the same way that the central nervous system was affected in his sister. As he grew and developed he received the innumerable and repetitive day-by-day instructions about being a boy. He easily established and maintained an intact sense of male gender identity. His behavior and interests were totally appropriate to the male role. This sense of identity, we must remember, is shown to us in a genetic female. And this sense was so strong that later evidences of physical feminization, including the development of female breasts and even the onset of menstrual bleeding through the penile urethra, did nothing to upset it. Rather, to use Dr. Money's words, "he viewed feminization as a disease or deformity and urgently wanted to be relieved of it. His treatment, surgical and hormonal, thenceforth was masculinization." In this case, as Dr. Money wisely notes, "Common sense dictates that the chromosomal and gonadal sex are here subordinate to the sex of physique, external genital anatomy, behavior, and to the gender identity, all of which declare the boy to be a heterosexual male." Thus, the prenatal androgenization of the central nervous system gave the boy behavior potentials which enabled him to accept without question the male role in which he was trained from the moment of birth.

Another concept of great interest and importance in this paper is the role of complementation in the process of sex-role learning. As Dr. Money points out, we have long been aware of the influence of identification with a same-sex parent or parent-surrogate. Such identification defines and reinforces positive concepts of appropriate sex-role behavior. The concept of complementation assumes that in addition to our same-sex models we also carry with us opposite-sex models—or programs of behavior. We use these opposite-sex models in a negative sense, to define behavior which is appropriate to the opposite sex but inappropriate to us. Furthermore, we use these complementary models to give us clues as to what to expect from the opposite sex. Perhaps a relevant example of such a situation is when we expect our wives to react in at least certain circumstances as we have come to expect our mothers to react. Likewise, the problems that arise when our wives fail to react in the expected fashion need no further elaboration here. Through the process of complementation the child learns to reciprocate, or to complement, the behavior of members of the opposite sex. I might wonder at this point what happens when two important members of the opposite sex display the wide variation we have already seen is possible in within-group optional behavior. A further implication of this concept is that in one-parent families the children still need strong figures of both sexes if the processes of both identification and complementation are to work successfully. As Dr. Money points out, "Inconsistency and contradiction on the part of parents and/or other leading identification and complementation models in a child's life induce inconsistency and contradiction into the child's own gender identity as it differentiates."

Finally, we come to the discussion of errors of gender-identity differentiation. We have seen that there are a multiplicity of gender-identity determinants, some inborn and some socially determined. There are many opportunities for failure of successful establishment of a gender identity that is consistent with and appropriate to the genital anatomy. Such failures result in the syndromes of transvestism, transsexualism, bisexualism, and obligative homosexualism and of transitions between them. Dr. Money defines these conditions in terms of the nature of the error of gender-identity differentiation: Transvestism is total and episodic; transsexualism is total and chronic; bisexualism is partial and episodic; obligative homosexualism is partial and chronic. In this paper Dr. Money does not specifically indicate which factors are involved in the production of each of these conditions. Still, our knowledge of the early age by which gender identity is established and the strength with which that identity persists at least helps us understand the difficulties that arise in the therapeutic setting when we try to alter gender identity in the adult patient. Such knowledge in transsexualism and obligative homosexualism lends credence to those who advocate supportive treatment rather than attempts to alter feeling and behavior into more gender-appropriate patterns.

In summary, Dr. Money has succinctly presented a coherent and experimentally-supported model for the development of gender identity. He has described factors that are nativistic and cultural, imperative and optional, phyletic and biographic. He has shown how these factors generally work together to produce a gender identity that is appropriate to the genital anatomy. He has also indicated how errors in the differentiation of gender identity result in certain well-recognized syndromes. He points out the fallacy of and, indeed, the danger of, the insistence on certain elements of the traditional cultural dichotomy between the ideal masculine and the ideal feminine models. It seems reasonable to hope that an understanding of the principles in this paper may lead to a society which will place more value on individual human expression than on tyrannical conformity.

3

Psychoanalysis Revisited in Terms of Experimental Primatology

WILLIAM T. MCKINNEY, JR., M.D.

WHETHER PSYCHOANALYSIS IS VIEWED as a theory of human behavior, as a method of treatment, as a research tool, or in any other fashion, it can be agreed that it is a discipline with roots firmly imbedded in a developmental context. The influence of various types of early life experiences on behavioral styles and methods of relating later in development has been a cardinal feature of much psychoanalytic theory since its inception. The mechanisms by which these early life experiences have differential effects have, of course, been the subject of considerable controversy. The most valuable contribution of experimental (laboratory) primatology to the behavioral, and especially clinical, sciences has occurred in the developmental context. There are striking parallels between the kinds of questions being investigated in the literature of both psychoanalysis and experimental primatology:

1. *What are the important variables in the development of a reciprocal mother-infant attachment bond?* Work with

The writing of this chapter was supported by a Research Scientist Development Award K01-MH-47353 from the National Institute of Mental Health. The research described was supported by Research Grants #MH-11894, #MH-18070, and #MH-21892 all from the National Institute of Mental Health, by #RR-0167 from the National Institutes of Health and by the Wisconsin Psychiatric Research Institute.

rhesus monkeys in a laboratory setting has helped clarify some of the early psychoanalytic theories regarding facilitation and inhibition of the development of this bond. This experimental work has led to a broadened—more enlightened—view of this attachment bond in humans.

2. *What are the short- and long-term differential effects of various rearing conditions on primate social behavior?* These conditions have ranged from mother-peer rearing to rearing in complete social isolation. The impact of these early rearing conditions has been documented in terms of their effects on a variety of social interactions including, among others, aggressive, sexual, and maternal behaviors.
3. *What role does separation have in the production of abnormal behavior, and what are the short- and long-term effects of separation from various affectional and environmental situations?* Separation has obviously been a key concept in the psychoanalytic literature, especially with regard to its possible involvement in the production of depression. Laboratory studies with several species of monkeys are contributing to our understanding of the effects of separation.
4. *What is the nature of the interaction between social and biological factors in producing abnormal behavior?* The emphasis here is on the manner in which social and biological factors interact, not on which are more important. Pioneers in the psychoanalytic field have contended that the study of this interaction was a proper field of inquiry for psychoanalysis from its beginning. Recent studies using primate models for human psychopathology attempt to get at the nature of this interaction in more detail than is currently possible in humans.
5. *What rehabilitative approaches are effective in reversing syndromes of abnormal behavior which have been produced in primates?* The above four areas relate to psychoanalysis as a theory of human behavior. Although there may be some treatment implications inherent in these areas of study, this has not been their primary focus. However, in the last several years there have been more direct studies of methods of rehabilitation of rhesus monkeys who have become abnormal through alteration of their early rearing conditions. Both successful and unsuccessful methods will be described.

In most of the above areas, the primary emphasis has been on observing the effects of rearing condition A on behavioral parameters B, C, D, etc. There is little firm data available to help in understanding the mechanisms by which condition A produces effects B, C, and D. In this sense, too, there are parallels between psychoanalysis and experimental primatology.

This paper will be largely limited to studies carried out in the conventional laboratory setting, with its limitations of space, housing, and animal care. It should be mentioned at the outset that there are at least two other major methods for investigating the behavior of primates. One method involves naturalistic field studies in which observations are made of groups of nonhuman primates living in their natural setting. In other words, one goes to their setting rather than bringing them to ours. This is a fertile and growing field which is quite vast in scope. Another method of studying the social behavior of nonhuman primates has been termed "semi-naturalistic" and involves studying such groups in large outdoor enclosures. Rather than go to them, we bring them to us but not into a laboratory as laboratories are generally conceived. Each of these methods of studying primates, that is, "naturalistic" field studies, "semi-naturalistic" studies, and "unnatural" studies in a laboratory setting, has its advantages and limitations and, hopefully, will be viewed as complementary rather than competitive, although currently this is not always the case.

Surrogate Studies (Mother-Infant Attachment Bonds)

The now famous (or infamous) Wisconsin surrogates entered into scientific history in 1958 and led Dr. Harlow to give an address to the American Psychological Association entitled "The Nature of Love." In that talk he pointed out that "the little we know about love does not transcend simple observation and the little we write about it has been written better by poets and novelists." The phrase "affectional systems" came to be used synonymously with "love bonds" to describe the attachments between rhesus monkeys, whether the bond be between mother and infant or between peers, and whether it be a heterosexual attachment or a parental attachment to offspring. Surrogates were created to allow direct experimental analysis of the relative importance of the stimulus variables determining the affectional responses in the neonatal and infant primate. That is, why does an infant attach to its mother? At that time the most prevalent psychoanalytic theory centered about the importance of drive reduction in determining this attachment. The so-called "secondary drive theory of attachment" stated that the child has a number of physiological needs which must be met, the most obvious of these being the necessity for food. The baby becomes attached to its mother as a result of the mother's meeting the baby's physiological needs and the baby's learning in due course that she is the source of its gratification. Though this was not the only theory presented prior to 1958, it was by far the most widely and strongly held. To quote John Bowlby, "From Freud onward, it has underlined much though by no means all psychoanalytic writing and has been a common assumption of learning theories." This theory is illustrated by representative statements such as: "Love has its origin and attachment in the satisfied need for nourishment;" and "Probably the feeding experience can be the occasion for the child to learn to be with others."

In the now classic surrogate studies done at Wisconsin, two kinds of surrogates were designed: the cloth mother surrogate and a wire mother surrogate. The cloth surrogate was made from a block of wood, covered with sponge rubber and sheathed in tan terry cloth. There was a light bulb behind her to radiate heat. It was designed so that a bottle could be placed at the height where the infant would normally encounter a breast. To quote Harlow, "The result was a mother, soft, warm and tender. A mother with infinite patience, a mother available 24 hours a day, a mother that never scolded her infant and never struck or bit her baby in anger. Furthermore, we designed a mother machine with maximal maintenance efficiency since failure of any system or function could be resolved by the simple substitution of black boxes and new component parts. It is our opinion that we engineered a superior monkey-mother although this position is not held universally by the monkey fathers." The other mother surrogate was made of wire mesh, a substance adequate to provide support and nursing capabilities. She also was warmed by radiant heat. The only difference between the two surrogates was in the quality of the contact comfort which was available. In the initial experiment, the *dual mother surrogate condition,* a cloth mother and a wire mother were placed in different cubicles attached to the infant's living cage. For four newborn monkeys, the cloth mother lactated and the wire mother did not. For the other four, this condition was reversed. In either condition, the infant received all its milk through the mother surrogate as soon as it was able to maintain itself in this way, a capability generally achieved within two or three days. Supplementary feedings were given until the milk intake from the mother surrogate was adequate to support the infant. Thus, the experiment was designed as a test of the relative importance of the variables of contact comfort and nursing comfort. During the first 14 days of life, the monkeys' cage floor was covered with a heating pad wrapped in a folded gauze diaper and thereafter the cage floor was bare. The infants were always free to leave the heating pad or cage floor to contact either mother. The time spent on the surrogate mothers was automatically recorded. The data indicate that contact comfort is a variable of overwhelming importance in the development of affectional responses, whereas lactation is a variable of negligible importance.

Also, with age and opportunity to learn, subjects with the lactating wire mother showed decreasing responses to her and increasing interest in the nonlactating cloth mother, a finding completely contrary to any interpretation of derived drive in which the mother form becomes conditioned to hunger-thirst reduction. In some ways it was not surprising to discover that contact comfort was an important basic affectional or love variable, but the extent to which it overshadowed the nursing variable was quite astounding. Indeed, the data were so striking as to suggest that the primary function of nursing as an affectional variable may be to insure frequent and intimate body contact of the infant with its mother.

One function of a mother, whether human or subhuman, and

presumably a mother surrogate, is to provide a safe base for the infant in times of fear and danger. The frightened or sick child clings to its mother, and the degree to which it does this in times of danger or stress may be used as a measure of the strength of affectional bonds. This kind of differential response was also tested in the original surrogate studies by presenting infants in their cages, in the presence of the two surrogate mothers, with various fear-producing stimuli, such as a moving toy bear. A typical response to the fear stimulus was to cling tightly to the mother. The data make it clear that at times of stress the cloth mother is highly preferred to the wire mother, and this differential selectivity is increased with age and experience. The variable of nursing appears to be of virtually no importance. In this situation, the infant consistently seeks the soft mother surrogate, regardless of nursing conditions.

Similarly, the mother or mother surrogate provides its youth with a source of security, and this is seen particularly when the mother and child are in a strange situation. This was tested in the original surrogate studies by introducing infants into the strange environment of a new room measuring six feet by six feet. This situation was called the "open field test" and contained multiple stimuli known to elicit curiosity responses in monkeys. The subjects were introduced into this situation twice a week for eight weeks with no mother surrogate present during alternate sessions, and a cloth mother present during the others. A cloth diaper was always available to the infant throughout all sessions. After one or two adaptation sessions, the infants always rushed to the mother surrogate when she was present and clutched her, rubbed their bodies against her, and frequently manipulated her body and face. After a few additional sessions, the infants began to use the mother surrogate as a source of security, a base of operation. They would explore and manipulate a stimulus and then return to the mother before venturing again into the new world of the strange room. The behavior of these infants was quite different when the mother was absent from the room. Frequently they would freeze in a crouched position. Emotionality indices such as vocalization, crouching, rocking, and sucking increased sharply. No differences between the cloth-mother-fed and wire-mother-fed infants were demonstrated under either condition. In the absence of the mother, some of the experimental monkeys would rush to the center of the room where the mother was customarily placed and then run rapidly from object to object, screaming and crying all the while. Continuous frantic clutching of their bodies, even when not in the crouching position, was very common. These monkeys frequently contacted and clutched the cloth diaper, but this action never seemed to pacify them. This same behavior occurred in the presence of the wire mother.

Thus, in the original studies, body contact was shown to be of overwhelming importance as a variable in determining mother-infant attachment. Also, even though the cloth mother was inanimate, it was able to impart to the infant such emotional security that the infant would, in the surrogate's presence, explore a strange situation and manipulate available physical or animate objects. Since the original surrogate studies, several modifications, and hopefully improvements, have been made in the design and function of the surrogate. To alleviate some practical cleaning problems inherent in the original cloth surrogate, a family of simplified surrogates was created. The simplified surrogate is mounted on a rod attached to a lead base four inches in diameter, angled upward at 25 degrees and projected through the surrogate's body for four inches so that heads may be attached if desired. The body of the simplified surrogate is only six inches long, two and one-half inches in diameter, and stands approximately three inches off the ground. Infants readily cling to the simplified surrogates' smaller bodies and decreased angle of inclination.

I have spoken of the important role of contact comfort in terms of determining an infant's attachment to its mother and of how the original surrogate study provided data which tended to negate much of what was then the current psychoanalytic thinking about the nature of this attachment bond. However, several other variables are probably important and should be discussed further.

1. *Lactation.* Given the existence of sufficient contact comfort, lactation becomes an important variable in determining infant preference to the mother. To demonstrate experimentally that activities associated with the breast were variables of significant importance, two sets of differentially colored terry cloth surrogates were constructed. A situation was arranged where the surrogate of one color lactated and the other did not. When, as in this study, contact comfort is held constant, the infant showed a consistent preference for the lactating surrogate. The importance of the lactation variable probably decreases with time, but one must be careful not to throw out the baby (or the milk) with the bath water.

2. *Facial variables.* It has been found that the type of face on the surrogate is not critical; however, what is critical is a change of the face to which an infant monkey has become accustomed. The infant monkey responds to the earliest version of the mother that he encountered and grows accustomed to this face. Subsequent changes introduced after the fear response matures almost invariably elicit fear.

3. *Body surface variables.* In an attempt to further analyze preferences for various materials, an exploratory study was performed in which each of four infants was presented with a choice of surrogates covered with terry cloth, rayon, vinyl, or coarse sandpaper. The infants, not surprisingly, showed a clear preference for the cloth surrogates and no significant preference differences among the other body surfaces.

4. *Emotion variables.* It has been repeatedly pointed out in the human literature and, to some extent, in subhuman primate literature that a rocking motion (proprioceptive stimulation) is a variable which might be important in binding the infant to the mother figure. This theory was measured with surrogates by comparing the time the infant spent on two identical planes, one rocking and one stationary, and on two identical cloth surrogates, one rocking and one stationary. The major finding was that the infant monkeys definitely preferred the rocking mothers or the

rocking plane prior to 140 to 150 days, with no clear preference being apparent thereafter.

5. *Temperature variables.* By the use of heating and cooling coils inside the surrogates, it has been possible to create warm and cold simplified surrogates, that is, cold and hot mamas. It became clear from this study that a simple linear model was not adequate to describe the effects of temperature differences of surrogates on infant attachment. Infants initially raised with a warm simplified surrogate to which they became attached, when exposed to a cold simplified surrogate, refused to spend time on it, but would spend time on the warm surrogate when it was returned. On the other hand, infants reared initially on cold surrogates to which they did not attach also did not attach when later given an opportunity to contact a warm surrogate. Apparently, being raised with a cold mother chills infant monkeys to mothers in general.

It is my impression based on talks with many groups that the surrogate studies are widely known but only superficially understood. There seems to exist a considerable amount of misunderstanding about the outcome of various surrogate studies and what their significance is in relation to psychoanalytic theory concerning infant attachment to its mother. Also, the studies represented one of the first illustrations of how work with primates in a laboratory can be used to operationalize certain psychoanalytic concepts for purposes of subjecting them to carefully controlled experimentation. In this instance, the results with primates have led to a clarification and broadening of our understanding of the forces which bind an infant to its mother.

DIFFERENTIAL REARING CONDITIONS AND LATER SOCIAL BEHAVIORS

There seems little doubt that differential early life experiences in a variety of animals influence later adult behavior. In rhesus monkeys, differential early life experiences produce seemingly permanent abnormalities which span the total behavioral repertoire. In this section the major rearing conditions which have been used at the Wisconsin Primate Laboratory will be briefly summarized and their effects on the later behavior of rhesus monkeys outlined.

The major rearing conditions include the following:

1. *Feral Monkeys.* These are monkeys born and reared in the wild and then captured and brought to a laboratory. Feral environments undoubtedly provide a richer source of stimulation than any of the laboratory conditions described below. However, the different laboratory conditions themselves can be graded in terms of the variety of available stimulation.
2. *Mother-Peer Rearing.* This is the most complex laboratory environment. In this playpen environment an infant basically lives with his mother in one of four corner units, but has access to the other infants in a central play area. The mothers can observe the infants playing with each other, but are not able to interfere. By appropriate manipulations of panels, any combination of infants can be allowed to interact together. Also, it is possible to further enrich this environment with a variety of stimulus objects.
3. *Nursery Rearing.* This involves taking the newborn infant from its mother at birth and housing it for its first 30 days in a carefully supervised laboratory nursery situation. During the first few days of life the infants are hand fed every two hours. They receive intimate physical contact with humans and at about 10 days of age are trained to feed from a bottle placed in a wire rack. They usually learn to feed themselves by 15 to 20 days of age.
4. *Peer-Only Rearing.* This so-called "together-together" situation provides social stimulation, but exclusively with age mates. These infants are taken from their mothers at birth, reared in the nursery for the first 30 days and then placed in groups of two, four, or six. The lack of mothering places this stimulus situation somewhat below that of mother-peer rearing in playpens. Animals reared in this peer-only situation eventually develop a normal range of social behaviors, although the maturational process is somewhat altered, in that more complex social behaviors are slower in developing than in the mother-peer reared infants.
5. *Surrogate-Only Rearing.* This condition, which has been

alluded to above, involves placing infants in enclosed cages with inanimate surrogate mothers after they have spent 30 days in the nursery.

6. *Social Isolation.* The technique of social isolation involves rearing animals from birth in either total isolation chambers where they have no social contact with other monkeys, or in bare wire cages, where their only contact is visual and auditory.

With the exception of the isolate monkeys, each of the rearing conditions mentioned above, although influencing the rapidity and/or nature of development of social behaviors, can be used to rear socially normal rhesus monkeys. Either partial or total social isolation early in life produces severe and persistent syndromes of abnormal behavior involving the major affectional systems. The mechanisms underlying the dramatic effects of social isolation are poorly understood, and there are virtually no data available about possible neurophysiological and/or neuroendocrinological substrates of the syndrome. Social isolation data are most extensive in rhesus monkey subjects and these will be summarized. However, the isolation syndrome has also been studied in dogs, in pig tail monkeys, and in chimpanzees. The measurement techniques differed from study to study in terms of the manner in which the effects of early social isolation were documented and also in that the specific techniques of isolation themselves varied. Nevertheless, one can make a general statement that in all species studied thus far, early social isolation has been a powerful method for inducing persistent patterns of abnormal behavior.

In rhesus monkeys, for example, subjects reared in total social isolation for the first six-to-twelve months of life exhibit upon emergence from isolation severe deficits in locomotive, exploratory, and social behaviors. The appropriate responses of grooming, play, and other social interactions are minimal in these subjects. They spend the majority of their time engaging in "autistic-like" self-clasping, stereotyped rocking and huddling, and self-mouthing behaviors. Appropriate adult sexual responses are virtually absent among isolate reared monkeys; the male monkeys do not seem to know how to approach or mount a female monkey appropriately. They attempt all kinds of unusual maneuvers, none of which achieves the desired effect. When approached by a normal male, female monkeys who have a history of early total social isolation do not emit appropriate sexual cues. They do not present their hind quarters appropriately, and when mounting attempts are made by the male, the females are completely uncooperative. Total social isolation for the first year of life may be one of the more effective ways to achieve zero population growth. In a monkey-breeding colony one does not want zero population growth and therefore artificial insemination is sometimes used to impregnate females with a history of early social isolation. Females so inseminated display grossly inadequate maternal behavior characterized by either indifference or brutality toward their first infants. The isolate rhesus mother might allow the infant to sit in a corner, but when the infant approaches her, will neither contact nor have anything else to do with the infant. Some infants are very persistent, however, and continue in their relentless attempt to establish sustained physical contact with the mother. This is almost uniformly unsuccessful and at times seems to frustrate or frighten the mother to brutality. On the other hand, the mother may be abusive to the infant from the outset, and in some cases infants have been killed by mothers before they could be removed. These animals have been termed "motherless mothers." This story is not complete, however, for if one impregnates these motherless mothers a second time, a modified tale emerges. The mothers who were indifferent, though not abusive, to their first infant often proved to be very effective mothers with their second infant. This change in their maternal behavior may be related to the sustained efforts of the artificially fed first infants to establish contact. On the other hand, there was a tendency for the mothers who were overtly abusive to their first infants to continue this pattern, although their behavior sometimes modified with subsequent infants.

Early social isolation also has severe effects on the rhesus monkeys' aggressive behavior. They often engage in self-aggression and have sometimes mutilated themselves to the point of requiring surgery. If the aggression is not self-directed, it is often inappropriately directed. For example, a chronologically mature social isolate will readily attack a neonate, an act rarely initiated by socially normal monkeys, or it may attack a dominant adult male, a blunder which few socially sophisticated monkeys are foolish enough to attempt. Socially isolated monkeys do not seem to be able to modulate their aggression. They either sit in a corner huddling, rocking, or clasping themselves, or out of the blue engage in unprovoked aggression against whoever happens to be around. This is probably part of their total inability to emit, or respond to, appropriate social cues.

Socially isolated monkeys have also been reported to exhibit extreme hyperphagia and polydipsia as adults.

Several variables are important in the production of the isolation syndrome. The most severe effects are produced when the isolation is total rather than partial, when it begins at birth, and when it lasts for a minimum of six months. Alteration of any of these factors is thought to produce a less severe and/or a less persistent syndrome.

The isolation syndrome, until recently, had been considered permanent. No technique that had been tried had been successful in reversing the syndrome. Such unsuccessful attempts included aversive conditioning type procedures, frequent social experience with peers, and prevention of the "emergence trauma" by prior adaptation. The first successful rehabilitation of social isolates was brought about by "monkey psychiatrists," a term that has come to refer to chronologically younger but normal monkeys who served as the therapists in the initial social rehabilitation study. The specific experiment to which I refer studied six-month male isolates and utilized three-month-old normal female animals as therapists. The isolates were allowed to interact with the therapist monkeys two hours per day, three days per week, as pairs (one isolate and one therapist) and two days per week in a group of four (two isolates and two therapists) in a playroom.

The isolates' initial response to both situations was to huddle in a corner, and the therapists' first response was to approach and cling to the isolates. Within a week in the home cage and two weeks in the playroom the isolates were reciprocating the clinging. Concurrently, the therapists were exhibiting elementary play patterns among themselves and attempting to initiate such patterns with the isolates. Within two weeks in the home cage and a month in the playroom the isolates were reciprocating these behaviors. Shortly thereafter, the isolates began to initiate play behavior themselves, and correspondingly, their disturbance activity, which originally had accounted for most of their behavioral repertoire, decreased to insignificant levels. By one year of age the isolates were virtually indistinguishable from the therapists in the amount of exploration, locomotion, and play behaviors. Not only have isolated monkeys responded to social treatment methods, they have also responded somewhat to chlorpromazine treatments. In a recent pilot study, rhesus monkeys subjected to partial social isolation for the first year of life, plus other traumatic experiences involving being immobilized or seeing peers immobilized, exhibited severe patterns of abnormal behavior, such as huddling, rocking, self-clasping, avoidance of other animals, and self-mouthing. When these subjects were two-and-a-half years of age, they were started on the adjusted chlorpromazine dosage of 7.5 mgm/kgm given once per day. Within four to eight weeks on this regime, the "active" self-disturbance behavior such as self-mouthing, clasping, huddling, etc., had decreased significantly, and even a few social encounters, such as play and social exploration, occurred in some subjects. These two rehabilitation attempts are currently being combined in studies using chlorpromazine plus social experience with younger therapists.

In terms of experimental models for human psychopathology, it is still unclear what human syndrome or syndromes may be represented by the isolation syndrome. We are currently hampered by a lack of understanding of the mechanisms by which early social isolation produces a severe and persistent effect on social behavior. Labels such as autism, schizophrenia, psychosis, and depression have been used by some professionals in describing the animals. A cautious approach to labeling is indicated at present. Certainly the behavioral parallels between these isolate monkeys and certain aspects of each of the above syndromes exist. Yet several criteria important for the production of animal models for human psychopathology have not been met or even approached. One criterion that is particularly critical to keep in mind is the comparability of inducing conditions. It is difficult to hypothesize a documentable human analogy to total social isolation, except for a few cases of drastic neglect of infants. Partial social isolation, on the other hand, has a clear analogue in the limited and stereotyped social input to children present in many institutions and families. There are virtually no biological data available on isolated monkeys that might help to understand the mechanisms or help with the definition of the syndrome. It has been said that rehabilitation studies can help clarify the syndrome, and within limits this is true. It appears that a socially induced syndrome can be reversed by appropriate social therapy and by use of antipsychotic drugs. The social therapy involves gentle physical contact and nonthreatening social interactions. However, did the drug therapy involve chlorpromazine's antipsychotic properties or did it facilitate social interaction by making the subjects less fearful of each other, or some combination of the two? What we can say at present is that differential rearing conditions in a primate laboratory produce differential effects on the developing social behavior of rhesus monkeys. To a group of psychoanalysts this is no big news, in the sense that this represents the cornerstone of much psychoanalytic theory and practice, that is, the dealing with the long-term results of differential early rearing conditions. However, such theories have been necessarily based on retrospective evidence. Laboratory studies of rhesus monkeys have provided direct evidence of how alteration of an organism's early environment can induce persistent behavioral effects. The monkey's life span is considerably telescoped in comparison to humans, and thus longitudinal studies have become more feasible than in humans. Rehabilitation work with animals devastated by early social isolation is relatively recent, but may hold some promise and some implications for approaches to humans who are severely abnormal due to early rearing conditions. It should be emphasized that additional investigations are crucial in order to clarify the mechanisms involved in the production of the isolation syndrome, which may in itself help clarify the significance of the syndrome as a model for human psychopathology.

Separation Studies

Separation experiences, i.e., object losses, are thought to precede the development of severe depression, as well as other forms of psychopathology in human beings. The theories that postulate the importance of separation are largely based on retrospective studies which start with the population of clinically depressed people who have undergone separation. There is little understanding of the mechanisms underlying the apparent close connection between separation and depression. The terms separation and object loss have themselves become well accepted phrases among clinicians. They have been used to describe many diverse states ranging from an infant's response to separation from his mother to an adult's loss of self-esteem when certain defense mechanisms are no longer effective, or when he is confronted with life-threatening illnesses. Unfortunately, separation is becoming a greatly overused term in the sense that its usage has far outstripped our basic understanding of its meaning. Separation is certainly more than just an event and needs to be defined in terms of many parameters. If this is not done, the risk exists that the term will continue to be used so broadly and loosely as to become meaningless. Many variables determine a response to separation and these need identification and study before the connection between what is called separation and depression can be understood. Also, depression is almost certainly not the only response to separation, or if it is, then depression may manifest itself differently depending on many factors, which almost certainly include genetic and neurochemical ones and possibly prior experiences with separations, the condition surrounding separation, and age, to mention only a few. It is in the area of clarifying the mechanisms underlying separation that primate models have perhaps been most useful thus far. Rhesus monkeys develop strong affectional systems and form close social bonds, factors which have facilitated studies of separation and depression. It was thought initially that these bonds were strong enough that they could be manipulated to produce dramatic changes in behavior. Results thus far have confirmed this belief.

The issue of mother-child separation and the mechanisms underlying the disturbances in the human infant have been discussed at length by John Bowlby (24), René Spitz (11), and others. In his writings concerning separation and grief and mourning in children and infants, Bowlby outlined six theories of separation and concluded that separation anxiety results from activation of the "component instinctual response systems" which form the basis of the infant attachment. He described three stages of the human child's response to separation: protest, despair, and detachment. Bowlby thought the protest stemmed from anxiety, the despair from grief, and the detachment from defensive reactions. Bowlby's theories, based on studies of the separation reactions of human infants, have provided a major portion of the theoretical underpinnings of the mother-infant separation work in primates. Also of key importance in stimulating the experimental work have been the observations of René Spitz on hospitalized young infants separated from their mothers. He termed their reaction anaclitic depression. Many infant monkeys undergoing maternal separation simulate the anaclitic depressive syndromes seen in human infants. A number of informal separation studies were conducted at the Wisconsin Primate Laboratory in the late 1950s on 30- to 90-day-old rhesus infants raised with their own mothers. It was noticed that separation which ranged from a few hours to a few days in duration resulted in acute disturbance of both mother and infant during the separation period and a marked increase in maternal protectiveness following reunion. In one case, the mother, after a three-day separation, kept her infant literally within her reach for a period of more than a month. These informal observations precipitated a more formal study of mother-infant separation which was reported in 1962 (12). The technique employed in the initial separations at Wisconsin involved the use of playpen apparatus. This apparatus allows mother-infant pairs to live together in each of four corner units. The central play area can be entered via an opening in each living unit by the infants, but not by the mothers. Separation is accomplished by merely closing off this opening while the infants are in the central part so that they can not return to their mothers. Plexiglass paneling is used to permit continued visual and auditory contact, wire mesh paneling to permit tactual contact, or masonite to allow only auditory communication.

In the original study, four infants and four mothers served as subjects. Two of the infants underwent maternal separation at 170 days of age and two at 207 days of age. The experiment was divided into three time blocks of three weeks each: preseparation, separation, and postseparation. In this study plexiglass dividers were used so that the infants could continue to see and hear all mothers. The initial reaction of all mothers and all infants after separation indicated a high degree of emotional disturbance. The infants' behavior included disoriented scampering around, high pitched screeching, cooing vocalizations, and huddling up against the barrier in closest proximity to their mothers. The mothers displayed an increase in barking vocalizations and in threats directed toward the experimenter. But the mothers' emotional response appeared to be both less intense and of shorter duration than that of the infants. Later during a separation period, most complex infant-to-infant social behaviors exhibited a drastic decrease in frequency of occurrence. For instance, noncontact play was for all practical purposes obliterated. Threats, approaches, and withdrawals also decreased. During the postseparation period, infant-mother clinging and mother-infant cradling rose significantly, and infant-mother nonspecific contact showed a significant decrease in three of the four infants. Interestingly, one of the infants showed a significant decrease in support contact, nipple contact, and nonspecific contact during postseparation as compared to preseparation. This initial investigation demonstrated that separating a rhesus monkey from its mother had striking behavioral effects, but with individual variation in terms of the nature of the response. In general, the sequence of stages seems to parallel the protest and despair stages described by Bowlby and to provide a powerful animal analogue for anaclitic depres-ion.

A study by Seay and Harlow (13) used eight rhesus mother-infant pairs separated at about 207 days of age. In contrast to the above study, masonite paneling was used during the separation stage so that the infants were not able to see any of the mothers. Behavioral changes were similar to those already described. However, the reactions seemed more severe when the infants could see their mothers than when they could not.

Jensen and Tolman (14), in one of the earliest separation experiments, studied the short-term effects of separation of mother-infant monkey pairs (Macaca nemestrina) for less than one hour and found that the infants screamed almost continuously during the separation. The mothers attacked their own cages and tried to escape. On return of the infant, there was a striking increase in the intensity of the mother-infant relationship. This study demonstrated that even an extremely short-term separation had severe effects on both mother and infant.

In a series of studies, Kaufman and Rosenblum (15) compared the separation reactions of infant pig tail monkeys (Macaca nemestrina) and infant bonnet groups (Macaca radiata). Their separation studies differed in several key ways from those previously described. In their studies, subjects lived in groups consisting of several adult females, at least one adult male and some adolescents. Separation was accomplished by removing a mother from the group, leaving her infant with the remaining members. Before separation, bonnet groups were observed to spend long periods of time in passive contact with each other, in contrast to pig tails, who did not make much physical contact, except to engage in active social interactions such as grooming, aggression, etc. Group mothering was common among the bonnet females, whereas the pig tails had a specific mother-infant bond with the infant rarely spending time with other adults. Following removal of the mother, the pig tail infants showed both the protest and despair stages. Unlike the pig tails, the bonnet infants showed only a slight protest and then became attached to the other adult group members. These studies were important in terms of the different methodology used to accomplish separation, that is, removal of the mother from a group rather than the infant from the mother, as well as in highlighting the importance of cross-species studies with respect to the relationship between the nature of maternal attachment, group attachment, and the effects of separation.

Hinde's group in England has focused its attention on the short- and long-term effects of short separations of rhesus monkeys (17). Their animals also live in groups consisting of a male, two to three females, and their young. Separation was accomplished by removing the mother from the infant's sight. In some of their original work, the age of the infants at the time of the original separation was 30 to 32 days, but the length of separation was six days. The infants responded to removal of the mother with behaviors similar to those described above for the pig tail infants, that is, both protest and despair behaviors. Upon reunion, three of the four infants returned to the preseparation level of activity within a week, but the fourth showed less activity up to four weeks afterwards. It was also noted that the less an infant had been in contact with his mother before separation, the less clinging he displayed on return and the more quickly he returned to behavior similar to that seen before separation. Hinde's work has demonstrated that the nature of the preseparation relationship directly affects the severity of the reaction to a six-day removal of the mother. Several other aspects of early separation have been studied by Hinde, including the length of separation and the long-term effects of early separation experiences. He found that the effects of a mere six-day absence of the mother at 30 to 32 days were clearly discernible in the behavior of the infant monkeys five months later. When the previously separated infants were confronted with strange objects, they were less likely to approach them than were the controls with no history of separation.

Other separation studies of importance have been done by Mitchell et al. (18), who studied the effects of separations of rhesus monkeys from their mothers at three different age periods: two months, three-and-a-half months, and five months. At all ages the infants exhibited signs of protest and despair even with a short separation period. This group reports that six of the 24 infants used in their studies showed clear signs of detachment when reunited with their mothers. That is, the mothers would try to retrieve the infants as usual, but the infants would screech and run away before establishing any ventral contact.

Without doubt, the mother-infant social relationship has received considerable attention. Mother-infant separation studies have been done many times with several species. The reaction of rhesus infants is surprisingly predictable, though there is certainly individual variation. Severance of the mother-infant bond in rhesus monkeys results in the development of a behavioral picture very similar to anaclitic depression. This picture varies with the species being studied, the nature of the mother-infant relationship prior to separation, the length of the separation, the conditions during separation, etc. In some ways this separation model may be a prototype for other depressions and, if so, a variety of social, biochemical, and rehabilitative studies could be successfully undertaken. In part, the usefulness of a model lies in these kinds of studies that may help elucidate the mechanisms underlying the abnormal behavior state produced.

The technique of peer separation has several advantages which make it a useful complement to mother-infant separation studies. In the case of peers, one is truly manipulating affectional bonds, and when a separation reaction occurs, it can be viewed more as an emotional reaction than as a survival or adaptive response.

Although mother-infant separation disrupts an affectional bond, it is complicated by the infant's dependence on the mother in terms of survival. The ensuing response upon separation has thus been frequently viewed as the infant's attempt at adaptation for survival. From a research standpoint, there was a serious question about the effects of disrupting peer bonds. Recent studies indicate that severe reactions can indeed be elicited via separation from objects other than mother. When infants are reared in a peer-only situation described above, and then subjected to repeated short-term separations from each other, they show a reaction very similar to that shown by rhesus infants separated from their mothers, that is, a protest and despair stage. When reunited following each separation, they show a great deal of ventral clinging.

Age is an extremely important factor in determining the form that separation reactions take following peer separations. When the age of the animal is under one year, they show the biphasic reaction described by Bowlby. However, when they are about three years of age and are subjected to repeated separations from each other, their separation reaction is characterized by hyperactivity; that is, protest, characterized by increases in locomotion and environmental exploration and decreases in passivity. These behaviors, which are typical of the protest stage, persist throughout a separation period as long as 14 days. There is no evidence available so far that three-year-olds exhibit behaviors typical of the despair stage following separation.

An overview would therefore indicate that separation studies thus far provide a useful model for certain aspects of a specific syndrome, i.e., depression. Separation is not the only technique to produce animal models for depression. One particularly interesting technique involves the production of a syndrome resembling "learned helplessness" described by Seligman (22), using dogs and rats. In the instance of mother-infant separation, the case for a monkey analogue for human anaclitic depression seems strong. This particular model is becoming sufficiently well defined behaviorally so that brain biochemical studies, psychophysiological studies, and both social and biological rehabilitative approaches can be tried. Great caution, however, should be exercised in viewing anaclitic depression as a prototype or model for all depressions. This is why separation studies have recently been extended to older subjects. Theories about separation and depression are incomplete if they fail to take into consideration the age of the organism as a factor in determining response to separation. Efforts to produce a despairlike state in older subjects are continuing, and the reaction of several more age groups to separation experiences needs to be determined. Also, the possible role of early separation experiences in predisposing a subject to more severe reactions to separations later in life is being pursued in rhesus monkeys.

An initial pilot study in this area suggests that rhesus monkeys which have undergone maternal separation plus a short period of environmental deprivation early in life respond quite differently to separation one to two years later than do control animals that have not had the early separation and deprivation experiences. The reaction of the early traumatized group to separation tends toward increases in most self-directed behaviors. On reunion with each other following separation, they do not engage in typical reunion behaviors such as clinging to each other. The control group without the early traumatic experiences responds to separation in terms of hyperactivity, and upon reunion they spend much of their time engaging in clinging and reunion type behaviors.

An Approach to Biological Studies in Primate Models

One of the reasons for creating primate models for behavior disorders is to facilitate direct biochemical studies. It is hoped to study rhesus monkey subjects with induced syndromes of psychopathology by directly examining the relationships between brain neurotransmitters and the abnormal behaviors exhibited. This area of research is in its infancy and this discussion is therefore largely an outline of approaches being used, rather than a presentation of specific data.

The basic idea is to use primate models to examine the critical relationship among brain, behavior, and peripheral metabolism. The general approaches can be divided into three areas: (1) experimental alteration of brain amines with the study of the subsequent behavioral effects and effects on urinary metabolites; (2) social induction of syndromes of abnormal behavior and study of consequent biological changes; and (3) biological rehabilitative methods following social and biological induction methods. Work in these areas is currently under way. Despite external pressures to do so, it would have been premature to engage in biochemical studies until the behavioral aspects of primate models had been sufficiently well established, since the weakest link in most behavioral biochemical research has been the behavioral aspect. It is also important to consider the problem of combining a social experiment, where it is necessary for animals to live or be tested together in groups, with the collection of biological specimens. For example, in some studies in other laboratories examining the relationship between brain biogenic amines and primate social behavior, the animals generally live together in small groups. Urine collection is accomplished by pulling an animal from the group and putting him in a restraining chair. This technique seems undesirable, since there are considerable data which indicate severe and persistent effects on primate group and individual social behaviors following removal and reintroduction of members. If group social behavior is used as the major index of drug effect, a hopelessly confused situation ensues.

Perspectives

The relationships between psychoanalysis and experimental primatology can be summarized as involving three major areas: (1) the effects of differential early rearing conditions on the development of a variety of social behaviors; (2) the operationalization of psychoanalytic concepts; and (3) experimental psychopathology. These three areas are obviously interrelated. One of the problems has been that most investigators doing research on the social behavior of primates do not have clinical background or experience. On the other hand, most people with a primary clinical interest do not want to spend their time doing experimental primatology in a laboratory setting, nor do they, in turn, have the expertise to do so. There are, however, some major changes occurring, in that there is a group of people who have both clinical interests and interests in animal behavioral research, including primates. It is quite important that this development be encouraged, since the two fields have much to contribute to each other's advancement. There have been many communication problems in the past between the two fields. Clinical terms have been used far too loosely by some animal behavior researchers, and there has been an excessive concentration on the use of conditioning techniques rather than more social paradigms. As a result of this and other philosophical issues, clinicians have often been uninterested in primate behavior.

In summary, the major areas of special interest for psychiatrists in primate behavioral research probably include the development of attachment behaviors, the effects of social isolation, separation studies, the possible experimental simulation of learned helplessness, and use of primate models to study the interactions between social and biological determinants of behavior. It is in these areas that work has been and is being conducted which may have potential clinical usefulness. Investigators may indeed be quite close to developing viable and acceptable animal models for depression which may facilitate a more comprehensive understanding of this particular syndrome and enable studies to be done which are currently impossible to perform utilizing human beings. The rest of medicine has long used nonhuman primates to advance knowledge, and there is no logical reason why psychoanalysis should not do the same.

References

1. Harlow, H. F. The nature of love. *Amer. Psychol., 13,* 673-685, 1958.
2. Harlow, H. F., and Suomi, S. J. Nature of love—simplified. *Amer. Psychol., 25,* 161-168, 1970.
3. Mason, W. A. The effects of environmental restriction on the social de-

velopment of rhesus monkeys. In C. H. Southwick (Ed.), *Primate Social Behavior.* Princeton: Van Nostrand, 1963. Pp. 161-173.

4. HARLOW, H. F. Early social deprivation and later behavior in the monkey. In A. Abrams, H. H. Garner, and J. E. P. Tomal (Eds.), *Unfinished Tasks in the Behavioral Sciences.* Baltimore: Williams and Wilkins, 1964. Pp. 154-173.
5. SEAY, B., ALEXANDER, B. K., and HARLOW, H. F. Maternal behavior of socially deprived rhesus monkeys. *J. Abnorm. and Soc. Psychol., 69*:4, 345-354, 1964.
6. MILLER, R. E., MIRSKY, A., CARL, W. F., and SAKATA, T. Hyperphagia and polydipsia in socially isolated rhesus monkeys. *Science, 165,* 1027-1028, 1969.
7. SUOMI, S. J., HARLOW, H. F., and MCKINNEY, W. T. Monkey psychiatrists. *Amer. J. Psychiat., 128*:8, 927-932, 1972.
8. HARLOW, H. F., and SUOMI, S. J. Social recovery by isolation-reared monkeys. *Proc. Nat. Acad. Sci., 68,* 1534-1538, 1971.
9. MCKINNEY, W. T., YOUNG, L. D., SUOMI, S. J., and DAVIS, J. M. Chlorpromazine treatment of disturbed monkeys. *Arch. Gen. Psychiat.* (In press)
10. ROBERTSON, J., and BOWLBY, J. Responsis of young children to separation from their mothers. *Courier du Centre International de l'Enfants, 2,* 131-142, 1952.
11. SPITZ, R. A. Anaclitic depression: An inquiry into the genesis of psychiatric conditions in early childhood. In *Psychoanalytic Study of the Child,* Vol. II. New York: International Universities Press, 1946. Pp. 313-342.
12. SEAY, W., HANSEN, E., and HARLOW, H. F. Mother-infant separation in monkeys. *J. Child Psych. Psychiat., 3,* 123-132, 1962.
13. SEAY, W., and HARLOW, H. F. Maternal separation in the rhesus monkey. *J. Nerv. Ment. Dis., 140*:6, 434-441, 1965.
14. JENSEN, G. D., and TOLMAN, C. W. Mother-infant relationship in the monkey, macaca nemestrina: The effect of brief separation and mother-infant specificity. *J. Comp. Physiol. Psychol., 55,* 131-136, 1962.
15. KAUFMAN, I. C., and ROSENBLUM, L. A. Depression of infant monkeys separated from their mothers. *Science, 155,* 1030-1031, 1967.
16. ROSENBLUM, L. A., and KAUFMAN, I. C. Variations in infant development and response to maternal loss in monkeys. *Amer. J. Orthopsychiat., 83,* 418-426, 1968.
17. HINDE, R. A., and SPENCER-BOOTH, Y. Effects of brief separation from mother of rhesus monkeys. *Science, 173,* 111-118, 1971.
18. MITCHELL, G. D. Abnormal behavior in primates. In L. Rosenblum (Ed.). *Primate Behavior.* New York: Academic Press, 1970.
19. SUOMI, S. J., DOMEK, C. J., and HARLOW, H. F. Effects of repetitive infant-infant separation of young monkeys. *J. Abnorm. Psychol., 76,* 161-172, 1970.
20. MCKINNEY, W. T., SUOMI, S. J., and HARLOW, H. F. Depression in primates. *Amer. J. Psychiat., 127,* 1313-1320, 1971.
21. MCKINNEY, W. T., SUOMI, S. J., and HARLOW, H. F. Repetitive peer separations of juvenile age rhesus monkeys. *Arch. Gen. Psychiat., 27,* 200-203, 1972.

22. SELIGMAN, M. E. P., and GRAVES, D. Non-transient learned helplessness. *Psychonomic Science, 19,* 191-192, 1970.
23. YOUNG, L. D., SUOMI, S. J., HARLOW, H. F., and MCKINNEY, W. T. Early stress and later response to separation in rhesus monkeys. *Amer. J. Psychiat., 130*:4, 400-405, 1973.
24. BOWLBY, J. *Maternal Care and Mental Health.* New York: Schocken Books, 1966.

Discussion

RICHARD G. VAN GELDER, PH.D.

There is always a sense of pleasure and righteousness, and even achievement, when members of another "religion" recognize that your gods may have some worthwhile attributes. This analogy seems applicable to the present exchange between psychoanalysts and primatologists. My remarks on Dr. McKinney's fine paper represent essentially the viewpoint of a fundamentalist, bearing approximately the relationship of a pantheist to a monotheist, of one who deals with 4,000 species of mammals to one who deals with a chosen one. I will discuss the use of animals, specifically mammals, as research subjects, and express some caveats concerning the use of animals in scientific investigations. To express it concisely, "Monkeys ain't men," and vice versa. Therefore, attempts to apply data derived from one group of animals to another group can be quite erroneous.

Why do we study primates? The unfortunate term "nonhuman primates" suggests that we study them because we believe we are thereby working with the animals closest to man. In what sense are primates most similar to man? Certainly we developed from the same evolutionary group, but branchings have taken place at different points. For example, rhesus monkeys diverged from the lineage of man considerably before the great apes—the gorillas, orangutans and chimpanzees. The essential point, however, is that they all diverged. We are studying groups of animals that have developed in different directions from man.

In selecting primates because they are evolutionarily derived at some point from the same group as man, we seem also to be assuming that they are man's closest behavioral relatives. This assumption presumes that all behavior is genetically determined, and precludes the possible influence of learning and culture upon behavior, conclusions with which most people would not totally agree. Therefore, monkeys and apes may not be man's closest behavioral relatives, leaving the choice of the rhesus monkey as the object for study open to scrutiny and question. We must take into consideration not only possible behavioral correlations between man and certain nonprimates, but also the vast number of behavioral variations among primates.

For example, in researching dominance, we tend to assume that male dominance is the rule. There are primates whose society is characterized by male dominance, but there are also primates whose society reflects strong female dominance. Female spider monkeys, for instance, are larger than the males and possess a clitoris as long as or longer than the male's penis. Their society is dominated by the females. In studying female dominance, one might investigate nonprimates, such as spotted hyenas. The society of the spotted hyena is also dominated by females. Hyenas seem to have rather catholic appetites, and in order to protect the young, the females may have had to grow big enough to fight off the males who would eat their own children. In hyena dens where cubs live, there is an opening large enough for the female, plus several small openings made by the young which allow them to escape being eaten by mothers in other clans (1).

Another animal whose behavior and society might be viewed as analogous to human behavior and society is the lion, particularly the Serengeti lion. Schaller (2) undertook the study of lions partly on the basis that it might be wrong to look for human prototype behavior in a species that is not carnivorous. He chose to examine the life of a carnivore, because it may be similar to how early man lived. Most of our monkeys, of course, are not carnivorous.

It might also be important to note that below the level of the great apes (the gorillas, chimpanzees, orangutans, and perhaps even gibbons), self-identity does not seem to exist. Given a mirror, a rhesus monkey makes social gestures as if there were another animal in the mirror. A chimpanzee, however, quickly learns to recognize that he is the animal in the mirror; he makes personal gestures, picks his teeth, explores his ears, and so on. An anesthetized chimp, experienced with mirrors, who has had his eyebrows and ears painted red, awakens and immediately recognizes that he is the animal in the mirror. He explores the places that have been altered. Below the level of the higher apes, such self-identity does not seem to exist. This may be of great importance in interpreting social behavior in animals.

Not only self-identity, but group identity, is an important consideration. Animals have culture; they transmit information from one generation to another, not only through genes, but through communication. For example, from cove to cove on the West Coast, sea lions talk different dialects. The implication here is that perhaps when we order a group of 50 rhesus monkeys of a certain age and sex, we are not getting as homogeneous a group as we might think. We have no idea of the previous history of these animals.

In cases where we do know the history of our experimental subjects, we must be careful to take this information into account and to accord it sufficient weight. An infant monkey bears the stamp of the background of its mother. Were the research monkeys taken from the wild, where one type of social structure existed, or had their ancestors been in captivity for several generations, where another culture had evolved? We probably know far more about rhesus monkeys in captivity than about these animals in the wild. In order to differentiate and define abnormal behavior, we must have a good idea of what is normal for the group. With regard to monkeys, normal would relate to the wild, free-living situation.

Just as the cultural derivation of the animal is relevant to the research study, so is the cultural placement. The animal is placed in a new environment, perhaps simulating a natural environment, perhaps not. The laboratory colony must, of course, be regarded as a culturally deprived group. Regardless of the living conditions of research animals, these conditions must seriously figure into the evaluation of data deriving from such research.

Thus far, I have attempted to raise certain issues which point up possible pitfalls in extrapolating data from research on certain mammals and interpreting it in terms of others. In other words, I have stressed the differences between man and even the "non-human primate," and differences in the focal points of the primatologist and the psychoanalyst. However, there is a relationship between the two fields, especially from the perspective of evolution. Obviously, both primatologists and psychoanalysts are dealing with mammals. Freud certainly grew up under the influence of Darwin, since Darwin was a common name in the household of any cultured family of that time. In his later writings, Freud focused on a fundamental aspect of evolution, that survival of the species requires reproduction, and survival of the young to the point where they, too, can reproduce. As a fundamentalist, I view the psychoanalyst's concern with sexuality as a proper concern, since reproduction is a fundamental part of evolution. Situations which cause sexual malfunction have no survival value for the species. If copulation does not take place because of psychological factors, reproduction will cease, and certain animals will be lost to the species and to the gene pool. If reproduction does occur, but psychological factors prevent good mothering, again the offspring may not survive to reproduce. It has been demonstrated that "poor mothers make poor mothers." From a fundamentalist point of view, I find the importance of sexuality a most significant contribution of Freud. Interdisciplinary studies in this area hold great promise for the future.

References

1. KRUUK, H. *The Spotted Hyena. A Study of Predation and Social Behavior.* Chicago: Univ. of Chicago Press, 1972.
2. SCHALLER, G. B. *The Serengeti Lion. A Study of Predator-Prey Relations.* Chicago: Univ. of Chicago Press, 1972.

4

Early Sexual Differences and Development

PETER B. NEUBAUER, M.D.

THE TOPIC OF PSYCHOANALYSIS AND SEXUALITY brings to mind two interrelated concepts: the original proposition of infantile sexuality and recent formulations concerning genital sex differentiation. Data from various fields, and particularly from investigations into developmental variations apparently related to sex differences, seem to confirm Freud's postulation of the presence of a sexual drive from earliest infancy.

The original theory of infantile sexuality was closely bound to the proposition of phases of development. Stages of development were outlined, at least in the beginning, from the viewpoint of libidinal organization. The drive organization led to the proposition linking phases of development to a biological core, assuming that the drive is, indeed, the biological expression of the need of psychic function. Thus, if one accepts phases of organization such as oral, anal, and phallic, one may accept, at least partially, the proposition that the stages of development evolve under the auspices of a hierarchy of influences within certain time periods of life in which specific conflicts occur.

It is not possible today to discuss sexuality in terms of the libidinal phases alone, since to do so would neglect the work of the last 30 years (1). Propositions previously considered from the viewpoint of libidinal or drive organization alone must now be considered in light of recent developments in ego psychology, which correlate the many variables of ego function. One can no longer speak of orality from the viewpoint of libido organization alone, but must consider the totality of the experience in which mother-child feeding and care take place. Similarly, one cannot speak of anality without taking into account various aspects of the child's internal-external functioning.

In the child psychoanalytic literature, differences between boys and girls are discussed more in terms of the vicissitudes of the libidinal stages and the conflicts associated with them than in terms of the end product in overt behavior. These differences in the end product are best observed during the latency phase. They are usually described in relation to the processes of gender identification resulting from the oedipal conflict. As to the preoedipal phase, the accent in the past has been on the similarities between boys and girls. However, with the advent of ego psychology and the concomitant interest in infant studies, several sex differences have been observed to occur in the early stages of development. These differences are of interest not only in relation to their bearing upon gender identification, but also in regard to their implications for identification and assessment of pathology and normality in boys and girls.

The distribution of certain types of pathology so clearly differs between the sexes that these clinical entities seem very closely linked indeed to the sex difference. Our inability to understand them better from the inference of early sexuality is somewhat amazing. We have not yet found in the treatment of such cases sufficiently clear genetic roots to link them to, and comprehend the significance of, the differential sex factor.

Among the familiar clinical conditions which occur significantly more frequently in boys than in girls are reading disorders, speech disturbances, difficulty in bowel control, hyperactivity, and aggressive behavior. Reading disorders, for example, present six to eight times more frequently in boys than in girls. On the other hand, there are specific disorders which appear more consistently in girls than in boys. These include problems of overdependency, emotional overcontrol, bowel retention, and anorexia. Analysis of the patterning of symptoms suggests that impulse control may be at the core of the problem in both sexes—lack of impulse control in boys, overcontrol in girls.

Research Studies

Having previously studied distribution and patterning of disturbances in relation to sex differences using boys and girls from clinical populations (2), we decided to use nonclinical populations for the present study. We thus hoped to be able to compare the degree to which children who do not come to our clinics share the variety of difficulties, conflicts, problems, or disorders with children who do come for our services.

We studied 50 children from a nursery school, following their development into late latency. Development was studied on a cross-sectional basis, using Anna Freud's profile to outline our data. The findings were criticized on the basis that they could not be generalized, since we used only New York middle-class children who suffered from specific conditions which were not generalizable. We therefore repeated the study with 50 children from a working-class population, so that we could note any substantial differences.

In profile, we grouped the children not according to disorders or diagnoses, but according to their ability to maintain their developmental progression. Symptoms were frequently present, but they did not interfere with the developmental process. The children were grouped around four developmental categories, which will not be discussed in detail at this time. Contrary to our expectations in using a profile of this sort, our findings seemed to fall naturally into boy-girl categories, and we were compelled to study the differences between the boys and the girls, aged three-and-a-half to approximately eight years, that is, into late latency. We especially investigated those categories which reflected significant differences between boys and girls.

From a large bank of data, we selected for examination items connected with the following: object relations, such as dependency, clinging, separation anxiety, as well as opinion of the self and idealization of objects outside the self; ego functions, such as impulse control, coordination, and language skills; and drive influences, such as those oral erotic aspects reflected in the various feeding disorders. We also considered affect, in terms of constriction or expansion, orchestration of affective interplay, sadness, moodiness, and so on. There exists a good deal of information about drive organization, but affect as a function of ego organization is relatively unknown. It must be examined, because the affective differences between the sexes become immediately outstanding and serve as criteria for the differentiation of developmental groupings of boys and girls.

Some of our results confirm findings already in the literature. For example, girls demonstrated a significantly greater amount of oral activity, such as thumbsucking, than did boys. From the age of three-and-a-half, girls also manifested a greater tendency toward daydreaming and social isolation, with behavior characterized by withdrawal, lack of participation in group activities, and inhibition of aggression. They did not hold their own when attacked, did not fight back, did not show anger. These observations were made by parents, teachers, and observers in our nursery schools, as well as by clinicians in individual interviews and by psychologists on the basis of psychological testing. Obviously, evidence of overcontrol of impulse was considerably greater in the girls than in the boys.

Affective considerations showed greater tendency among girls toward mood swings, sad expression, crying, sensitivity, and inability to openly express their feelings with others. By contrast, the behavior of the boys was outwardly directed. They engaged in such activities as fighting and running, which signaled greater interplay of self and environment, self and peers, and which permitted greater expression of aggressive impulses.

Discussion

In our research with clinical populations of children, we found that on the whole, girls were brought for treatment at an earlier age than boys. The age difference was small, but significant. This seems to suggest that the mood swings and withdrawing behavior of girls are more upsetting to parents than the aggressive, outwardly directed behavior of boys. There is obviously a tendency to interpret the data presented above as evidence of greater pathology in girls. However, the regularity with which these behaviors manifested themselves in the nonclinical population of girls we were studying convinced us that this was not so.

The girls were placed in developmental groupings which seemed to indicate greater conflicts with less resolution of conflict. This forced us to question our procedures. Were our data correct? Were they biased? Were we assessing girls as if they should behave like boys, and if they did not, were we considering them deviant, not from the norm, but from the behavior expected of certain age groups? Or were we indeed dealing with organizational shifts in girls which should have provided us with clues concerning the possibility of additional stages or steps in the development of the girl?

One cannot help but feel that, as the child enters the phallic organization and sex differences occur, there may indeed be some shifts in orientation of conflicts—shifts, not increases. The boy may run, shoot, play cowboy, and so exercise his assertiveness and experience his own functioning in relationship to his environment and his peer group. The girl, on the other hand, may use as the arena of her functioning the area of internal sensitivity, the area of feeling exploration, of social refinement, of evolvement of an image beyond the behavioral expression of the internal mental and emotional picture. These shifts did not show the persistency characteristic of certain affective modalities or behaviors deriving from oral fixation. Rather, these differences, considered longitudinally, appear to be transient.

We concluded that it is important for the clinician—and not only for those who study normal development—to have two developmental scales, one for the boys and one for the girls. Boys and girls are sufficiently different that, in assessing a child, we should not have in mind a single scale of normal development against which we check the developmental readiness of that child. We cannot use a systematology which does not sufficiently take into account the significant differences which are sex-determined—the different stages, conflicts, rates of resolution and progression in the developmental process.

Conclusion

Although the data linking variations in the normal development of boys and girls to sex differentiation are interesting and important, we do not at the present time have sufficient knowledge to link the sets of information deriving from the study of earliest infancy to factors which would explain their psychic relevance. Still needed is an outline of the internal steps which lead from the earliest sensitivity of skin conduction, to differences in touch responses, to motor skill. A genetic continuum has to be established. For instance, there are congenital factors affecting different areas of function. Infant girls have a lower threshold of jet stimulation, a higher basal skin conductance at birth than do infant boys. These factors suggest a sex difference in the regulation of internal impulses and the dawn of ego functions. The girl obviously has a more rapid maturation, which is confirmed in faster bone and tooth growth. Speech development seems to occur earlier, and toilet training is generally achieved earlier.

Freud stressed the role of constitutional factors affecting differences in drive vicissitudes between the sexes. He described suppression of the component of aggression in women and suggested that more constraint is applied to the libido when it is pressed into the service of feminine function. Thus, one must take into account the contribution of aggressive strivings to sex differentiation and to gender identity. How do congenital factors recognizable in earliest infancy lead to reading disorders or speech disorders? How do they contribute to gender identity?

We know from our vast accumulated knowledge of the development of infants that there is complexity from infancy on. Research into the development of sex differences and gender identification must take into account the sensory and autonomic functions of the early ego involvement, and the fact that these functions soon become part of the totality of the baby's functioning and his selective relationship with the environment—his selecting from the environment those stimuli which fit his own needs. These processes determine not only the ego variation from infant to infant, but also those variations which seem to be connected with the sex differences. The interplay of the variety of ego functions—sensory, autonomic, affective—with the libidinal drive organization contributes to the overall development of the child and to the process of gender identification.

References

1. Stoller, R. The bedrock of masculinity and femininity: Bisexuality. *Arch. Gen. Psychiat., 26,* 207-212, 1972.
2. Neubauer, P. B., and Beller, E. K. Sex differences and symptom patterns in early childhood. *J. Amer. Acad. Child Psychiat., 2:*3, 417-433, 1963.

Discussion

Eleanor Galenson, M.D.

Dr. Neubauer has discussed certain differences he found in relation to the development of boys and girls, and has raised the question of the regularity of phasic emergence. I will present findings concerning these issues in a younger age group, in infants during their second year of life.

In 1966 Dr. Roiphe and I established a research nursery at the Albert Einstein College of Medicine in order to investigate sexual behavior and the development of symbolic functioning of children during the second year of life. By the end of June, 1972, we completed six full years of operation and have thus far studied in detail 43 children.

To the best of our knowledge, this is the first research effort to study this specific area in a comprehensive and systematic manner. We have followed the emergence of awareness of anal and urinary functioning and have uncovered evidence of endogenous sexual sensations, interest of the child in his own genitals, and reactions to the anatomical difference between the sexes. In some children, we have found evidence of mutilation fears arising from this discrimination. Furthermore, we have discovered considerable relationship between these body image developments and the emergence of symbolism both in play and speech.

General Statement of Research Hypothesis and Some General Findings

Roiphe (1) postulated that at some time between the ages of 16 and 24 months children *normally and regularly* would show evidence of sexual sensation, interest in their own genitals, and reactions to the anatomical difference between the sexes (which was referred to as an "early genital phase"). In general, we have found that ordinarily a child will pass through this phase with only moderate behavioral reflections of the underlying sexual arousal. These behavioral reflections include significantly increased frequency and intensity of manipulation of the genitals, including frank masturbatory activity and interest not only in their own genitals but in those of other children and adults as well.

Reflections of this sexual interest and arousal have appeared in play behaviors which include such sequences as visual and tactile examination of the genital area of dolls and toy animals. *We have noted certain structural similarities* between the bodily experiences mentioned previously and many sequences of play behavior. For example, the child who fills and empties containers, or builds towers, or pushes at protuberances, or plays with faucets and puddles is thereby reproducing some internally experienced sensation. Through the tracing of such play patterning, we have studied the derivatives of anal, urinary, and genital sensations and concerns. In some of the more advanced children, verbal symbolization provides further evidence of the effect of such body schematization.

Some children have shown evidence of profound mutilation fears arising from the discrimination of the anatomical differences between the sexes. These fears, on the basis of our work carried out thus far, are reflected behaviorally in increased general irritability, mood changes, loss of bowel and bladder control, fear of the flush of the toilet, and a variety of other fears. In the more verbal child, there is the expressed fear that the penis will fall off and be flushed down the toilet. Play behavioral reflections of these mutilation anxieties are abundant. A little girl places a stick between her legs, points out and is distressed by broken crayons, misses small parts of toys, examines dolls' genital areas with evident discomfort and shifts her interest upwards to other body areas, such as the umbilicus. She also adopts a doll as a constant eating companion; it is not only a *boy* doll in appearance, but is named "boy" in contrast to her other dolls. A little boy examines his teddy bear and other animals repeatedly in the perineal area, and ends up by masturbating with this bear.

In several children, boy/girl differentiation, which had already been established in relation to pictures in children's books and on puppet figures, has been lost. Under the impact of the anxiety concerning the genital difference, some children regress in their symbolic functioning, both in the verbal and nonverbal areas. Whereas this is a transient affair in most children, we do not yet know whether there are any long-term effects of such symbolic distortion.

Mutilation fears seem to arise when there is a confluence of the following three conditions:

1. Temporally, after there are indications of the normal sexual arousal, some time between 16 and 24 months.
2. The child, in the context of his sexual arousal, has had the opportunity to observe the anatomical difference between the sexes.
3. The child has earlier had some experience which severely disturbed the stable body schematization (such as severe physical illness, pain, surgical intervention), or any experience which interfered with the developing mental image of the mother (such as loss of a parent or maternal depression).

Data Analysis of Fifteen of the Children

All were exposed to parents' nudity regularly, although this ranged from occasional exposure to prolonged play with naked parents. All were exposed to parental toileting at times.

In regard to the initial discovery of the genitals, this occurred in boys some time between the fifth and eighth months, in contrast to the girls, where this occurred between 10½ and 14 months of age. This first discovery seems to be part of the general body exploration and schematization. Having once discovered the genitals, the boys continue to touch them fleetingly, whereas most of the girls do not.

Then, at about 15 to 18 months, there is the period of increased genital handling which we have described, following very closely upon the emergence of anal and urinary awareness, with which it is intimately intertwined. In the girls, resumption of genital manipulation tends to emerge somewhat later and then is replaced in many by indirect genital stimulation—rocking on horses or other objects, or thigh pressure. In the boys, the genital manipulation has never really ceased since its first emergence at five to eight months, and continues on after the intensification during the early genital phase of 15 to 18 months.

Most of the boys both pointed at and acquired a word for the penis during the early genital phase, whereas none of the girls pointed to their genitals and only two had a word label for the vagina.

Data concerning the emergence of patterns of anal and urinary awareness, as well as the complex effects of genital awareness and awareness of the genital difference, have been analyzed and will be presented elsewhere.

The emergence of genital awareness, along with anal and urinary body schematization during the second half of the second year of life, seems to have a far-reaching organizing influence upon other areas of development, including object relations, the separation-individuation process, and nascent ego functions.

Reference

1. Roiphe, H. On an early genital phase, with an addendum on genesis. *Psychoanalytic Study of the Child*, Vol. XXII. New York: International Universities Press, 1968. Pp. 348-365.

5

Latency, Its Tasks, and Its Settings: Overview

MIO FREDLAND, M.D.

THE DISCOVERY OF INFANTILE SEXUALITY and the impact of its vicissitudes in later life was Freud's major contribution. But, to the surprise of Freud, the intensity of the infant's and young child's first years of libidinal drive was not sustained. Rather, it was followed by an interim period of apparent sexual quiescence, which is unique in the human species.

Latency is understood in our society to comprise a period of childhood between six and twelve and is assumed to possess certain features: there is a reworking of the ego-superego structures, and with the development of new defenses come a capacity for a higher degree of sublimation and a possible diminution of instinctual drive. Numerous contemporary authors use the term latency to mean a period of complete cessation or absence of all sexual activity.

The tasks of latency include: (1) the renunciation of direct instinctual gratification; (2) increasing the emphasis on reality; (3) the establishment of secondary process; (4) the furthering of achievement and sublimation; and (5) the establishment of moral and ethical standards.

Latency, as so defined, applied in a stable western civilization, as Freud knew it. But changing society, particularly in the United States where numerous subcultures now form a significant segment of the population, has prompted a reexamination of Freud's views.

Freud's position on latency and some subsequent views will be considered. Latency in other cultures will be compared with the traditional western one. Some possible alternative hypotheses will be presented.

Freud's Views of Latency

Freud discussed, over a period of more than 40 years, how and why latency comes about. His two main views were that it occurs (1) because of the ontogenetic and phylogenetic "clock," including here the drive-diminution theory,* and (2) as the result of a constellation of ego defenses, in which cultural standards and expectations play a part.

In 1925, in *Inhibitions, Symptoms and Anxiety,* Freud put forth his phylogenetic views. "Something momentous must have occurred in the vicissitudes of the human species which has left behind this interruption in the sexual development of the individual as an historical precipitate" ** (1). In 1923, in "Two Encyclopedia Articles," he stated, "This diphasic development of the sexual function—in two stages, interrupted by the latency period—appears to be a biological peculiarity of the human species. . . ." (2). In 1919, in *A Child is Being Beaten,* he said, ". . . These incestuous loves probably pass away because their time is over, because the children have entered on a new phase of development in which they . . . recapitulate from the history of mankind the repression of an incestuous choice" (3). In the same paper he added, "The origin of the Oedipus complex itself and the destiny which compels man, probably alone among all animals, to begin his sexual life over, first like all other creatures in his early childhood and then, after a long interruption, once

---

* See below for a discussion of this theory.

** Freud was referring to Ferenczi's speculations that the glacial periods had a catastrophic and inhibiting effect upon primitive man and that this is recapitulated as latency in our individual lives (19).

more at the age of puberty are problems connected with man's archaic heritage."

In 1924, in "The Dissolution of the Oedipus Complex," he stated, "Another view is that the Oedipus complex must collapse because the time has come for its disintegration just as the milk teeth fall out when the permanent ones begin to grow. Although the majority of human beings go through the Oedipus complex as an individual experience, it is nevertheless a phenomenon which is determined and laid down by heredity and which is bound to pass away when the next preordained phase of development sets in. This being so, it is of no great importance what the occasions are which allow this to happen, or, indeed, whether any such occasions can be discovered at all" (4).

Although there is a great deal of controversy at present around the entire concept of drive, for the purposes of this discussion it will be assumed to mean that in every human being there is a set of impulses such as exist in lower animals, but which are coupled with an affective component. Thus, drive has an aim, an object, and an energic factor. Drive, therefore, leads the person from a state of unpleasure to pleasure through a diminution of tension.

Freud made a number of contradictory statements on the subject of drive in latency at different periods in his work. The idea that latency is an actual period of "biological lessening of drive activities" was stated specifically by Freud once, in 1926, in *The Question of Lay Analysis:* [During latency] . . . "Sexuality normally advances no further; on the contrary, the sexual urges diminish in strength" (5).

He restated this idea in two of his last works—*Moses and Monotheism,* in 1939 (6), and *An Outline of Psychoanalysis,* in 1940 (7). The germs of sexual impulses are present in the newborn, they continue to develop for a time (*Three Essays*), but, at or about the fifth year, there is a halt and retrogression in sexual development which deserves to be called a period of latency.

Among the defenses which contribute to the onset and continuance of latency, repression plays a major part. Freud first mentioned repression in connection with latency in 1896, in a letter to Fliess (letter 46, 5/30/96) (8). He wrote that he thought there were two transitional periods "during which repression usually takes place, from about 8-10 years and 13-17 years." The first period was called latency by Fliess. Six months later Freud refined his view (letter 52, 6/12/96) (8), placing the period of repression between ages 8-14. Later, latency was revised to extend from the end of the fifth year (9)* until puberty at around eleven.

Freud's speculations regarding the ontogenetic and phylogenetic development of man led him to the following consideration of repression. In 1897, in letters 55 and 75 (8), he reflected that a crucial organic factor in repression was prehistoric man's assumption of an upright posture. Sight then replaced smell as the principal means of perceiving his environment. "The nose is lifted from the ground and hitherto meaningful and exciting sensations become repellent and even evoke disgust. Sexual excitation may awaken memories having to do with such old abandoned zones. This results in a release of unpleasure analogous to disgust . . . to put it crudely, the current memory stinks just as an actual object may stink; and just as we turn away our head and nose, so do the preconscious and our conscious apprehension turn away from the memory. This is repression."

In 1905, in *Three Essays,* he examined other defenses which appear in latency: "It is during this period of total or only partial latency that are built up the mental forces which are later to impede the course of the sexual instinct . . ."; ". . . germs of sexual impulses are already present in the new-born child and . . . develop for a time, but are then overtaken by a progressive process of suppression . . ."; and "Nothing is known for certain concerning the regularity and periodicity of this oscillating course of development." Then, speaking of sublimation and reaction-formation, he emphasized that "the activity of those [sexual]

---

* Deutsch (1944) (23) and Anna Freud (1949) (21) noted that latency is shorter than Freud had assumed, overlapping with the last year or two of the infantile sexual stages, and extending to pre-puberty only.

impulses does not cease even during this period of latency, though their energy is diverted, wholly or in great part, from their sexual use and directed to other ends" (10).

In 1908, in *Character and Anal Erotism,* he goes further: "During the period of life which may be called the period of sexual latency . . . reaction-formations, or counter-forces, such as shame, disgust and morality are created in the mind. They are actually formed at the expense of the excitations proceeding from the erotogenic zones." And, "One vicissitude of sexual excitation arising from erotogenic zones is that they become deflected from sexual aims and directed to others. This is sublimation" (9).

Sublimation was considered by Freud to play a paramount role in the development of the human species. Sublimation is a way in which instinctual demands can be met without repression. In 1909, in *Five Lectures,* he described sublimation as the "energy of infantile impulses having a higher and perhaps no longer sexual aim" (11). In *Three Essays,* he discussed sublimation extensively: "Sublimation begins in latency, and it is a diversion of sexual aims to new ones. . . . Some sexual activity may persist through the whole duration of latency. Reaction-formation is a sub-species of sublimation and in favorable conditions continues throughout life" (10).

He noted, in his 1914 study *On Narcissism,* that the component impulses have a special capacity for sublimation. In this paper he also stated that repression must be lifted in order for sublimation to occur, and that premature repression makes for grave interference with later sublimatory attempts (12).

In his consideration of the energic aspects of sublimation, he stated, in 1923 in *The Ego and the Id,* "When an object has to be given up there may be ego alterations by identification. This means a transformation of object libido into narcissistic libido which implies an abandonment of sexual aims, a desexualization, a kind of sublimation. This may be the universal road to sublimation . . . through the mediation of the ego." And "Every identification, including formation of the superego, is in the nature of a desexualization or even a sublimation" (13).

In 1924, in "The Dissolution of the Oedipus Complex," he posited that it was the abandonment of the original goal of the Oedipus which was central to the start of latency. When the Oedipus fails in its aims, "The child's ego turns away from the Oedipus complex by replacing object cathexes by identifications. The superego is formed by the introjection of the father into the ego. The superego takes over the severity of the father and perpetuates his prohibition against incest. Libidinal trends are in part desexualized and sublimated and in part are inhibited in aim and changed into impulses of affection. This process preserves the genital and paralyzes it. This is more than repression; it is destruction and abolition of the Oedipus complex. If it were only repression it would exert a pathogenic effect later" * (4).

In 1925, in *Inhibitions, Symptoms, and Anxiety,* he stated that the Oedipus "is not simply repressed, it is literally smashed to pieces." This is explained by the fact that "The danger situation in latency [is] anger of the superego" (1).

Fantasy formation was considered by Freud to be an adaptive defense during latency. In 1911, in *Formulations on the Two Principles of Mental Functioning,* he observed, "About the time the ego instincts are forced to obey the reality principle, the sexual instincts succumb to a wave of repression in latency and remain bound to the pleasure principle. Thus there is a close connection of ego instincts and reality and sexual instinct and fantasy" (14).

Freud noted, as well, that the stage of latency was subject to cultural influences and to variations. In 1935, in *An Autobiographical Study,* he said, "[Latency] can give rise to a complete interruption of sexual life [only] in cultural organizations which have made the suppression of infantile sexuality a part of their system. This is not the case with the majority of primitive peo-

---

* The concept of the superego has been expanded beyond Freud's original definition to include both parents and other important authority figures as introjects. Moreover, it should be noted that Freud in his later writings made a distinction in the psychosexual development of boys and girls. (*Consequences of the Anatomical Sex Distinction,* 1925, Standard Edition 19; *Female Sexuality,* 1931, Standard Edition 21; *New Introductory Lectures on Psychoanalysis,* 1933, Standard Edition 22.)

ples" (15). For, as he wrote in *Three Essays,* ". . . some sexual activity may persist through the whole duration of the latency period until . . . puberty"; ". . . [it is] an educational ideal from which individual development usually diverges at some point and often to a considerable degree" (10).

Post-Freudian Concepts of Latency

A number of excellent articles have been written on the diagnostic and therapeutic issues in latency. Here, however, only a few authors who have discussed concepts of latency will be cited.

As evidence that there is no such thing as a "true" latency in terms of drive-diminution, Malinowski (16) and Reich (17) in 1929 and 1932 described societies where children did not renounce sexual play or masturbation during latency. Muensterberger (18) expressed the same opinion later. Ferenczi (19) observed in 1913 that among the lower classes the children engaged in sexual practices throughout latency. Recently Money (20) stated that there was no complete psychosexual latency, citing as evidence a number of primitive societies where latency-age children of the second period * play at adult sexual behavior. This occurs only sporadically, however, in contrast to the more frequent sexual play until the age of five. He emphasized the absence, until puberty, of any romantic attachments in these games. Money prefers to call it a period of privacy, rather than latency.

In the writer's unpublished study of more than three hundred primitive societies, only 12 were discovered in which there is any discussion of childhood sexual practices, and most of these referred to later latency (i.e., the period from age 8 to 11). These 12 societies are alike only in the tolerant attitude of the adults to the sexual play of the children, as Money also found.

A review of 2,200 papers in the *Index Medicus* did not reveal any mention of latency sexual practices in children belonging to indigenous subcultures in the United States. This is a paradoxical finding in view of the widespread latency sexual practices known to exist by all who have worked with ghetto children.

Among many child analysts and others who work with children, there is a strong feeling that there is no diminution in sexual drive during latency. Rather, they believe, it is maintained intact from the Oedipal period, but subjected to different ego and superego mechanisms. They cite the ready availability of the sexual fantasies, and also the nearly ubiquitous practice of the playing of sexual games by latency children when circumstances permit.

Anna Freud in 1949 describes the child's struggle against masturbation as reaching its climax with the onset of latency, and the need to masturbate reasserting itself periodically throughout latency (21). One could infer from this that she believes the strength of the drive remains undiminished.

In 1965, however, she asserted the theory of the primary diminution of drive activity. "Extreme castration fear, death fears and wishes, together with the defenses against them, which dominate the scene at the height of the phallic-Oedipal phase, and which create the well known inhibitions, masculine over-compensations, passive and regressive modes of the period . . . disappear as if by magic as soon as the child takes the first steps into the latency period. . . . as an immediate reaction to the biologically determined lessening of drive activity" (22).

Many others have agreed. Among these, Deutsch referred to latency as ". . . a period of weakened sexual urges" (23). Bornstein stated that "sexual demands have become less exerting" in latency (24). There is probably a "biological diminution in the libidinal drive" (25). All of them have emphasized as well the importance of the maintenance of the new ego defenses, and training and education, in furthering adaptation to reality and socialization.

Closer to Freud's view was Buxbaum, who stated she had "not seen any child with a complete latency of sexual feelings," but

---

* Cf. A. Freud (21) and Bornstein (24), who divide latency children into two groupings, the first from 5½ to 8, the second from 8 to 10.

that "the child's reduced interest in sexual matters seems to be at least in part the result of repression . . . reinforced through compulsive-obsessive defenses" (26).

Erikson, in 1950, stated: "Infantile genitality, of course, is destined to remain rudimentary, a mere promise of things to come. If not specifically provoked into precocious manifestation by special frustrations or special customs, it is apt to lead to no more than a series of fascinating experiences which are frightening and pointless enough to be repressed during the stage which Freud called the latency period, i.e., the long delay of physical sexual maturation" (27).

Lampl (28), in 1953, reintroduced the idea of endocrinological changes. He reviewed the earlier views on the evolution of somatic phenomena and their importance in latency. In support of Freud's phylogenetic theory regarding the somatic pause in latency, he cited the theories of Darwin and others on variations which could be inherited. Lampl postulated a period in the evolution of the human race when every instinctual need was met with a minimum of effort. But this period ended when, with the coming of the glacial age, man was rudely evicted from paradise and, in order to survive, had to think. He cited the work of Bolk,* an endocrinologist, who attributed the pause in man's sexual development to certain endocrine and anatomical changes, noting, for example, the arrest in the growth of the ovaries between four and fourteen. Lampl postulated the endocrine change as following from an inhibition of the instincts, as is frequently seen in certain psychological states.** He summarized it schematically: (1) uninhibited primitive man; (2) glacial period; (3) man who has evolved inhibitions of instinctual drives; (4) hormonal changes; and (5) latency period and the development of present-day man. Hence, he concluded, the decisive factor is the mental

---

* Bolk, L., *Das Problem der Menschwerdung.* Jena: Gustav Fischer, 1926.

** He cites Thomas Mann's novel, *Die vertauschten Kopfe,* in which a dull robust man and a sensitive educated weakling exchange heads. Soon the influence of the head is seen in a reversal of their earlier body states.

change which has become permanent and is transmitted. In other words, mutation and selection are responsible for the ego as we know it, and this in turn brings about latency.

We know that the hormonal system is affected in many emotional conditions. Recently Bernstein demonstrated in rhesus monkeys a rise or fall in blood testosterone levels when a monkey was elevated to or removed from an alpha position (29).

Discussion

Freud himself, as well as most authors who followed him, was not certain of what constituted the primary mechanism in latency. For example, in "The Dissolution of the Oedipus Complex," he states that latency comes about because it is a "preordained phase in development" and that the process of desexualization and sublimation usher in latency. He finally resolved the uncertainty by postulating an ontogenetic and phylogenetic history which produced an ego structure which may bring about latency in cultures where it is fostered.

Subsequent authors have been divided in their opinions. Certain tentative hypotheses suggest themselves on the basis of some later anthropological and laboratory data.

MacLean (30) recently postulated three phyletic systems in man's brain: (1) the innermost, which is like the reptiles'; (2) the paleomammalian cortex or limbic system which would place man in mammalian mating behavior, but lower than a rabbit; and (3) the outermost system, the neomammalian or cerebral cortex. The last accounts for his capacity to think (and to delay gratification of libidinal impulses).

The "biological clock" of hormonal maturation is programmed in the old part of the brain, the limbic system. The limbic system, which is relatively larger in man than in other mammals, is concerned with sexual behavior and with motivation, as well as emotions such as rage and fear. The final common pathway is via the hypothalamus, through which the pituitary gland is programmed to secrete gonadotropic hormones, stimulating the gonads to secrete sex hormones (31). In addition, other pituitary hormones, such as ACTH and growth hormone, affect central nervous structures involved in motivational, learning, and memory processes (32) (33).

These findings could be taken as possible support for Bolk's hypothesis. However, one can infer from these studies only the possibility of the same evolution occurring in human beings, and it is hoped studies will be forthcoming in this area.

It is interesting to note that in all civilizations, where permitted, sexual activity increases toward the end of latency but preceding the actual advent of puberty. Many psychoanalysts explain this as the result of a relaxation in the ego-superego prohibitions against the emergence of direct sexual fantasies.

The increase in activities resembling mature mating practices is seen, as well, in infrahuman primates, and in many lower mammals. In chimpanzees, for example, Goodall has observed sexual "practicing" to appear several months before actual puberty (34).

In the hypocampus of female rats, there are special receptors for estrogen, which remains at the same concentration in the cytoplasm from days 20-25, appearing in the nucleus only at about day 25. Puberty occurs between days 30-37. Similar rises in intranuclear estrogen have been found in rhesus monkeys (Personal communication from Bruce S. McEwen and Linda Plapinger. Detailed material will appear in *Acta Endocrinologica,* November, 1973). Pre-pubertal sexual practicing behavior occurs in both species. The nucleus of the neurone is close to the gene, and might therefore influence behavior.

The gonadotropins, FSH and LH, remain at approximately the same level in human beings from age five until nine or ten, when they begin to rise (35). (Assays before the age of five are unknown to the author.)

So it would appear that increased sexual activity in primates and lower mammals correlates with increased levels of central and/or peripheral gonadotropins. This would appear to lend support to Freud's theory of variations in the energy of the libidinal drive. But possible verification of these energic phenomena requires hormonal studies of children before and during the Oedipal phase.

It is rather striking that, of the more than 300 societies reviewed in the author's study, there was discussion of latency sexual play in only 12. In Money's transcultural studies, references are made to sexual play up to the age of five, then, again, after eight or nine. In the author's review of 2,300 papers on ghetto-reared children, there were no references to latency sexual activity. Bornstein (24) has said (speaking of our culture), "The child's behavior during the latency period might be described as one of persistent denial of the struggle against the breakthrough of instinctual impulses, a denial which extends into adulthood as a partial amnesia for this period. This may be one of the reasons why one learns relatively little about latency from the analysis of adults."

Therefore, the relative lack of data in various studies on latency sexual practices, and the tendency to report only later latency behavior, may be explained on the amnesia basis, that is, that the scotoma may be in the eye of the observer. What is more, since many societies have rules against sexual practices, anthropologists have often had their informants tell them how it is supposed to be, rather than how it is. It may also be that there is in fact such significant diminution of sexual play during this early period that it is not noted in studies. This could be seen as corrobation for the drive diminution theory.

To view latency period sexual experimentation in other societies as a sign that there is no drive diminution ignores the differences between sexual play and mating behavior from puberty onward. Sexual object choices are usually varied and fickle, and long term romantic attachments are hardly ever seen. This would suggest that perhaps the hormonal latency is at least partially reflected in the transient nature of the romantic attachments.

Fenichel conjectured that sexual play in children constitutes a kind of ego learning, that through self-established sexual tension the child learns how to deal with sexual stimulation (36). This might be compared with childrens' games involving frightening personages or experiences, and also with many other forms of play connected with mastery of difficult tasks. Buxbaum suggested that "a certain amount of libidinally induced tension [is] necessary in order to keep up a sustained effort, be it in sublimation or personal relationship" (26).

In primitive cultures where latency sexual play is present, the children are progressing simultaneously in their acquisition of skills and social information relevant to their society. This usually takes the form of "incidental education"—there is no formalized education, but rather an intimate daily contact between adults and children in which imitation is the principal mode of instruction. In this setting, the sexual play does not appear to constitute an interruption of latency.

By contrast, Dale Meers (37) cited cases in which there were severe disturbances in learning, memory, synthesis, and other ego functions. The children in his study had lived through and continued to experience severe psychological traumas in the form of aggressive sexual or hostile assault or exposure. Freud's reference to the interruption of latency by seduction would appear to apply in these cases (10).

What seems to make the difference between the capacity for learning and other sublimatory activities during latency is not the presence or absence of sexual play, but rather the nature, intensity, and degree of the child's control of sexual experience.

The essential element in the establishment of psychological latency is said to be the dissolution of the Oedipus and the crystallization of the superego. The classical view of the decisive factor in the dissolution of the Oedipus is that the boy fears castration. Hartmann (38) has suggested that, even where there are no explicit threats, "castration is in the air" as a kind of archaic memory residue.

However, many present-day child analysts feel that the major impetus to the advent of the latency period is the child's fear of humiliation, and that it is that which turns him away from his oedipal goals and replaces them with an increased desire for mastery and expertise in other spheres.

In certain primitive societies where there is a more permissive attitude toward childhood sexual activity, the resolution of the Oedipus may take many forms not present in our culture (39). Perhaps in these circumstances one does not see the "crystallization" of the superego, as manifested in rigorous efforts to stop masturbation, in social behavior characterized by avoidance of the opposite sex, in transitory obsessive-compulsive symptoms, in reaction-formations, and so forth. Rather, there may be a gradual growth of the superego, the child's peer group representing attenuated versions of the oedipal figures, with continued sexual play as a direct equivalent of the transformed and disguised fantasies seen in children of other societies.

It is felt by most child analysts that the style of the "nursery superego" in large measure sets the tone for the post-oedipal superego. If it is true that "[the child] will tend to judge in later life his genital activity in terms of his parents' attitude toward his anal erotism" (22), then it is also to be expected that the greater permissiveness toward all pregenital libidinal activities in most primitive societies would be followed by the freer sexual play in latency.

Latency assumes the existence of a conflict-free ego sphere, which enables the child to grow and develop in relation to both the internal and external worlds (37). In assessing the success of the attainment of sublimatory goals, it is important to add that in most primitive societies the moral system, the sublimated activities, and the ego goals have been much less assailed by ambiguities than in our own society. This is especially true in many aspects of ghetto life.

Conclusion

It appears that when sexual play takes place with a peer group, latency—in the sense of a period for reworking of defenses and the development of the capacity for sublimation—continues as it would in the presence of aggressive play, for example. It is also important that a balance be maintained with the other activities in the child's life. This is substantiated by the author's investigations of primitive societies. Only when the character of the sexual activity changes, it may become overwhelming because of (1) active seduction by an older person; (2) too vivid correspondence to earlier frightening fantasies; or (3) the degree to which sexual play takes over the child's life, interrupting the growth and development of ego functions which are essential for maturation and mastery of the inner and outer world.

There are laboratory data and ethological studies which appear to lend support to Freud's ultimate view of changes in drive intensity.

We are still in a relatively dark age in the understanding of latency. As Freud said in *Three Essays,* "We must not deceive ourselves as to the hypothetical nature and insufficient clarity of our knowledge concerning . . . latency. . . ." Hopefully this will be illuminated through studies in the future.

References

1. Freud, S. Inhibitions, symptoms, and anxiety (1926). *Standard Edition,* Vol. 20. London: Hogarth Press.
2. Freud, S. Two encyclopedia articles (1923A). *Standard Edition,* Vol. 18. London: Hogarth Press.
3. Freud, S. A child is being beaten (1919). *Standard Edition,* Vol. 17. London: Hogarth Press.
4. Freud, S. The dissolution of the Oedipus complex (1924). *Standard Edition,* Vol. 19. London: Hogarth Press.
5. Freud, S. The question of lay analysis (1926). *Standard Edition,* Vol. 20. London: Hogarth Press.
6. Freud, S. Moses and monotheism: Three essays (1939 [1934-38]). *Standard Edition,* Vol. 23. London: Hogarth Press.
7. Freud, S. An outline of psychoanalysis (1940 [1938]). *Standard Edition,* Vol. 23. London: Hogarth Press.
8. Freud, S. *The Origins of Psychoanalysis.* Letters to Wilhelm Fliess, Drafts and Notes, 1887-1902. Edited by Marie Bonaparte, Anna Freud, and Ernst Kris. London: Imago, 1954.
9. Freud, S. Character and anal erotism (1908). *Standard Edition,* Vol. 9. London: Hogarth Press.
10. Freud, S. Three essays on the theory of sexuality (1905). *Standard Edition,* Vol. 7. London: Hogarth Press.
11. Freud, S. Five lectures on psycho-analysis (1910 [1909]). *Standard Edition,* Vol. 11. London: Hogarth Press.
12. Freud, S. On narcissism: an introduction (1914). *Standard Edition,* Vol. 14. London: Hogarth Press.

13. Freud, S. The ego and the id (1923B). *Standard Edition,* Vol. 19. London: Hogarth Press.
14. Freud, S. Formulations on the two principles of mental functioning (1911). *Standard Edition,* Vol. 12. London: Hogarth Press.
15. Freud, S. An autobiographical study (1935) (1925 [1924]). *Standard Edition,* Vol. 20. London: Hogarth Press.
16. Malinowski, B. *The Sexual Life of the Savages.* London: Routledge, 1929.
17. Reich, W. *Der Einbruch der Sexual Moral.* Berlin: Sexpol verlag, 1932.
18. Muensterberger, W. Biopsychological determinants of social life. *Psychoanal. and Soc. Sci., 4,* 7-25, 1955.
19. Ferenczi, S. *Sex in Psychoanalysis.* New York: Basic Books, 1950.
20. Money, J., and Ehrhardt, A. A. *Man and Woman, Boy and Girl.* Baltimore: Johns Hopkins Univ. Press, 1972.
21. Freud, A. *Certain Types and States of Social Maladjustments. Searchlights on Delinquency.* New York: International Universities Press, 1949.
22. Freud, A. *Normality and Pathology in Childhood.* New York: International Universities Press, 1965.
23. Deutsch, H. *Psychology of Women.* New York: Grune and Stratton, 1944.
24. Bornstein, B. On latency. In *The Psychoanalytic Study of the Child,* Vol. VI. New York: International Universities Press, 1951. Pp. 279-285.
25. Friend, M. R. In *The Latency Period.* S. Kaplan, Reporter (Scientific Proceedings, Panel Reports). *J. Amer. Psych. Assn., 5,* 525-538, 1957.
26. Buxbaum, E. A contribution to the psychoanalytic knowledge of the latency period. Workshop, 1950. *Amer. J. Orthopsychiat., 21,* 182-198, 1951.
27. Erikson, E. *Childhood and Society.* New York: W. W. Norton, 1950.
28. Lampl, H. The influence of biological and psychological factors upon the development of the latency period. In R. M. Lowenstein (Ed.), *Drives, Affects and Behavior.* New York: International Universities Press, 1953.
29. Bernstein, A., Rose, R., and Gordon, T. Leaders made, not born. Excerpts from Emory University Research, July 1973. *Newsweek,* August 27, 1972, p. 50 (Status seeking hormones).
30. MacLean, P. D. The brain in relation to empathy and medical education. *J. Nerv. Ment. Dis., 144,* 374-382, 1967.
31. Ramaley, J. A., and Gorski, R. A. The effect of hypothalamic deafferation upon puberty in the female rat. *Acta Endocrinol., 56*:66, 674, 1967.
32. Goy, R. W. Early hormonal influences on the development of sexual and sex-related behavior. In Quarton, Melnechuh, and Adelman (Eds.), *The Neurosciences, Second Study Program.* New York: Rockefeller Univ. Press, 1970. Pp. 196-207.
33. DeWied. Effects of peptide hormones on behavior. *Endocrinology, 84,* 157-168, 1969.
34. Lawick-Goodall, J. van. The behavior of chimpanzees in their natural habitat. *Amer. J. Psychiat., 130*:1, 1-13, 1973.
35. Johanson, A. J., Guyda, H., Light, C., Miglon, C., and Blizzard, R. M. Serum luteinizing hormone by radioimmunoassay in normal children. *J. Pediat., 74,* 416-424, 1969.

36. Fenichel, O. *The Collected Papers of Otto Fenichel, Second Series.* New York: W. W. Norton, 1954. P. 168.
37. Meers, Dale R. Contributions of a ghetto culture to symptom formation: Psychoanalytic studies of ego anomalies in childhood. In *Psychoanalytic Study of the Child,* Vol. XXV. New York: International Universities Press, 1970. Pp. 209-231.
38. Hartmann, H. *Ego Psychology and the Problem of Adaptation* (1939). London: Imago, 1958.
39. Le Barre, W. *The Ghost Dance.* New York: Doubleday, 1970.

6

The Couples Model in the Treatment of Sexual Dysfunctions in the Single Person

CLIFFORD J. SAGER, M.D.

HIGHLY EFFECTIVE METHODS based on working with the married couple as a unit have been developed for the treatment of sex dysfunctions. The disorders most amenable to this approach are: in the male, premature or retarded ejaculation, and impotence; in the female, vaginismus, general lack of sex pleasure and arousal, and orgastic problems.

Single persons, since they do not have a spouse, continue to present difficult therapeutic problems whether treatment is on an individual, couples, or group model. This paper deals with the experience of treating single persons with sex dysfunctions by means of the couples model.

Patients who do not have a committed partner are a particularly troublesome problem. The therapeutic alternatives available to them have been discussed elsewhere by the author. Those who cannot establish a close relationship with others may have emotional problems that require psychoanalysis or some other form of general psychotherapy before they are prepared to venture into a sustained intimate sexual relationship.

The couples model of sex therapy has been explicated by Masters and Johnson (2) and Kaplan (1). The latter, in addition to innovating variations in technique from the Masters and Johnson model, has also evolved an excellent eclectic conceptual framework for sex therapy. Briefly, sex therapy using the couples model is joint treatment of the couple sharply directed toward removal of the sex dysfunction, utilizing assigned tasks to be conducted in the privacy of the home. The conjoint session with the therapist deals with the specifics of the assigned tasks, as well as the feelings and reactions they engender. In these sessions resistance to the tasks and to progress are dealt with in a variety of ways so that the primary goal of therapy—adequate sexual functioning—can be achieved. This method of treating married couples yields an overall effective rate of about 80% (2) as compared with 43% positive results with the long-term individual insight methods of psychoanalysis or psychoanalytic psychotherapy (3).

Not all married couples with sex dysfunctions are suitable candidates for sex therapy. Sager (4) has developed five criteria for evaluating a couple's interpersonal status to determine their suitability for sex therapy:

1. Relative freedom from basic feelings of hostility. If either partner is consistently angry with the other there is no basis for sex therapy, as they will be unable to cooperate sufficiently. Such a couple should have marital therapy first.

2. General acceptance of each other as a sex partner. If this condition is not met, sex therapy cannot be undertaken.

3. Each has to be motivated to help himself and to see the value of therapy for him or herself, as well as for the partner. A self-sacrificing or patronizing approach is destructive. It is desirable for each partner to become aware of his own role in causing or perpetuating the dysfunction and to perceive the mutual benefits of an improved sex life.

4. Ability of each partner to postpone sexual gratification. It may be necessary when treating a female dysfunction for the man to temporarily put aside his gratification, or vice versa.

5. Therapy may also have to be initiated in a non-demand ambience acceptable to both spouses. The wife of an impotent man, for example, must be able to put aside any overt or im-

plied demand that her husband enter her, maintain his erection, and have effective coitus with her, and to eschew any implication that anything else is distasteful or repugnant. Similarly, the husband of a non-orgastic woman has to accept the fact that she may not be orgastic for a while longer, and that her failure to achieve orgasm is not a reflection on his masculinity.

These criteria, plus others that will be discussed later, have to be employed when working with unmarried couples where we employ the conjoint model or brief, goal-directed and task-oriented sex therapy.

THE CONJOINT COUPLE MODEL WITH SINGLE PERSONS

Masters and Johnson (2) define two types of partners for single persons: the *surrogate partner* whom they provide and the *replacement partner* selected by the single patient. The former is a volunteer who has been carefully chosen and trained by the therapists. The replacement partner is one whom the dysfunctional person brings to the Reproductive Biology Research Foundation. Couples with a replacement partner have to meet the criteria of being seriously involved with each other and to have been referred together by the referring authority. Their relationships were all found to be of six months duration or longer.

I prefer not to use the term *replacement partner* because "replacement" suggests someone who is taking the place of someone else. Even for people who are divorced or widowed, replacement suggests carrying over the memory and history of another person rather than establishing a new relationship that stands on its own. Hence, I prefer the term *consenting partner*. The major emphasis of this presentation is on consenting single partners. I have not worked with surrogate partners, hence have nothing to say about this approach except that it has demonstrated its value, although beset by many psychological and legal ramifications.

OUTCOME

Over an 11-year period Masters and Johnson accepted for treatment 16 consenting single couples, 13 male dysfunctionals and

3 female. They found that results were about the same as with married couples, i.e., about 80% favorable. The results with surrogate partners were similar.

Working in New York City with residents of the Greater New York Area, I conducted conjoint couple sex therapy with single patients and their consenting partners. I have employed some techniques that differ from those of Masters and Johnson. For example, patients were not isolated from their usual environment and problems. Sessions were held once or twice a week spread over roughly 2 to 12 weeks rather than two or three weeks of daily sessions. I rarely worked with a cotherapist except for occasional specific contra-gender problems. Most important is the utilization of my knowledge and experience as a marital therapist, psychoanalyst, and group therapist in order to work through rapidly or bypass resistance to the tasks and goals of treatment.

The outcome of my first series was not as positive as Masters and Johnson's in their work with replacement partners. In working with married couples I have been able to achieve an overall 80% positive response, similar to Masters and Johnson's results. However, in working with consenting partners in this first series the success rate for the entire group was only 50%. I am now on a second series of singles with consenting partners, and indications are that the outcome will be better as a result of my experience with the first series.

In the first series there were 11 patients with consenting partners. Of the 11 couples, 10 males and one woman complained of sexual dysfunction. Seven completed the full course of treatment, the others discontinued for reasons indicated below. The 50% failure rate includes the entire group.

SEX THERAPY WITH CONSENTING PARTNERS

Treatment Terminated Prior to Completion of Therapy

The only female primary patient was a woman who was not orgastic, either with her lover or by herself. She was an extremely independent person in many ways. Her partner had been her lover for a year, in addition to being involved with her in a business enterprise. We had had only one session together and had scheduled a second, when she telephoned and broke the appointment. I wrote and received a response from her in my routine follow-up.

As I considered her follow-up response in light of the data from the first and only session, it became clear that she had been involved in a power struggle with her lover, which had very deep psychological significance for her. She indicated in the follow-up that she *did not want* to have an orgasm with him, and that this was why she was withdrawing from treatment. She felt that for her to climax with him would give him a means of control over her which she did not want him to have. Unfortunately, she did not return to treatment, where we might have been able to work this out. I recognized the essence of the problem only when cued by the follow-up response, and then it was too late.

Another patient who withdrew was a young man with primary impotence who first saw me for two sessions by himself. I indicated to him that if we were to get anywhere in treating his problem he would have to have a partner who would join him in the therapeutic program. He called me a month later and said that he had a friend who had agreed to help him. I saw them together. Both were in their mid-twenties. She was a very lovely, gentle woman who appeared to be anxious and very tense; I suspected an underlying schizophrenic process. I outlined the program and what was involved, and she agreed to participate.

By the third joint session the young woman was manifesting a great deal of anxiety. She was very upset by her own lack of sexual responsiveness and pleasure, to the extent that she found it impossible to carry out the assigned sex tasks. By the fourth session it had become clear that she was on the verge of decompensating; the pursuit of sex therapy had been harmful to her and she was more involved emotionally than she had anticipated. She felt exploited by her friend because there was no commitment to a long-term relationship, even though she had agreed to the conditions of treatment. Understandably, their joint effort had seduced her into desiring more of a commitment than he was willing to make. This lack of commitment, in addition to confrontation with her own sexual difficulties and the realization that she too would have to be treated in the process, upset her terribly. She was caught between her feeling that she should not be in this situation with him if he did not love her and her desire to please him and not lose him. The prospect of overcoming her own inhibitions frightened her, particularly since she felt exploited and distrustful of his motives.

I reassured her that this was a situation she need not be in, that she really had no way of anticipating what feelings the situation would engender, and that it was marvelous of her to try to help her friend. Conflicting feelings were surfacing, as often happens, and she was absolutely correct in wanting to withdraw. I supported her in this and assured her she need not feel guilty. Had she not been a participant in even these four sessions he would not have gotten as far as he had. She had given him a gift, but at too great an expense to herself. I made the decision to discontinue the sex therapy, which greatly relieved her.

The next patient was also a young man in his mid-twenties who was seen for three sessions before we were able to define his problem. It finally became clear he had primary impotence and that he was in a sense defending himself by utilizing homosexual preoccupation and obsession. He, too, searched for a partner and found a young woman in his office with whom he had previously had a limited sexual experience. He had kissed, necked, and lain down with her three times during the past year, although they had not had intercourse and his penis had remained flaccid throughout their physical contacts.

When I first saw them together the young lady told me that she had had excellent sexual experiences with many men. She thought she would be a perfect partner for this type of therapy because she did not want to become involved with or tied down to anyone. She clearly understood my admonition that there be no covert hopes or expectations contingent on successful treatment. She assured both of us that she was a cool person and intended to remain isolated, with only casual and brief contacts with men. This appeared to fit in very well with the needs of the young man, who also feared closeness. Treatment began.

Again, at the fourth session we had to discontinue sex therapy. During the third session the woman complained that he wanted to see her three times a week, and that this was too much. Couldn't they make it just once a week? I agreed that we might try once a week and see how it worked out. When they returned the following week she complained about the new schedule. He became upset and angry at this session, stating that she was not honoring her part of the agreement and he felt cheated. He saw her attitude as proof that there's no point in giving anything to women because whatever you give them they don't want, they step on you, etc. He incorporated this experience into his somewhat paranoid attitude toward women. I decided that therapy should be discontinued because of her mounting resistance as her defenses became threatened. To have attempted to continue treatment would have been disastrous for both of them.

The next time I saw him alone. He told me that he wanted to continue treatment and had another woman waiting in the wings with whom he thought he would now try sex therapy. I refused to see him with his new partner and suggested that he wait awhile to see how their relationship worked out. I told him that I thought he should make a commitment to the woman before trying again, that we both had a great deal to learn from this experience. I cautioned him not to choose a woman who would keep him at a distance unless he was determined to prove his thesis that women cannot be trusted.

The fourth case that did not complete treatment was a 28-year-old unmarried man who appeared to have secondary impotence and brought two partners in turn to treatment. His first partner felt he was sexually demanding because he wanted sex every night, and sometimes two or three times per night.

After a short interval he appeared to be making some gains in therapy and to have achieved a functioning plateau without consistently realizing full erectile adequacy. Not always attaining a full erection, he felt justified in not making a complete commitment to his partner. Unconsciously he used his penis like litmus paper, to see if his partner had the correct pH in which he could flourish. The reading, however, could never be an accurate assay because unconsciously he feared the intimacy and loss of control that he believed would result from any real commitment. His penis merely followed the dictates of his anxiety-laden unconscious.

The first partner he introduced me to disagreed several times about the state of his erection and said he often had a better erection than he admitted. Because of underlying mutual negative feelings that now surfaced they stopped seeing each other. I regarded this as an insurmountable resistance to progress in treatment that sprang from the core of his anxiety over closeness and being controlled. He informed me that there was another woman with whom he had had a sexual relationship, who now was free, and whom he would like to bring into sex therapy. Never having treated a situation of this complexity, I was curious and thought we might act on his request to work with the second partner, particularly as he had known her previously. I made it clear to the first woman that I felt a sense of obligation to her too, and certainly would be willing to continue helping her with her problem.

The patient returned with his new partner. This woman knew him somewhat better than the first. She was very emphatic that he did have a full erection most of the time during intercourse. He became very angry with her. I saw each of them alone in an effort to get at the facts. She was very definite that he had a full erection nearly all the time, sometimes two or three times within 24 hours. He was equally insistent that she was overrating him because she wanted to marry him.

He became angry when I interpreted his demand to be considered impotent as an attempt to present himself to the world as an inadequate man. Actually he was unusually sexually competent. I seriously questioned that he was impotent at all, in view of the testimony of both of his partners. He informed me heatedly that his two friends had ulterior motives (i.e., they wanted to marry him) and that he was going elsewhere to work with a therapist who would supply him with a surrogate partner who would have no designs on him.

I question whether this man had more than a mild relative and episodic impotence. I suspect his sense of impotence was more subjective than objective and represented a means of allaying the anxiety of threatening deeper involvements. If he were impotent he need not commit himself, but if he found a woman with whom he did not feel impotent, she would be the maiden whom the glass slipper fit, who would automatically become his bride. At any rate, whether his symptoms were subjective or not, they did cause him sufficient pain to seek help and had to be respected. A form of psychotherapy aimed at resolving his underlying anxiety and conflicts was more appropriate than conjoint couple sex therapy, and this was recommended to him.

These four uncompleted cases were rated as therapeutic failures.

Treatment Completed

Of the seven cases that completed treatment, one patient with secondary impotence eventually had a poor result; another with secondary impotence apparently had a poor result on termination, but on follow-up was found out to be successful; and a third with secondary impotence had only a fair result. On the other hand, four cases of premature ejaculation had successful outcomes. The cases that will be presented are those that illustrate problems peculiar to treating unmarried couples. Those cases with good results that are not discussed in detail proceeded with only the usual problems that might be encountered in the treatment of married couples.

In one case where treatment initially produced good results, the patient was a man with secondary impotence. He and his partner had been together for about a year, during which time the man was impotent. The consenting partner was an unusually attractive woman, who was open about her sexuality and enjoyment of sex. The couple progressed very well and, upon completion of treatment, were doing fine. During the next six months, however, their sexual relationship deteriorated, as did his erectile functioning, not totally, as before, but to the extent that only one time out of four was he able to have satisfactory sex. Other parameters of their relationship deteriorated, too.

During the course of conjoint sex therapy, there had been some stormy periods, and on two occasions I had confronted them with the possibility of terminating treatment because of subtle, but important, hostile elements in their interaction, In order to allay her anxiety about her own sexuality and sense of worth, the woman was overtly demanding that her partner function well as a lover. She felt that all she had to offer was her sensuality and that if her lover did not respond properly, it must be because he found her lacking. Although all the men she had known previously had been sexually effective, the woman idealized the patient as the perfect male, except for his impotence. They had originally come to therapy with the hidden agenda that if they were able to have good sex together, they would marry. At the time the deterioration set in after treatment he had just received his divorce and was free to remarry. His previous obsessiveness and spectatoring during sex returned, and he again became impotent.

Another couple was a man in his late 40's and a widowed woman in her mid-40's. After his wife had left him he had functioned adequately until he had a herniorraphy, after which he became impotent when with a woman, but not if he masturbated.

Examination revealed no evidence of neurological damage. The consenting partner with whom he came to treatment was extremely hostile. His agenda called for marriage if therapy was successful. She was not certain that she wanted to get married again and refused to commit herself until after she had spent considerably more time with him. "We have only known each other for three months. I'm not sure, but I do want to help him if I can." He kept insisting throughout therapy that he wanted his "penis to work" because he wanted to marry *her,* and could not be shaken from this attitude.

It wasn't just her hostility that circumvented successful coitus, it was his uncanny ability to arouse these hostile reactions in her because he perceived her similarity to his overbearing ex-wife. *He did not want treatment to be successful or he would have to marry her!* In reality, he achieved near success in their sexual relationship and then drove her away by frustrating her in a variety of ways. At one point they appeared to be doing so well that I announced that the next session would be the last. After that everything blew up. He immediately demanded that they marry. She turned on him and listed his faults: he was too passive, did not earn enough money, was not as verbal (i.e., intelligent) as her friends, etc.

We decided to discontinue therapy and I referred him to a behavior therapist * to help him overcome his passivity. His therapist has informed me that the patient has found another partner who is not hostile or controlling and he is able to maintain an excellent sexual relationship with her. He has become generally more assertive and found a new and more rewarding job. Apparently sex therapy brought him to the point where he gained sufficient confidence to drive his unsuitable partner away. With the help of assertive training he was then able to find a more appropriate woman for himself, as well as to advance his career. This case was changed from failure to positive result on follow-up.

This case history illustrates how detrimental commitment to marriage can be when it is contingent on successful therapy. Ambivalence about marriage on the part of either partner is likely to lead to sabotage of treatment when improvement occurs and marriage looms as a consequence. However, a commitment to marry if treatment is successful is not a contraindication to sex therapy when there is no conscious or unconscious ambivalence about the marriage.

The following case illustrates a rather unusual factor that contributed to the etiology of the dysfunction.

This couple involved a widower of 63 and his consenting partner of 55, a woman who was comfortable with her sexuality.

---

* Dr. Herbert Fensterheim

I thought at first that this man's secondary impotence was due to guilt about being "unfaithful" to his deceased wife, with whom he had functioned very well sexually. However, circumstances were such that this couple could not marry. They had been enjoying sex without living with each other for two years. They were truly in love with one another; their mutual tenderness and consideration were very moving. They lived in a rural community where he could not spend the night with her without raising gossip and both had sensitive positions. As a result, he had to sneak out of her house during the night and was very disturbed because they were not married. Working through his feelings about the illicitness of their relationship improved his ability to maintain an erection but he remained subject to episodes of impotence whenever circumstances recalled their unmarried state. In this instance, contrary to the usual situation, the illicit quality deterred rather than enhanced his performance.

DISCUSSION

Results for this first series of consenting partners are not as satisfactory as those of Masters and Johnson, who also have reported on a series of consenting partners (2). My favorable results are about 50%, theirs about 80%. Neither series, of course, can be considered statistically significant; they had 16 cases over 11 years, I had 11 over one year. Yet, it cannot be denied that there is a difference between 80% and 50% when the outcome for all dysfunctions is considered together. It is important to account for this difference, particularly because in treating married couples my results are so similar to theirs.

Two major factors may account for the discrepancy. First, when a couple travels to St. Louis for two weeks, they make a large investment in terms of time, money, and commitment. The partners are involved in a serious relationship and have been screened for this by the referring authority. Often they plan to marry if treatment is successful. All of these couples have had a relationship of six or more months duration. In many of the couples I treated, the partners had no such commitment either emotionally or timewise. The two young men with primary impotence and the

28-year-old with questionable secondary impotence were not involved in relationships of intimacy or long standing intensity, despite the fact that they may have known their partners for years. Several couples in my series had a very incomplete relationship, for example, the case in which the woman wanted to remain isolated from her partner and see him only occasionally. These couples did not consist of persons who were sharing a life and sharing the problems of living together. Those couples that were successfully treated in my series all had meaningful relationships; conversely, most of those whose treatment failed did not have a relationship with commitment. If I were to exclude from my series those couples who did not have a relationship with serious commitment the outcome rate of these seven cases was 80% too. These observations lead to obvious conclusions regarding selection criteria.

Second, the issue of covert expectations played a large part in the interactions of the couples I saw. The contracts of many of the couples in my series were not very clear or open. For example, marriage was frequently part of a hidden agenda. The wish to marry is not a *verboten* desire at all. In fact, when the contingency for marriage is adequate sexual functioning, and when there is no ambivalence about marrying, the prospect of matrimony may be a motivating factor or added incentive for successful completion of therapy. In several of the couples I treated, however, one or both of the partners were very ambivalent about marrying. In such cases, making marriage a consequence of successful treatment is destructive to the therapeutic process. As improvement takes place, the partner who is ambivalent about marriage invariably resists or sabotages progress.

CRITERIA FOR SEX THERAPY WITH SINGLES

How to set up criteria for consenting partners that would better assure effective treatment without exploiting or injuring either partner is a perplexing problem. Is it preferable to offer therapy to new couples, rather than to let them first become set in ways of failure with each other? Should we try to work with them before such patterns become conditioned or well established? Another approach would be to encourage new couples to live together for at least a six-month period, despite the quality of their sexual functioning. They would thereby have demonstrated a serious commitment to the survival of their relationship. In the process they would get to know each other better and develop an emotional history. They can refer to their life together and have a backlog of positive credits they can draw upon as they get into the stress of treatment. I don't know if either approach is preferable in all cases, and have concluded that it is wiser not to set up rigid rules regarding how long partners have known one another or how complete their relationship need be. The most important factor is motivation. Why does each want to participate with the other in this most trying project? It should be noted that treatment of premature ejaculation may not necessitate as many positive relationship criteria as does that of impotence. Data where the woman is the primary patient are too scant to allow for the drawing of any conclusions.

The partner who has the sexual dysfunction obviously wants someone to help overcome it. But why does a person wish to help another who has such a dysfunction? There may be a variety of reasons. Good motivation may also, of course, be multidetermined.

First are the personal determinants. Sometimes it's love. They witness their partner's pain and their own frustration. The dysfunction is likely to be regarded as blocking a fuller relationship. They may want to marry or live together. Occasionally, a consenting partner acts out of gratitude for what he or she has received from the other. Some, on another level, simply have a desire to save a sufferer. A few have been curious or titillated by the idea of sex therapy, or it has played into various types of role fantasies. Whatever the consenting partner's motivation, the couples have to meet the five criteria mentioned earlier for married couples if we are to recommend sex therapy.

The second group of criteria relates to the interplay of intrapsychic and transactional factors. How do these two people treat one another? Are their mutual transactions based on good feelings, cooperation, and consideration? What are the intrapsychic forces that influence their behavior toward each other? What is the role of the symptom for the dysfunctional partner, and how is the symptom used? What is the attitude of the person who is helping? What effect does this motivation have on the other partner? This aspect of the evaluation includes the intrapsychic status of each individual and the ways in which their transactions may initiate defensive reactions, particularly hostile, paranoid, or distancing maneuvers.

The third category of criteria deals with the contract each person makes in his own mind regarding his expectations from the other and what he is willing to give to the other. Another set of contract "clauses" deals with what each really wants from therapy and the therapist. Sex therapy exerts a profound influence on the relationship of any couple. Hence, it is necessary to bring into the open their contracts with each other and with the therapist—what are their purposes for entering sex therapy? Presumably they are there for treatment of the sexual dysfunction, and for that alone. However, because of the vulnerability of sex functioning to psychological influences, and vice versa, it is impossible to treat just the sex dysfunction without affecting in various ways the persons involved and their relationship.

Fourth, I explain what the treatment is likely to consist of, and in general what each partner has to do. I don't go into details, because therapy never follows a cookbook type recipe, but varies according to conditions that reveal themselves as we proceed. However, I can and do give the couple an idea of what they may expect and give specific examples. My accounting of what to expect and what is expected of them in treatment causes some to realize they do not wish to be involved in a program that involves their feelings and responses so intimately.

I find it increasingly important to deal with the woman's and man's attitudes toward their own and the opposite gender. Almost inevitably the filtering down to the general population of women's liberation and male supremacist attitudes makes it important to get feelings about gender roles and exploitation out in the open. If it is the dysfunctional male who brings the couple to treatment, it is incumbent on the therapist to point out that the man may have to act like a "male chauvinist pig" for a while; if it is a dysfunctional woman, the man may have to take the backseat for a while and postpone his sexual gratification.

Can the male accept direction in sensate focus, acknowledge the fact that the woman knows better what pleases her, and, therefore, let her instruct him how to touch her at a particular moment? I attempt to clarify attitudes related to these questions as they arise and to bring feelings to the surface in order to better assess the underlying attitudes, fears, resentments, and competitiveness that may exist. Furthermore, I make it clear to both partners that we will have to work on whatever sex problems the consenting partner may reveal, as well as the problems of the presenting dysfunctional partner. The consenting partner immediately becomes a patient and receives the same consideration for his/her needs as the primary patient. A careful sex history is taken from each patient, usually in the presence of the other. Each is equal in the treatment situation, and the therapist must be careful not to be partisan. Those trained in couple or family therapy are familiar with the systems model, and the need for removing the onus from the "identified" patient.

After explaining what is entailed, I allow at least one week for the couple to think over the conditions and caveats of treatment before agreeing to proceed.

The final special consideration affecting the therapist's decision to proceed with sex therapy already has been alluded to: his responsibility to both partners. Professionals are responsible for the welfare of the consenting partner as well as that of the primary patient. The consenting partner is usually not fully aware of possible consequences of the situation he/she is getting into, and must be protected. For example, I felt a tremendous obligation to the woman with an incipient schizophrenic reaction, regarded her as a patient who had to be protected from a situation which, unfortunately, I had helped to create by stressing her defensive system. In practice the dysfunctional patient who brings in the consenting partner is usually the one who pays the practitioner's fees. This fact, of course, cannot be allowed even in subtle fashion to make the therapist partisan. I take the trouble to point out this obvious fact because awareness is the therapist's best defense against being drawn into subtle prejudicial behavior (countertransference?).

This discussion has dealt with sexually dysfunctional single persons who can find a partner of their own choice with whom to develop a therapeutic emotional and sexual relationship. When such couples have a serious commitment their likelihood of success in treatment is the same as for married couples. Those who cannot find such a partner must be treated by other means.

Individuals who have not been able to form a meaningful relationship with another are among those who suffer the greatest psychic pain. Whether sex is involved or not, such persons may merely be timid, or their lack of contragender involvement may be due to varying degrees of psychopathology. These individuals should be seen for evaluation to determine whether they need some form of psychotherapy. Others may have attempted sex but displayed evidence of dysfunction and are afraid to risk the humiliation of another failure. There are a wide variety of reasons for coming to therapy without a partner. Individual and group methods available for treating these non-partner singles require further exploration.

References

1. Kaplan, H. S. *The New Sex Therapy*. New York: Brunner/Mazel, 1974.
2. Masters, W. H., and Johnson, V. E. *Human Sexual Inadequacy*. Boston: Little, Brown, 1970.
3. O'Connor, J. F., and Stern, L. O. Results of treatment in functional sexual disorders. *N.Y. State J. Med., 72*:15, 1927-1934, August 1972.
4. Sager, C. J. Marital discord and sex therapy. Chapter 24 in H. S. Kaplan, *The New Sex Therapy*. New York: Brunner/Mazel, 1974.

Discussion

EDRITA FRIED, PH.D.

Sex therapy consists of a mixture of various prevalent treatment methods. Since the mixture is well thought through and astutely blended, it sets an example of how much can be accomplished if effective techniques of therapy are applied conjointly with judgment and in the best sense of an eclectic approach. The following methods stand out:

(A) Precise physiological-psychological diagnosis (1, 2) concerning locus of problem, type of nervous excitation, and release processes involved in a particular form of dysfunction.

(B) Dynamic understanding of obstructive emotional problems in one or both partners, and thorough treatment prior to sex therapy. This requires familiarity with psychoanalytic principles of diagnosis and therapy. Much sexual anxiety, for instance, is attributed to existing hostility. Whether such hostility is overt or defended against by such methods as passivity, withdrawal, reaction formation or denial is to be discerned and treated by the psychoanalytically experienced practitioner.

(C) Ego therapy (3) of a psychoanalytic kind is the third treatment outlook involved in sex therapy. The prime emphasis is on present and future behavior with the therapist understanding genetic factors but not necessarily demanding that the patient unearth them. Control and decontrol of release functions which are of a physiological-psychological nature are emphasized, though the experience of control or its opposite is not necessarily a conscious one. Anxiety which is known to obstruct sexual functioning, for instance, in premature ejaculation, is removed by experiences of mastery. The failure to ejaculate, where it stems from fear of performance (2), is removed by establishing a series of success experiences through ingenious construction of control methods.

(D) Focusing and localizing are part of behavior therapy as they are part of ego therapy. Let us in this context recall that Balint (4), a psychoanalyst, recommended localizing in short-term treatments. Positive accomplishments, in accordance with behavior therapy (5), are reinforced by sensations of pleasuring. Repetition, part of all human learning, is stressed in behavior and sex therapy. Of course, in a more sophisticated way it is also an essential factor in the working-through of psychoanalytic therapy.

(E) Sex therapy takes place in vita. It does not encourage mere talk about corrective sexual experiences, rather, their performance and achievement in the privacy of "at home" are expected and the after-the-fact reports are an important part of treatment. This is one of the trump cards of the method. I pointed out some time ago (6) that change is often encouraged by encouraging its occurrence in part or whole before insight. The gestalt therapists rightly attribute their successes largely to a method which elicits corrective life experiences in the treatment session and encourages their repetition until they become part of awareness (7). The suggestion of appropriate mental exercises between sessions is also part of the gestalt technique (8), as the circumscribed physical-psychological tasks are part of sex therapy. My own approach has been to ask patients at appropriate moments: "What have you done about the things we talked about?" In this connection one is reminded of an anecdote, probably true, told about Sigmund Freud. One day he said to one of his patients who was simultaneously one of his most brilliant collaborators: "Now that we've talked about this fourteen times, my dear Herr Colleague, why don't you go out and practice?"

(F) Finally, sex therapy relates itself to group process (because the dyad, not the single partner, is treated) and to consideration of systems theory, inasmuch as generally two separate though interrelated systems are treated. If the homeostasis between the two systems is subjected to a fair degree of tension, pleasure is nevertheless forthcoming, as in some sado-masochistic arrangements. But if the tension is very high, violent, and abrupt, the homeostatic equilibrium will not hold up sufficiently to produce pleasure.

We see in Dr. Sager's paper, with its highly interesting topic, that most of the dyadic systems he studied broke down because the homeostasis between the partners was disrupted.

With the couples model so astutely blended in sex therapy, it is no wonder that Dr. Sager has attempted to use it for single patients who come to treatment originally because of a sexual disturbance. If they can bring a "consenting" partner along, they are given the benefits of couple therapy. Dr. Sager must be commended for opening up his clinical "books" freely, offering case material that can start us off on answers. I regret that he does not provide more female cases with sexual dysfunction. In the treatment of frigidity, sex therapists frequently advocate as the first step toward orgasm that the woman practice autoerotic stimulation, then introduce the dyadic approach as the second step, recommending a transition from the autoerotic to heterosexual (or two-sexual) stimulation. Sex therapy proceeds in this way from the single to the dyadic situation. It would be interesting to have systematic reports on how this progression works.

The disappointing results obtained by Dr. Sager can be explained in terms of the mentioned integration of six divergent but reconciled treatment approaches. They can be explained also by considering Dr. Sager's own five criteria for the applicability of the couples model. The demand for a cooperative atmosphere with little or no hostility, as is called for in Dr. Sager's criteria 1 and 5, is not satisfied in Cases 1, 5, and 6. The same cases offend the demand of psychoanalytic therapy that neither open nor veiled defensive hostility be prominent if interactions between two people, including especially sexual relations, be successful. In terms of the emphasis which behavior therapy places on repetition of new learning at close intervals, one wonders what prompted Dr. Sager to meet at considerable intervals with his original patients and their partners. The intrapsychic, group process, or systems principle that two people or systems, in order to remain attached, need a certain degree of homeostatic peaks and a level of homeostatic permanence is actually only satisfied in Case 6. Dr. Sager's call for future tryouts with couples who have achieved a good deal of permanence appears to be a central prerequisite for success if an original patient and a consenting partner are to be treated with the couples model.

Finally, a special appeal to Dr. Sager and others who practice and study sex therapy. One of the essential techniques of sex therapy is the stop and start approach which Dr. Helen Kaplan characterizes as mild teasing. I have often wondered why sado-masochistic character tendencies, muted but recognizable, appeal distinctly to persons with neurotic and sexual problems. Does this appeal rest on the premise that people expect the teasing, stop and start manifestations on a flirtatious and social level to have a parallel in the sexual responses they expect from teasers? I have found many times that, for example, people with a passive, reactive, withdrawn character structure, and a distinctly neurotic one at that, go for teasers who carry on flirtatious stop and start games. These games create suspense, animation, titillation. They free general and sexual energy, though all too often they also raise the anxiety level to an intolerable high. Do those who like to be recipients of the teasing look forward to concomitantly provocative, stop-start, now I'm here/now I'm not sexual conduct? Do they intuitively look for an amateurish kind of stop-start/start-stop sexual experience in the unconscious hope that it will improve physical functioning?

REFERENCES

1. MASTERS, W. H., and JOHNSON, V. E.: *Human Sexual Inadequacy*. Boston: Little, Brown, 1970.
2. KAPLAN, H. S.: *The New Sex Therapy*. New York: Brunner/Mazel, 1974.
3. FRIED, E.: *The Ego in Love and Sexuality*. New York: Grune and Stratton, 1960.
4. BALINT, M., ORNSTEIN, M., and BALINT, E.: *Focal Psychotherapy*. Philadelphia and Toronto: Tavistock Publications, J. B. Lippincott, 1972.
5. FRANKS, C. M., and WILSON, G. T. (Eds.): *Annual Review of Behavior Therapy: Theory and Practice*. New York: Brunner/Mazel, 1973.
6. FRIED, E.: Change before insight. *Int. J. Group Psychother.*, No. 3, 1962.
7. PERLS, F.: *The Gestalt Approach and Eye Witness to Therapy*. New York: Science and Behavior Books, 1973.
8. POLSTER, E., and POLSTER, M.: *Gestalt Therapy Integrated*. New York: Brunner/Mazel, 1973.

7

Authentic Feminine Orgastic Response

NATALIE SHAINESS, M.D.

THIS SYMPOSIUM IS DEVOTED to what is new in psychoanalytic thinking about sex. Changes presented to the public and the professional community have been rapid and insistent, and the devotion to change has been of an almost compulsive nature. Change is inevitable, yet reevaluation may disclose different reasons for retaining what is valuable but subject to new conceptualization. I wish to consider what to hold on to, in the face of new beliefs.

My title implies a consideration of the female sexual act and its climax as a totality, as something genuine and non-manipulative, as a response within the woman to another person, to the interaction between the two—as an endpoint to a chain of events within the woman—and starting *before* the sexual encounter, in terms of physical desire and pleasurable anticipation (1, 2, 3). I do not, in this conception, include the terminologies of what I have come to call "the great orgasm debate," although I hope to make certain distinctions clear.

In the past we have been told, by psychoanalysts as well as others, that women do not experience sexual release as men do, but that the sex act is completed with delivery or motherhood (4, 5, 6, 7, 8). Others have asserted that the pleasure of being held close, or the pleasure of serving the men they love is sufficient for women, Deutsch concluding that the female has no orgastic component at all.

Freud insisted that there is a difference between "clitoral" and "vaginal" orgasm (9). To be specific, in "The Transformation of Puberty" he says, with regard to the clitoris: "Its role is to conduct the excitement to the adjacent genital parts; it acts like a chip of pinewood which is utilized to set fire to the harder wood. It often takes some time before this transference is accomplished. . . . This anaesthesia (vaginal) may become permanent if the clitoris refuses to give up its excitability. . . . If the transference of the erogenous excitability from the clitoris to the vagina succeeds, the woman then changes her leading zone for the future sexual activity." While I have abandoned many of Freud's theoretical concepts, let me bow in the direction of his superb understanding of feminine sexual mechanics—with the clarification that I do not think he meant that the clitoris had to give up its *total* excitability, but rather, its major role in the genital experience. And now, on to current views.

Masters and Johnson gave great impetus to the idea of a single major erotic site in women as there is in men—in this case, the clitoris (10, 11, 12). I attribute this to the fact that an orgasm *can* occur from purely clitoral stimulation, and that for their purposes, they made no distinction between masturbation and intercourse in women, in point of fact, expressing their *preference* for masturbation. In effect, they were telling Little Red Riding Hood "All the better to see you, my dear." This elimination of the vaginal, or some equivalent of it, simplified matters—for the doctor, the research subject, the psychoanalyst, and the problematic patient or nonpatient. Quick to latch on to this view was Mary Jane Sherfey,* who spun a very complex but unsubstantial web around it in her *Evolution and Nature of Female Sexuality* (13). Judd Marmor asserted (14, 15, 16) along with Harold Lief that anything other than clitoral orgasm was a myth. Such also seems to

---

* Letters published in the *New York Times* in response to Dr. Sherfey's articles of Nov. 13, 14, 1972, headed "See Here, Dr. Sherfey," revealed an educated lay public much more critical than the professionals, calling her work shoddy, and stating that if she is actually a practising psychiatrist, she furnishes a prime example of why the public is increasingly distrustful of her profession.

be the view of Leon Salzman (17) and many others, including Polatin (18), who cites Masters and Johnson saying "an orgasm is an orgasm no matter where the emphasis." Not so—not only because of location and activity, but because no two sexual experiences are ever exactly alike.

It is interesting to observe that many of the more militant feminists found this single clitoral response pleasing. It resulted in the now well-known paper by Anne Koedt (19) called "The Myth of the Vaginal Orgasm"; and Ti-Grace Atkinson called the vaginal orgasm a "mass hysterical survival response" (I interpret this as meaning that women give men what they want to believe sexually, in order to survive socially). It also made lesbian activity seem more "natural."

Strangely, others with completely opposing views have found support in the non-corroborated models of Masters and Johnson as well. Burness Moore, acknowledging his appreciation to them, feels (5, 6) he cannot reconcile the fact that "aggressive, masculine women experienced intense vaginal orgasm, while loving, giving, maternal and happy women did not." He feels that, taking woman's reproductive function into account, "it seems logical that . . . interest in the clitoris and its sensations becomes secondary to a passive, receptive interest in receiving the penis and a child through her vagina." He adds that "it is conceivable that a more mature, realistic and adaptive reaction is that of impaired orgastic response . . . (since) an overwhelming orgastic reaction would be threatening to her mate." Here one cannot help but reflect that this is a rather self-serving view of woman's sexual role. Subservient impotence (frigidity) is preferred to possibly less complaint and more challenging potency in women (20). Others, like Schimel (21), agree with the alleged provocations of "egalitarianism" (a blown-up word for equality?) in sex.

This is the gamut of views, expressed mostly by men, who seem to have no doubts about their understanding, not only of the psychology of female sexual response, but its biophysiology as well. As a corollary of this, most seem convinced of another representation of Masters and Johnson—the superiority of the female sexual capacity, in terms of multiple orgasm (10)—a questionable honor and capacity in women, of unproven validity, but one that may feed male fantasy of endless indulgent acceptance by women. And to complicate the picture even further—if that is possible—along has come Seymour Fisher with his huge book on *The Female Orgasm* (22), in which he denies any relationship between psychological health and orgastic response, while at the same time indicating in his findings from a questionnaire-survey of women that many women had indeed experienced essentially two different kinds of orgasm.

In a previous paper titled "A Re-assessment of Feminine Sexuality and Erotic Experience" (2), I dealt with factors both psychological and physiological as well as anatomical, which helped to explain the observations of a seemingly dual site of orgasm in women. Before reviewing the psychological aspects, let me expand on the physical. First, to set the range of feminine responses in perspective, the first illustration is a graphed spectrum of my view of feminine orgastic responses, individually, but also indicating a historical cultural prevalence at a particular time, reflecting the values and styles of the era.

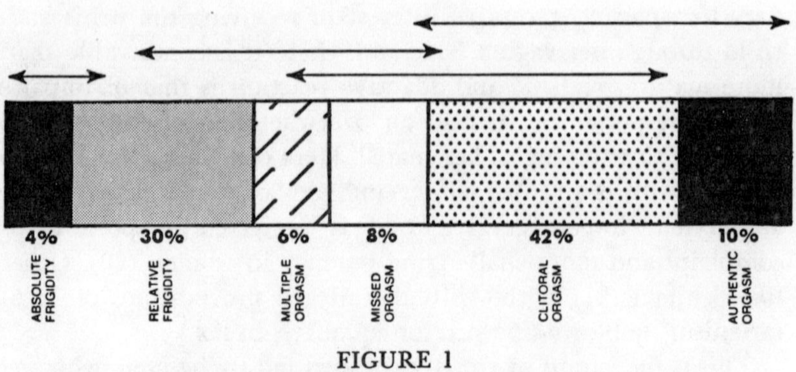

FIGURE 1

Spectrum of Feminine Erotic Response

This spectrum has been estimated as an approximate breakdown of 100 percent. The arrows indicate the range of possible shift, either spontaneously or with treatment. There is a range of responses within each woman, depending on the processing of the variables for each sexual engagement. But as indicated above, there is a limit to the range of shift.

This spectrum ranges from absolute frigidity (that is, under any circumstances) of approximately 4%; to relative frigidity (approximately 30%); to multiple orgasm—a fantasy misinterpretation of multiple erotic sensations in a given sexual interaction, equivalent to gain and loss of erection in the male and also based on erectile response, since turgid tissue is more responsive to stimuli (approximately 6%); to "missed orgasm"—an "almost" response (about 8%); to clitoral orgasm—about 42%, and the prevalent response of our time (alienated, mechanical sex); to the authentic ("vaginal") orgasm, possibly as high as 10%. The second largest category, "relative frigidity," was probably greater in Freud's time, not only because of sexual codes and woman's more dependent position, but also in good measure due to the lack of adequate means of birth control, with its subsequent fear and sometimes anger (at the need to comply sexually with the threat of pregnancy ever-present). The arrows indicate the range of shift in any given woman (beyond the early immature sexual experiences) with treatment or growth—or retrogression. There is a comparable spectrum for male responses (22).

Figures 2 and 3 show comparable sections of genital anatomy in male and female (these sketches are not accurately scaled to size). Observe that much more than the clitoris is included as an equivalent of the glans. Location of the different specialized sensory nerve-endings is based on Kinsey's excellent neuroanatomical description (24). The clitoris is heavily endowed with endings responding to light touch. These continue in considerable numbers to the vaginal introitus—the site of major sensibility—and a bit beyond in the anterior wall; while endings responding to deep pressure predominate in the vagina. The radial markings on the sketch surrounding the vagina and uterus suggest the stretch on ligaments and other organs, and pressure on some when the vagina is expanded by the penis, indicating that kinaesthetic and somaesthetic sensation via stimulation of autonomic nerves are also involved.

This indicates perhaps more clearly from a neuroanatomical vantage point what I have tried to demonstrate before: that the

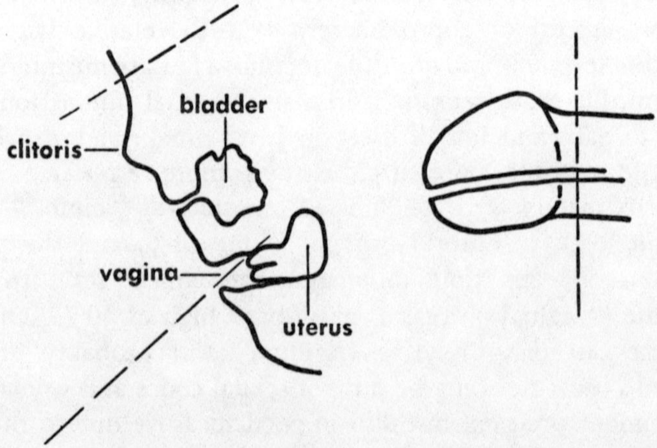

FIGURE 2

Comparable Sensory Areas for Male and Female

Sagittal section showing comparable genital areas, from embryological development and anatomically, and served by the pudendal nerve.

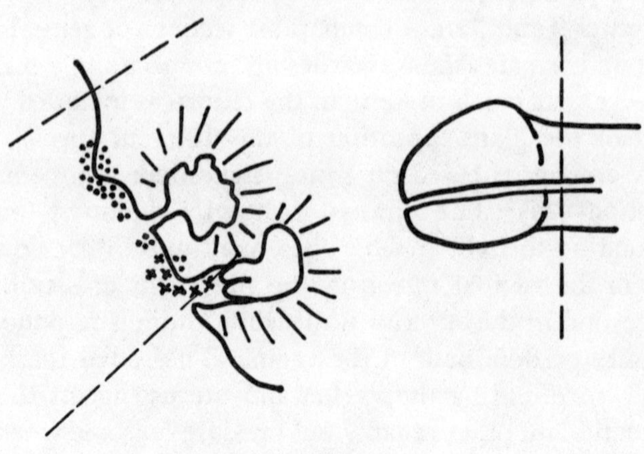

FIGURE 3

Comparable Sensory Areas

Dots indicate endorgans responding to touch and light pressure. Crosses indicate endorgans responding to deep pressure. Radial lines indicate stretch, autonomic nerves mediating kinaesthetic and somaesthetic sensation.

clitoral response is a *partial* response (to stimulation of only part of the pudendal nerve which serves the genital area; also, it excludes autonomic sensation) in which persistent—and therefore irritant and pathological—overstimulation of a particular and easily accessible site finally triggers an orgasm (accounting for Masters and Johnson's "plateau" finding—an artefact). But this orgasm, coming from an organ intended primarily for arousal, is less satisfying than the more total response for many reasons.

First, in describing the differences in physical sensation—and this seems to be borne out by Fisher's reports (22)—the clitoral sensation seems to be qualitatively different from the so-called vaginal or authentic: the clitoral feeling is reported as sharper, yet lacking in depth, in a woman who has experienced both. It is also less satisfying (2). Some women who have made this "transfer" report that they simply cannot return to clitoral satisfaction—it doesn't seem to "work." And they have observed in their sexual maturation transitory situations in which "missed orgasm" occurred—a condition in which an "almost" feeling suddenly disappeared, and there was a loss of interest in further sexual activity, but no sensation of orgasm, that is, a central nervous system alteration without completed genital sensation.

They also reported occasions when there seemed to be a waxing and waning of erotic sensations which almost, but not quite, eventuated in orgasm. This could be construed as "multiple orgasm," indicating insatiable need only because of failure of total satisfaction. Bose, in an early paper (25) considering the duration of coitus, stated that "the woman who experiences repeated orgasms during a single intercourse is not a normal person," adding that the woman who has one *satisfying* orgasm finds further sexual activity unwelcome. I believe this to be correct. We have yet to be presented with real proof to the contrary. Because it supports denial of inadequacy, it has caught on.

In considering the validity of woman's experiencing orgasm as a result of *genital* interaction, I believe that the "orgastic pretense," so well considered by Rosenbaum (26), would never have become a temptation for women to act out, if they did not realize

—and men of wide experience *know*—that an orgastic equivalent in the female does occur. Turning to the psychological, giving up the need to compete or control is a big factor in orgastic success. This does not preclude activity—it requires it. It may be true to some extent, as Fisher reports (22), that there is no easily discernible connection between mental illness, or its absence, and orgastic capacity. However, my observations lead me to conclude that there *are* definite personality correlates and responses representative of certain types of interpersonal transaction. I have observed that after the initial interview with new patients (both men and women) I can quite reliably predict their sexual responses, which are later confirmed.

Down through the centuries, women have been preoccupied with their sexual desirability. This, of course, has biological as well as social roots. They have also been aware that their sexual desirability and the social use of their sexuality has for the most part determined their fate. This has been carefully considered by Halleck (27) in the current framework in which many problems are viewed—that of power. He says: "Viewing sexual behavior in the context of power relationships provides insight into many sexual disturbances." Woman's weaker position has affected her sexual responses in many ways, one of the major ones being that it has deflected her attention from her own needs and feelings to the outer-directed pleasing of men, and so has served to obscure her responses. Those who have been able to keep their own sexuality intact, rather than subverted to other purposes, are more likely to experience an authentic response—an expression of potency and authenticity in personality as well as sexually. Perhaps this translates into Burness Moore's "masculine, aggressive woman," who is allegedly less mature because her response threatens her mate. But is this a really tenable explanation?

As a last point in relation to women's difficulties sexually, Ash has pointed out (28) that Freud, in a recently found brief paper on "Feminine Identity," emphasized that women come into analysis looking for a penis, as well as relief from symptoms. She wondered, as did Clara Thompson (29), whether they were not really looking for self-worth, which to them meant an honorable or masculine identity. Perhaps *this* is the problem of sexual passivity and of clitoral orgasm, with its hints of competitiveness—a sexual acting-out of penis envy, with its implication of being exactly like a man, because of the failure to become authentically feminine.

Yet according to Salzman (17): "One of the unfortunate consequences of the clitoral-vaginal orgasm notion is that it tends to encourage discontent in the female, who experiences orgasm when there is clitoral stimulation either by the finger or by the penis before or during sexual intercourse. She assumes that her orgasm is inferior and that she is sexually immature, even though it may have been pleasurable. She has (rightly) insisted on having vaginal orgasm, and either blames herself or her husband for her failure to experience it. Since there appears no validation for this whole notion, there is no reason to assume that an orgasm which is achieved by clitoral stimulation with either the finger or penis is inferior or imperfect, or that it can be improved by psychoanalytic therapy." He goes on to say that recent studies of female sexual behavior also fail to support this notion of clitoral vs. vaginal orgasm, quoting Sherfey and the ubiquitous M & J.

The curious fact is that all the concern about the clitoral response being belittled strikes one as a bit absurd. One of the sad facts about human sexual behavior is how frequently competition dominates—even in bed. And anxiety or indifference so dominate the sex act in men—even those who are reasonably potent—that often they have little notion of what is going on in their partner. Manual clitoral fiddling is push-button sex, and sex fixated upon passivity, sex deprived of spontaneity.

What psychoanalysis can offer is greater capacity to be self-assertive, free and spontaneous, to be daring and risk-taking, by striking off the bonds of irrational fears, as well as the need to maintain control of self and others. It cannot always succeed, but often it can. The woman who experiences authentic orgastic response needs no reassurance, has no doubts. Actively participant, involved in the "sexual dialogue," but not apart and intellectualizing, nor obsessively ruminating, nor fantasying special conditions, nor anxiety-ridden, nor narcissistically "on stage," nor competing with her partner—she feels her passion grow, dares to respond in a way that increasingly heightens her sensations, becomes aware of a time when an almost automatic rhythmic movement takes over, and experiences the full flood of release, with its various central nervous system changes; and then the stillness, with its backwash of gratitude and appreciation of the partner—the tenderness in the wake of the storm. She needs no reassurance about whether her orgasm is real, superior, or anything else. She knows, because in this sexual area she is completely autonomous.

Robert Browning was another man who, like Freud, had great insight into feminine response—the meaning and effect of clitoral arousal (foreplay) and of the total sex act, enhanced when also an act of love. In his poem from the group "Pippa Passes," which symbolically describes the two phases of the sex act, she speaks to her lover:

> The moth's kiss, first!
> Kiss me as if you made believe
> You were not sure, this eve
> How my face, your flower, had pursed
> Its petals up; so here and there
> You brush it, till I grow aware
> Who wants me, and wide ope I burst.
>
> The bee's kiss, now!
> Kiss me as if you entered gay
> My heart at some noon day,
> A bud that dare not disallow
> The claim, so all is rendered up,
> And passively its shattered cup
> Over your head to sleep I bow.
>
> *The Moth's Kiss, First!*
> Robert Browning—1843

This poem indicates that there are two stages in the sexual act: the first of arousal, the second of genital interaction. It suggests the need for a tentative approach initially—for the activity leading to arousal—the purpose of the clitoris. When mutual acceptance and arousal have occurred, then caution is thrown to the winds and complete abandon, complete involvement, and free activity of a genital nature take place, permitting the woman to be drained, "shattered," content. Often the need to be deeply penetrated in the final moments before orgasm reaches a conscious level, impelling the attempt to satisfy it. No clitoral stimulation can accomplish this.

The more sex is trivialized, the seemingly easier it becomes; the more it is cut off from appropriate physiological action, as well as from human meaning and relationship, the less seems to be its value and reward. Increasingly we are altering norms and values, and even concepts relating to physiology, to fit the patient or individual in society to lie in a particular Procrustean bed. But no area is isolated—each is a thread in the complex fabric of life. We should think carefully about our own orientation. Is it not possible that we do not have an answer to every mystery? A cure for every malaise including the sexual? On the other hand, as we elide the nuances from sexual expression, may we not invite the woman to give up too readily, to settle for less too quickly, or to accept the fact that there is nothing more, when in fact there may be? Are we removing *emotional* satisfaction from sexual experience? We need to take time out from the rush of change to examine some of these issues.

References

1. Mann, E. C. Frigidity. *Clin. Obstet. & Gyn., 3,* 739-757, 1960.
2. Shainess, N. A re-assessment of feminine sexuality and erotic experience. In J. Masserman (Ed.), *Science and Psychoanalysis,* Vol. X. New York: Grune and Stratton, 1966. Pp. 56-71.
3. Shainess, N. The therapy of frigidity. In J. Masserman (Ed.), *Current Psychiatric Therapies,* Vol. VIII. New York: Grune and Stratton, 1968. Pp. 70-79.
4. Heiman, M. Sexual response in the female. *Psychoanal. Quart., 30,* 615, 1961.
5. Moore, B. E. Psychoanalytic reflections on the implications of recent physiologic studies of female orgasm. *J. Amer. Psychoanal. Assn., 16,* 569-587, 1968.
6. Moore, B. E. Psychoanalytic meaning and treatment of frigidity. In P. J. Fink and V. B. C. Hammett (Eds.), *Human Sexual Function and Dysfunction.* Philadelphia: F. A. Davis Press, 1969.

7. Benedek, T. *Psychosexual Functions in Women*. New York: Ronald Press, 1952.
8. Deutsch, H. *Psychology of Women*, Vol. I. New York: Grune and Stratton, 1944.
9. Freud, S. The Transformation of Puberty. Three Contributions to the Theory of Sex. *Basic Writings*. New York: Random House, 1938.
10. Masters, W. H., and Johnson, V. E. The human female: Anatomy of sexual response. *Minnesota Med., 43,* 31-36, 1960.
11. Masters, W. H., and Johnson, V. E. Treatment of the sexually incompatible family unit. *Minnesota Med., 44,* 466-471, 1961.
12. Masters, W. H., and Johnson, V. E. *Human Sexual Response*. Boston: Little, Brown, 1966.
13. Sherfey, M. J. Evolution and nature of female sexuality. *J. Amer. Psychoanal. Assn., 14,* 28-129, 1966. Also, *Nature and Evolution of Female Sexuality*. New York: Random House, 1972.
14. Marmor, J. Some considerations concerning orgasm in the female. *Psychosom. Med., 16,* 240-245, 1954.
15. Marmor, J. Sexual frigidity. In H. I. Lief et al. (Eds.), *The Psychological Basis of Medical Practice*. New York: Hoeber, 1963.
16. Marmor, J. Changing patterns of femininity. In S. Rosenbaum and I. Alger (Eds.), *The Marriage Relationship*. New York: Basic Books, 1966. Pp. 31-46.
17. Salzman, L. Psychology of the female. *Arch. Gen. Psychiat., 17,* 195-203, 1967.
18. Polatin, P. The frigid woman. *Med. Aspects of Hum. Sexual., 4,* 8-13, 16, 21-24, August 1970.
19. Koedt, A. *The Myth of the Vaginal Orgasm*. Radical Feminist Press, 1970.
20. Shainess, N. Review: The Feminine Mind and Body, D. Chapman. *Amer. J. Psychother., 22*:4, 123, 1968. Also, review: Frigidity: Dynamics and Treatment, F. Kant, *Amer J. Psychother., 25*:6, 135, 1971.
21. Schimel, J. L. Psychopathology of egalitarianism in sexual relations. *Psychiatry, 25,* 182, 1962.
22. Fisher, S. *The Female Orgasm*. New York: Basic Books, 1973.
23. Shainess, N. The distaff side of impotence. *Med. Insight, 5*:4, 34-41, 1973.
24. Kinsey, A. C., Pomeroy, W. B., Martin, C. E., and Gebhard, P. H. *Sexual Behavior in the Human Female*. Philadelphia: W. B. Saunders, 1953.
25. Bose, G. The duration of coitus. *Int. J. Psychoanal., 18,* 253, 1937.
26. Rosenbaum, S. The significance of the orgastic pretense. In S. Rosenbaum and I. Alger (Eds.), *The Marriage Relationship*. New York: Basic Books, 1968.
27. Halleck, S. L. Sex and power. *Med. Aspects of Human Sexual., 3,* 8-24, October 1969.
28. Ash, M. Brief communications: Freud on feminine identity and female sexuality. *Psychiatry, 34,* 322-326, 1971.
29. Thompson, C. Penis envy in women. *Psychiatry, 6,* 123, 1943.

Discussion

SILVANO ARIETI, M.D.

In her relentless search for authenticity, Dr. Natalie Shainess engages herself in the analysis of many controversial issues and courageously espouses unpopular points of view.

Human sexuality is one of the major areas of her research. She is a non-Freudian who in this instance happens to be Freudian, and, not to be forgotten in this particular case, she is a woman. All these prerequisites make her particularly suitable to express an authentic point of view about the authentic female orgastic response.

Dr. Shainess's presentation seems quite convincing to me. At a time when many people are overtaken by the popularity of Masters and Johnson's mechanical approach and easily accept that the clitoral response is just as satisfactory as the vaginal, Dr. Shainess's voice is one of the few to warn us against embracing pseudosolutions and facile explanations. In her paper she has given sufficient physiological evidence that the clitoral sensation does exist as a strong feeling which may even be sharper than the vaginal but remains a partial one.

Some of the phenomena that Dr. Shainess has described in her paper have been expressed to me by many patients. Thus in reading her paper I experienced a sense of familiarity which I do not often experience in reading articles on similar subjects. For instance, I was glad finally to see reported in a psychoanalytic paper the fact that when a woman has made the transfer from clitoral to vaginal orgasm, she simply cannot return to the clitoral response except with a sense of dissatisfaction. The multiple orgasm, as an indication of a need which seems insatiable because of failure of total satisfaction, is a condition repeatedly expressed to me by a large number of patients. I agree with

Dr. Shainess that manual clitoral fiddling is push-button sex, or sex fixated upon passivity.

Her description of the woman who experiences the vaginal response is accurate, beautiful, poetic. Listen again to a few lines of Dr. Shainess's description of this woman: "Actively participant, involved in the sexual dialogue, but not apart and intellectualizing, nor obsessively ruminating, nor fantasying special conditions, nor anxiety-ridden, nor narcissistically 'on stage,' nor competing with her partner—she feels her passion grow, dares to respond in a way that increasingly heightens her sensations, becomes aware of a time when an almost automatic rhythmic movement takes over, and experiences the full flood of release, with its various central nervous system changes, and the stillness, with its backwash of gratitude and appreciation of the partner—the tenderness in the wake of the storm. She needs no reassurance about whether her orgasm is real, superior, or anything else. She knows, because in this sexual area she is completely autonomous."

This description gives us the sense of authenticity.

One wonders why we doubt so easily; why so many of us are taken in by push-button techniques. Maybe because it is easy to push buttons; how much easier than to reconstruct one's total personality! The vaginal response does indeed require a total participation.

Because of my special interest I want to report two facts concerning vaginal orgasm in schizophrenics or former schizophrenics. It is a popular belief that for these patients it is even more difficult than for other persons to eventually achieve vaginal orgasm. The concept of unhedonia formulated by Rado has acquired large acceptance, but does not correspond to clinical findings. Many recovered schizophrenics are able to experience a full vaginal orgasm. The myth that they cannot is so rooted in the traditional didactical knowledge of many psychiatrists that they refuse to believe the evidence. I have reported elsewhere the case of Geraldine, an intelligent and very sensitive patient who had several schizophrenic episodes of long duration, with hallucinations and delusions. She recovered, and at the age of 35 she got married. She was a virgin until her wedding night. From the beginning, she experienced full, authentic vaginal orgasm. I was invited to give a series of lectures to a Kleinian psychoanalytic institute in Buenos Aires and reported in detail the case of Geraldine. The audience was skeptical, and I would add sardonic, though within respectful limits. Many discussants said it was impossible for my patient to have the authentic experience. Two of them suggested that Geraldine was still actively schizophrenic and was hallucinating having vaginal orgasm. Rather than accepting the evidence offered by my prolonged treatment of Geraldine, they stuck to their belief; and in order to do so, they had to think she was still hallucinating.

Actually there is a good reason why a considerable number of schizophrenics easily achieve vaginal orgasm when they recover. When they were little girls these patients did not masturbate as other more normal girls do, before they had discovered the existence of the vagina. Thus whereas normal or not so disturbed girls learn to stimulate their clitoris, the candidate for schizophrenia often does not. So she is not so prone later to adopt the quick response.

I want to refer now to a very dissimilar experience, and I would like Dr. Shainess to help me with suggestions for similar circumstances. A vaginal orgasm, achieved for the first time by a very disturbed patient who had previously experienced only clitoral orgasm, may indeed precipitate a schizophrenic psychosis. Several patients have reported to me that the overt psychosis started exactly then, and I do not believe this is delusional either. Of course, the ground was prepared for the psychosis. A patient of mine who had been very disturbed or prepsychotic throughout her life remembers that while she was achieving for the first time in her life vaginal orgasm with great intensity and abandon, she heard telepathic messages transmitted from her sexual partner. The telepathic message was saying, "I, your partner, am a genius to make you feel it this way." And the word genius, genius, genius was incessantly telepathically repeated. That was the first symptom of the psychosis.

Full delusions and hallucinations, not manifestly related to sexual matters but actually oedipal in content, followed in this case. Examples of this type, of course, do not speak against the vaginal orgasm. On the contrary, they indicate that this is a very deep experience capable at times of disrupting the equilibrium of a person not prepared for such depth.

On one point I disagree with Dr. Shainess. Maybe I do not disagree, as she expresses herself in terms of a question; but in asking the question she seems to imply that we know the answer. At the end of her excellent paper she asks whether it would be better for the woman to be nonorgastic and symptomatic rather than part-achieving asymptomatic and emotionally dead. In other words, she asks whether it wouldn't be better to have no orgasm at all rather than a clitoral one. My answer is that if the woman, for whatever may be the reason, is really incapable of shifting to the vaginal orgasm, and we are not able to help her with psychoanalytic therapy, a clitoral orgasm is better than nothing. I may be labeled a down-to-earth pragmatist in this case. But I do believe that some ideals may crystallize us into static or absolute positions which are not compatible with the human situation, human anguish, and human compassion. We have to aim at the best possible form of sexuality; but if we unfortunately cannot achieve it, some other forms of sexuality may be acceptable and beneficial.

Finally, I really do not like to describe the woman who achieves only clitoral orgasm as "emotionally dead." In my opinion she is not emotionally dead at all. Often the fact that she cannot have the authentic experience leads her to other intense emotions, undoubtedly poor substitutes, and some of them negative and regrettable, but indicating nevertheless an intense emotional life. Perhaps Dr. Shainess does not always use her words literally and has used the expression "dead" at the end of her paper only to stress a point for stylistic emphasis. If she did so for this reason, I want to tell her that it was not necessary. Her paper, so rich in content, controversially vibrant, and so valuable for the unusually given data, does not need this hyperbole.

8

Biosocial Roots of Childhood Sexuality

IRVING BIEBER, M.D.

IN 1958, MY CRITIQUE OF THE LIBIDO THEORY was published (1); in 1966, my discussion of Robert White's paper on competence and the growth of personality (2) included an appraisal of ego psychology; and in 1972, my critique of the superego concept appeared (3). Thus, it is only fitting that I complete the cycle with a critique of the genetic theory. Of all the components of Freud's metapsychology, the genetic theory is supposed to be the one most rooted in biology. In elucidating what I believe to be the shortcomings and failures in this theory, I will also be describing my own views.

Freud first presented his genetic theory in the *Three Essays on the Theory of Sexuality* in 1905 (4). This paper marked his departure from a reliance on observable data which was the hallmark of his brilliant discoveries as they appeared in *The Interpretation of Dreams* in 1900 (5). He now chose, instead, to concentrate on the often mystical and speculative theories that characterize his metapsychology. It is in the *Three Essays* that he first enunciated his concept of orality as a psychosexual developmental phase, a concept that he wrote was based upon ". . . my) regarding thumb-sucking as a sexual manifestation and choosing it for our study of the essential features of infantile sexuality." The reasons Freud gave for claiming thumb-sucking as a sexual phenomenon deserve review:

1. "Sensual sucking involves a complete absorption of the attention and leads either to sleep or even to a motor reaction in the nature of an orgasm." Thus, one way he attempted to establish sucking as sexual was to compare it with orgasm in adults. His thinking here is clearly more related to poetic metaphor than to logic. Sucking may indeed absorb a child's attention but attentiveness does not equate a behavioral sequence with sexuality. Many sorts of stimuli may command attention, such as dangling a colored object in the crib, smiling and nodding, or rocking the child, activities in no way sexual. Further, sucking does not necessarily lead to sleep, nor, incidentally, does orgasm in adults. But even if sucking invariably did lead to sleep, this would not prove sucking to be a sexual phenomenon. Eating is often followed by drowsiness or sleep; exercise, too, may promote sleep. As for infantile sucking leading to orgasm—I have never observed it, nor has any pediatrician with whom I have discussed it.

2. Freud stated, ". . . (sucking) is not infrequently combined with rubbing some sensuous part of the body such as the breast or the external genitalia. Many children proceed by this path from sucking to masturbation." Sucking and grasping are associated movements in infancy and childhood, and Freud referred to this association in the *Three Essays*. In 1936, I reported a study of neonate sucking and grasping (6, 7), where I emphasized this association. I hypothesized that the association of sucking and grasping represented our mammalian heritage from primates where the clinging response of infants to the mother enabled them to nurse. In 1938, Fulton and I reported our neurophysiological experiments on primates which established that grasping was part of the postural reflex system (8), thus supporting my earlier hypothesis. The rubbing movements which Freud referred to are associated hand movements to the sucking, akin to associated grasping. As for the parts of the body rubbed, Freud chose the breast and genitals—sexual organs—as the involved areas. The origins of his choice of blocks in his theory building are extremely interesting. Freud obtained his material from a Dr. Lindner who did not, however, describe the breast and genitals as

the usual areas rubbed. Lindner named those children who rubbed a part of their body while they sucked, "suckers with combination." Later, the word "combined" reappeared in Freud's description, "(Sucking) is not infrequently *combined* with rubbing some sensuous part of the body." Lindner had stated that "all ordinary (simple) suckers can increase their pleasure of sucking by active assistance; the index fingers of one or both hands rub any sensuous spot (erogenous zone) on the head, the neck, the breast, and the abdomen, or pelvis, or thighs." As Lindner stated it, "the most sensitive points of the head are the hairy scalp, one or both sides of the nose, one nostril, one or both earlobes, and one or both lips simultaneously. The most sensuous points on the neck are the areas of the larynx. On the chest it is the nipple, on the abdomen it is the navel, and in the pelvic area, the genitals are chosen." Of the 69 cases of thumb-suckers described by Lindner, only four rubbed their genitals and, of these, only two did it consistently. Freud's mention of only breast and genitals as areas the child rubs was not exactly accurate reporting. When he attempted to support the sexual character of sucking in his conclusion that genital rubbing associated with sucking leads children from sucking to masturbation, his argument became an obviously specious one. Firstly, only a small percentage of the suckers rubbed their genitals. Secondly, in a careful study of 500 children, Lindner found only 69, that is 13.8%, who were suckers. It seems clear that since all children masturbate, sucking is not the route that usually brings them to genital activity. The argument that sucking is a sexual phenomenon because it leads to masturbation, can, in all fairness, be dismissed.

3. Freud stated in the *Three Essays,* "in the nursery, sucking is often passed along with other kinds of sexual 'naughtiness' of children." I don't think parents or their surrogates tend to view sucking as sexual or even naughty. It seems to me sucking is viewed more as undesirable, inappropriate, infantile, and so forth, but not sexual.

4. Freud stated, "Lindner himself clearly recognized the sexual nature of this activity and emphasized it without qualification."

This is inaccurate. Lindner did not regard sucking as sexual nor did he emphasize it without qualification, although there were indications that he thought there might be some connection. The *Three Essays* went through four editions: 1905, 1910, 1915 and 1920. The statement about Lindner appeared in the 1915 edition. In the 1905 and 1910 editions, Freud wrote, "No observer has felt any doubt as to the sexual nature of this activity," but it seems to me that Freud had some gnawing doubts himself about the sexual nature of sucking. In the 1920 edition, he included the following footnote: "In 1919 a Dr. Galant published under the title of 'Das Lutscherli' the confession of a grown-up girl who had never given up this infantile sexual activity and who represents the satisfaction to be gained from sucking as something completely analogous to sexual satisfaction particularly when this is obtained from a lover's kiss." Freud then quoted Dr. Galant as saying, "Not every kiss is equal to a lutscherli—no, no, not by any means. It is important to describe what a lovely feeling goes through your whole body when you suck; you are right away from this world . . ." How sure was Freud about the sexual nature of sucking during childhood if, 15 years after he originally proposed his theory, he used this farfetched example of an adult woman to substantiate his views?

To return to Lindner. Freud's remark, "Lindner himself clearly recognized the sexual nature of sucking and emphasized it without qualification," appeared in the 1915 edition. Now who was Lindner? Lindner was a Hungarian pediatrician who in 1878 published a very good study on pleasure sucking (9) or what we today refer to as nonnutritional sucking. It might well be one of the first pediatric statistical studies. Because Freud had placed so much weight on this study, I asked Dr. Martha Schon to translate it for me. The following were the only allusions to sexuality in Lindner's paper: the terms, "excited," "exalted," and "ecstatic" were used to describe one type of sucker; for example, "the six-year-old son of a cigar store owner who sucks his right thumb, digs his nostril with the little finger of the same hand until the blood comes and runs down over his lips." Lindner then mentions the four children who rubbed their genitals while sucking, adding, "There is no doubt about it that as the years go on the tickling of the genitals can lead to proper masturbation." In a footnote there appeared the statement that quiet suckers who need no rocking or singing to put them to sleep rub pleasure points which are the same as one finds in adults as their erotic areas. These are Lindner's only allusions to sexuality. He demonstrated statistically that thumb-sucking or pleasure sucking has no connection with too much or too little breast feeding or too much or too little exposure to pleasurable pacifiers. Freud's later formulation that oral eroticism had an experiential base in too much or too little oral gratification finds no support in Lindner's study.

In elaborating secondary developments, Freud stated, "It is not every child who sucks in this way (pleasure sucking). It may be assumed that those children do so in whom there is a constitutional intensification of the erotogenic significance of the labial region. If that significance persists, these same children when they grow up will become epicures; in kissing they will be inclined to perverse kissing (probably a reference to French kissing) or if males, will have a powerful motive for drinking and sucking. If, however, repression ensues they will feel disgust at food and will produce hysterical vomiting." This summarizes Freud's basic assumptions underlying his hypothesis that there is normally an oral sexual phase in childhood development.

From a physiological viewpoint, the responses consequent to sucking are almost the opposite of what occurs when an adult is sexually stimulated orally. In sucking, there is a quieting of all excitation; there is a decrease in heart rate, heart rate variability, respiratory rate, and motoric phenomena. In adults, kissing and other oral erotic stimuli trigger increasing arousal with concomitant physical excitation. Sucking can also be viewed as a mechanism for tension release. Bridger and Birns (10) have shown that if an infant is exposed to a noxious stimulus, like immersing a foot in icewater, sucking behavior is initiated even in children who have just been fed. This type of stimulation and the ensuing behavior are not sexual.

Since Freud, no one has offered any more solid data than he

had in support of his hypothesis that infantile sucking and orality are sexual. This idea has been accepted as if it had been methodologically established. And it continues to be accepted and taught as proven doctrine. From time to time I have discussed this matter with colleagues who have the "classical" point of view. They argue, firstly, that my view of sexuality is too literal; that theirs is the broad view, though this broadened view has developed out of an unsupported and, I believe, erroneous assumption that infantile orality is sexual. Secondly, they propose that even if it were not sexual, orality still represents the dominant way in which infants symbolize their relationship with the mother, as well as other aspects of the world as they perceive it. Undoubtedly, the feeding relationship between mother and child is very important; it is, however, only one variable in the immensely complex growth process. Surely psychological development cannot be reduced to orifice-phallus psychology. The mother-child bond may be variously symbolized in terms other than oral. I have, for example, seen maternal deprivation appear in dream scenes of coldness and barrenness, which are thermal and visual symbols.

The anal phase. Freud based his concept of an anal phase following an oral phase on the fact that the anus could be used as a sexual organ in both homo- and heterosexual activity and that many individuals experienced erotic sensations in this area. Again, using adult sexuality as a model, he viewed the anus as a type of vagina and the fecal column as a phallic substitute. Since the feces could stimulate the receptive anal mucosa, this potential gave it great value. The child then became reluctant to part with valued feces and when he did, he sustained a sense of loss, i.e., castration with the loss of feces. Traits of stubbornness, rebelliousness, and stinginess were presumably the derivates of anxiety associated with this sense of loss. My own observations do not support Freud's schema. I have been able to delineate three psychodynamic processes associated with the bowel and anus. Two are connected with sexuality; the third is not. The first has to do with anal odors and is a component of the Oedipus complex;

the second has to do with the use of the anus as a genital substitute after genital functioning has been inhibited. I shall discuss both mechanisms later on. The third process concerns power relationships between parent and child. Bowel training used to be, and in many families still is, the first major area of a power struggle between mother and child. A dominating, controlling mother demands action and rapid returns; a rebellious, stubborn child refuses. Traits of stubbornness and rebelliousness, when rooted in bowel training disturbances, are the by-products of power dynamics.

Sexual development. The earliest behavior that I have been able to identify as possibly sexual is the infantile manipulation of the genitals which begins in the male between the sixth and ninth month. As far as I know, there are no recorded observations as to when this begins in the female. Shortly before his death, Bela Mittelman told me he thought it occurred somewhat later in females, closer to the end of the first year. Recently, I obtained two observations on female infants. In both, the behavior was present at nine months. If not interfered with, such behavior continues into a masturbatory pattern during childhood, preadolescence, adolescence, and adulthood. In Freud's era, infantile manipulation and childhood masturbation were almost always interrupted as soon as they were detected. In the *Three Essays,* Freud has this to say: "The masturbation of early infancy seems to disappear after a short time; but it may persist uninterruptedly until puberty and this would constitute the first great deviation from the course of development laid down for civilized men. At some period of infancy, as a rule before the fourth year, the sexual instinct belonging to the genital zone usually revives and persists again for a time until it is once more suppressed or it may continue without interruption."

I referred to infantile manipulation of the genitals as possibly being sexual, since the genitals are involved in the activity. Freud observed and reported that stimulation of the infant's genitals produced a quiescence. Because of this, he noted, unscrupulous nursemaids quieted children in this manner. I myself have not verified this observation but if it checked out, as I believe it would, then the physical responses to infantile genital manipulation are similar to those following sucking and the opposite of what occurs in later life when the genitals are stimulated. Whether or not an infant's manipulation of his genitals is sexual, the parents interpret it that way so that from a sociobiological viewpoint, it can be termed sexual behavior. It is important for heuristic purposes to determine when the physical response to genital stimulation changes from quiescence to excitation. One would think that with the volumes written on infantile sexuality, we would have known this by now. We do know that by the fourth year, genital manipulation produces arousal and excitation. I observed a three-and-a-half-year-old genitally masturbating who came to orgasm and I have a patient who assures me that by the age of five, certainly, he was able to come to orgasm by masturbating. Kinsey (11), in his volume on female sexuality, reported the case of a five-year-old girl who was observed by her mother masturbating to orgasm. During this symposium, Dr. Eleanor Galenson reported that she had observed erections in a male child as erotic responses to his mother when he was two years old. This may well be the earliest age at which such a reponse has been recorded.

The evidence is very suggestive that the arousal reaction to genital manipulation develops with the Oedipus complex. Freud termed infantile masturbation "autoerotic" because it was not initiated by other objects nor did the behavior depend upon a relationship with other objects. Object-related sexuality begins with the Oedipus complex somewhere between the ages of two and five. From birth on, the child participates in ever increasingly complex social interactions with parents and others. I do not consider such interactions as sexual before the Oedipus complex develops. A sexual system can be defined just as one can define a respiratory, cardiovascular, or gastrointestinal system, each with its own anatomy, physiology and biology. The genitals are clearly part of the sexual anatomy as are the organs of reproduction—uterus, tubes, gonads, and those organs that represent secondary sexual characteristics such as breasts and so forth. Those parts of the nervous system specifically identified with sexual arousal and behavior, such as parts of the limbic lobe, are part of the sexual anatomy. Physiological aspects of sex include processes operant in arousal and release in orgasm as described by Masters and Johnson (12) and include specific hormone function. Waxenberg, Drellich, and Sutherland (13) have demonstrated that a minimal level of sexual steroids was essential to maintain the sexual function. In their study, women who had been deprived of all steroids, estrogens, and androgens by oophorectomy, hypophysectomy, and adrenalectomy lost all capability for sexual arousal or interest. Sexual elements disappeared even from their dreams. These women did, however, maintain a wish to be held and be shown affection by their husbands, thus clearly distinguishing between a sexual and an affectional system. The women had lost their sexuality but not their desire for an affectionate relationship.

As to the Oedipus complex—this phenomenon may be divided into two components consisting of (1) the initiation of heterosexual responsivity, and (2) the rivalry with same-sex individuals. This type of division may be more persuasive for those who do not accept the Oedipus complex as a constellation of observable data but see it merely as metapsychological theory. These days, analysts of varying viewpoints seem agreed that the capability of responding to the opposite sex with specific sexual interest and excitation does not begin as late as puberty. Most of us can clearly recall our own interest in the opposite sex, certainly by the age of six. I have had many patients, male and female, who remember being sexually interested by the age of four or five; in males it often included responding with erection. If we are agreed that children indeed respond heterosexually at such an early age to their peer mates, this capability must also extend to all members of the opposite sex, in particular, those in one's intimate family environment; for boys, it is the mother and sisters; for girls, it is father and brothers.

In 1959, I published a paper entitled "Olfaction in Sexual

Development and Adult Sexual Organization" (14). I advanced the hypothesis that olfaction was a primary modality in the initiation of heterosexual arousal in humans, and I offered supporting data. For clarification, an explicatory digression is indicated. A male dog of three months has an acute sense of smell but will not respond to the odor of a bitch in heat. He will respond when he is nine months old. Somewhere between the third and ninth month, a development has taken place in his central nervous system that makes possible a response to an olfactory stimulus, known among odor researchers as a pheromone. I believe that the same phenomenon occurs in humans. The capability of reacting with a specific response to olfactory stimuli from the opposite sex is established somewhere between the ages of two and five. Once the olfactory response occurs, all other sensory modalities are rapidly integrated into the sexual system—vision, touch, hearing, and so forth. In 1963, Kalogerakis reported the only case in the literature on the olfactory sexual experiences of a child during his oedipal phase (15), including a description of the development of a foot fetish in this boy. He initially began to enjoy smelling the feet of his young aunt who lived with his parents. He was clearly turned on by the experience. His response became generalized to other women but never to men. Then he began to look with interest at, and become excited by, the ads of women's stockings in the newspapers. A reaction which was initially olfactory thus became integrated with another sensory modality, vision. Kalogerakis' subject was not only turned on by the odor of women but he was turned off and nauseated by the odor of a male, in particular, his own father. Kalogerakis extended my hypothesis. Not only was olfaction operative in the excitatory response to the heterosexual object, but it was also operative in the rivalry response to the same-sex object as demonstrated by the aversive olfactory reaction. Since 1959, I have gathered a great deal of additional supporting data. I have had at least five male patients who recalled a negative reaction to their father's odor. Toby Bieber has reported one male homosexual who could immediately turn off a homoerotic response by recalling a male's anal odor (16). Female odors pleased and excited this patient. Freud postulated that there was no instinctual mechanism to determine heterosexual object choice. I think that all humans, excluding those with chromosomal, hormonal, and gonadal anomalies of the type described by Money and the Hampsons (17), have an inborn mechanism involving olfaction that guarantees heterosexual responsivity. This phase of the Oedipus complex is biologically determined. I think, too, that same-sex rivalry is also biologically rooted. It is identifiable in infrahuman vertebrates and, most probably, humans are no exception.

As to anality in connection with olfaction, I have obtained information, mostly from men, which indicates that anal and body odors, their own and their mother's, play a role in oedipal development. A recent clinical experience is illustrative. A patient who was in love with an erratic woman knew that marriage to her was unwise. When he communicated his doubts to her, she broke off their relationship. As a consequence, he became acutely agitated and depressed. During the depth of his reaction, he had the following dream: He was a child back in the kitchen of his parents' home. His mother was cooking chicken soup and its wonderful aroma pervaded the room. The patient himself was sitting on the potty, defecating, and emitting unpleasant odors. From this dream, the following material emerged: There had been four women in his life, apart from his mother, with whom he had had a profound emotional relationship—his first wife who died some years ago, her mother, another woman some years his senior with whom he had had an affair for many years, and his recent amour. He clearly remembered that the mother of his first wife smelled like his own mother; his wife had smelled like her own mother, and the other two women had smelled like his wife. In short, although the patient did not describe it directly, each woman had smelled like his mother. Olfaction had played an important role in his choices and emotional reactions to these women. The dream in which he is defecating suggests that anality is a determinant of his sexual response to his mother and is operant on an oedipal level. After the dream was analyzed, the patient's agitation and depression disappeared with dramatic suddenness, relief that lasted for several days, to be followed by mild hypomanic excitement as a reaction to his discovery.

The anal component in the sexuality of men and women seems to differ. Male patients not infrequently contribute clear evidence of interest in their mother's anus and of an unconscious wish to have had anal intercourse with the mother. Certainly most adult males find female buttocks sexually arousing, yet a comparable interest in men's buttocks seems not to be present in most women, a difference in sexual behavior well worth further investigation.

As to the use of the anus as a substitute genital: in both sexes the proximity of the anus to the genitals and the similarity of innervation makes the anus particularly suitable as a paragenital organ. The anterior wall of the rectum is in close approximation to the sexual organ in both sexes. In the female, the anterior wall of the rectum and the posterior wall of the vagina are palpated as one structure and in the male the anterior wall is adjacent to the prostate and seminal vesicles. When genital masturbation is suppressed or extinguished, children may discover anal masturbation as a substitute. Genital masturbation may be interfered with or entirely extinguished by direct prohibition or by a boy's own castration fears about handling his genitals; or, in the case of a girl, fears about vaginal injury. After the oedipal phase has been established, arousal by the cross-sex parent or siblings may stimulate genital masturbation. Generally, there is no consciousness that the stimulus is an incestuous object. If fear of retaliation is great, genital functioning may be suppressed and the anus may then take on the function of the genital. Some male homosexuals are incapable of genital insertion and they use the anus as a receptive genital organ. In these men, their anus may become symbolic of a vagina. Several heterosexuals whom I have treated have masturbated anally. With the restoration of their genital functioning, including the capability of genital masturbation to orgasm without anxiety, anal masturbation disappeared.

A recurring question concerns the relationship between the oedipal constellation and psychopathology. Why is it, many ask, that the Oedipus complex is so much more important in some individuals than in others, yet the complex is ubiquitous? Freud never directed himself centrally to this question. The only explanation he offered concerns constitutional factors such as exaggeration of partial impulses, oral or anal, or excessive passivity in the male. In researching the problems in homosexuality, my colleagues and I found that the factors determining the outcome of the biosocial maturational phase known as the Oedipus complex are directly linked to family influences, particularly the parents (18). Freud concerned himself with the child's sexual responses and rivalries toward parents, not with parental responses to their children. Parents who do not become disturbed by their sexual responses, do not disturb their child's emerging sexuality. I have noted that, in the main, fathers have more anxiety about their sexual responses to daughters than mothers to sons. In one case, a father rejected his daughter when she reached adolescence. He brought in a dream in which he and his daughter were climbing up the side of an active volcano. The volcano was erupting and the lava threatened to destroy both. Though the patient was analytically sophisticated, he had not the vaguest notion of the obvious meaning of his dream when he reported it.

Normally, youngsters become rivalrous with a same-sex parent; it is altogether inappropriate for parents to become rivalrous with children. If a parent's rivalry is significantly acted out, or if it precludes an affectionate relationship, serious psychopathology, sexual and nonsexual, develops in the child. The various ongoing studies of the family and family systems should continue to illuminate the highly complex and varied ways in which parents respond to their child's oedipal development and the ways in which a child adapts to parental reactions to his or her gender and sexuality.

Freud's discovery of the Oedipus complex is, in my view, among the truly great contributions to the understanding of human behavior. His theories, however, are badly in need of revision and change. This paper is an effort in that direction.

References

1. Bieber, I. A critique of the libido theory. *Amer. J. Psychoanal., 18,* 52, 1958.
2. Bieber, I. Discussion of "Competence and Growth of Personality" by R. W. White. In J. Masserman (Ed.), *Science and Psychoanalysis,* Vol. II. New York: Grune and Stratton, 1967. P. 49.
3. Bieber, I. Morality and Freud's concept of the superego. In S. C. Post (Ed.), *Moral Values and the Superego Concept in Psychoanalysis.* New York: International Universities Press, 1972. P. 126.
4. Freud, S. Three essays on the theory of sexuality (1905). *Standard Edition,* Vol. 7. London: Hogarth Press.
5. Freud, S. The interpretation of dreams (1900). *Standard Edition,* Vols. 4 and 5. London: Hogarth Press.
6. Bieber, I. Grasping and sucking. *Arch. Neurol. and Psychiat., 37,* 704, 1937.
7. Bieber, I. Grasping and sucking. *J. Nerv. Ment. Dis., 91,* 31, 1940.
8. Bieber, I., and Fulton, J. F. Relation of cerebral cortex to grasp reflex and to postural and righting reflexes. *Arch. Neurol. and Psychiat., 35,* 1208, 1938.
9. Lindner, S. Ludeln. *Jahrbuch für Kinderheilkunde,* Leipzig, *14,* 68, 1878.
10. Bridger, W. H., and Birns, B. M. An analysis of the role of sucking in early infancy. In J. Masserman (Ed.), *Science and Psychoanalysis,* Vol. II. New York: Grune and Stratton, 1968. P. 156.
11. Kinsey, A. C., Pomeroy, W. B., Martin, C. E., and Gebhard, P. H. *Sexual Behavior in the Human Female.* Philadelphia: W. B. Saunders, 1953.
12. Masters, W. H., and Johnson, V. E. *Human Sexual Response.* Boston: Little, Brown, 1966.
13. Waxenberg, S. E., Drellich, M. D., and Sutherland, A. M. The role of hormones in human behavior changes in female sexuality after adrenalectomy. *J. Clin. Endocrinol. and Metab., 19,* 193, 1959.
14. Bieber, I. Olfaction in sexual development and adult sexual organization. *Amer. J. Psychother., 13,* 851, 1959.
15. Kalogerakis, M. The role of olfaction in sexual development. *Psychosom. Med., 25,* 420, 1963.
16. Bieber, T. Group therapy with homosexuals. In H. I. Kaplan and B. J. Sadock (Eds.), *Comprehensive Group Psychotherapy.* Baltimore: Williams and Wilkins, 1971. P. 527.
17. Money, J., Hampson, J. S., and Hampson, J. L. Imprinting and the establishment of gender role. *Arch. Neurol. and Psychiat., 77,* 333, 1957.
18. Bieber, I., et al. *Homosexuality—A Psychoanalytic Study of Male Homosexuals.* New York: Basic Books, 1962.

9

Ludeln

S. Lindner

THE SUCKING OF FINGERS, LIPS, AND SO ON, in childhood, a long known peculiarity, has drawn the attention of physicians only insofar as it is a common bad habit of children. As far as I know, there has been no scientific study investigating "sucking for pleasure"—if one can classify it as such. Therefore, it is justified to report some observations and consequences of this behavior.

"Ludeln," better called "sucking for pleasure," means in the strict sense of the word either sucking of the mouth itself or sucking of an object which is introduced into the mouth. These objects are either parts of the human body or objects which may or may not be edible. Even if the object can be eaten, the one who sucks it has no intention of eating or digesting it.

In this sense the proverb "ludeln and dudeln" applies if someone sings a song. Similarly, a tobacco pipe is nicknamed a "ludel." Suckers, therefore, can be classified as (1) the ordinary, simple sucker, and (2) the combination sucker. Simple suckers become "combination suckers" by means of "active assistance" and "passive assistance." Each type of sucker, the simple as well

---

The sucking of the fingers, lips, etc., in children. *Jahrbuch für Kinderheilkunde,* Leipzig, *14,* 68-91, 1878.

as the combination, can also be an occasional sucker, a sucker with various methods of sucking, and an excited sucker.

The Simple (Ordinary) Sucker

The ordinary sucker sucks his lips, tongue, fingers or thumbs, back of the hand, arms, or foreign bodies. In mouth sucking, one sucks either with closed lips, or with the tip of the tongue touching the upper or the lower lip so that one can see clearly the tip of the tongue between the lips. The first type we call the lip sucker, the second type, the tongue sucker.

Those who suck on their own body usually choose—like the old god Harus—one thumb, more often the right one, and sometimes two or three fingers of the same hand. Usually, the second and third fingers are chosen, sometimes the second and ring fingers, or the three middle fingers; very rarely the big toe is selected. The remaining few suck on the back of the hand or the arm. Thus we have finger or thumb suckers, back-of-hand suckers, and arm suckers.

Sometimes the position of the hand is such that the insides of the second and fourth fingers face the front; this is uncomfortable, at least for older children. When the second and fourth fingers are sucked, they are stretched and brought closer to each other, whereby the middle fingers have to be bent more or less. For known anatomical reasons, if these fingers are stretched, it is impossible to bend the middle finger or the little finger without involving the fourth finger. Sooner or later, severe pain develops between the third and fourth fingers, and between the fourth and fifth fingers.

Artists tend to portray children with only one finger in their mouth, namely the second finger of the right hand.

Those who suck objects usually suck bread or the nipple of their bottle or a part of their clothing. For example, every night before going to bed, the six-year-old son of a watchmaker asks for a clean shirt, which he sucks until he falls asleep. I would classify him as an "occasional sucker" because he only sucks when he can get hold of the particular object he wants to suck; he does not suck any other time.

It has been observed that any type of "sucker" can be switched over to a different type, that is, one who sucks his lips can become a tongue sucker, and vice versa. Furthermore, most of those who suck their lips can become "occasional" suckers of objects, because they get, by chance, pieces of bread between their lips and they suck on these pieces of bread. Those who suck on their lips may also suck the back of their hand and their arms. An eight-year-old daughter of a businessman usually sucked her left thumb, but she also sucked her right thumb and left toe. Those individuals who are able to switch from one sucking method to another, I call "suckers with an ability to change": "Ludler mit Wechsel in Ludeln."

The Combination Sucker

All ordinary (simple) suckers can increase their pleasure of sucking by active assistance: the individual fingers of one or both hands rub any sensuous spot (erogenous zone) on the head, the neck, the breast, the abdomen, pelvis or thighs. The most sensitive areas of the head are the hairy scalp, one or both sides of the nose, one nostril, one or both earlobes, and one or both lips.

The most sensuous point on the neck is in the area of the larynx; on the chest, it is the nipple; on the abdomen, the navel; and in the pelvic area, the genitals.

Children usually rub the lips with an object. If the object is delicate and light, like the corner of a bed sheet, then this object moves visibly. However, if the object is rough and heavy, like the sleeve of a cloth coat, then the movement is hardly noticeable. Obviously, a gentle touch tickles the sensitive lips, which have many nerve fibres and blood vessels and a thin epidermis, more than the touch of a coarse object. Sometimes the sensitive spot lies in the active hand which helps out. The middle finger might rub the back of the neighboring second finger; or the friction might take place between the touch corpuscles of the middle finger and the thumb of the same hand; or the sensitive spot may lie within the tips of all fingers which are rubbed against a pillow.

Whenever the combination sucker is taken into the arms of a person, or sleeps with someone, he has the odd habit of transferring his special sensitive spot to that person. For instance, he touches the ears or breast of the other person. It is unlikely that the active helping hand will travel toward the lower part of the body. Small children cannot reach that area; bigger children will not dare such a maneuver because it will only bring about disapproval.

Just as there is a switch from one type of sucking to another, there are also changes in the active helping hand and in the sensitive spot. Not only does the helping hand alternate, but often a new sensitive spot is chosen, very often on the genitals.

In contrast to active assistance is passive assistance. The duty of the passive helping hand is either to hold the sucking object or to support or hide it.

Small children sometimes hide the sucking objects with their hand out of fear; adults hide it because they are ashamed. This kind of sucker may be called the "sucker with the mask." Unfortunately, as time goes by, every mask becomes a habit and consequently a kind of active help. The 11-year-old daughter of a manufacturer, whom I have observed since she was five years old, originally was sucking with closed lips. Later she masked the mouth with her right hand every time she was afraid of being caught. Today, she could not suck at all, or only with difficulty without the mask, because she became a tongue sucker due to the assistance of the mask. The passive helping hand is usually quiet and acts as a support for the object which assists actively and is in motion more or less.

Suckers who increase the value and intensity of the pleasure by inflicting pain on themselves or by procedures which are unpleasant or distasteful to other children can be considered "excited suckers." The following four cases are representative of this group:

The six-year-old son of a cigar store owner sucks his right thumb and digs his nostril with the little finger of the same hand until the blood comes and runs down over his lips.

The 14-year-old daughter of a landowner sucks her tongue and finds extreme pleasure in pulling one hair out from her scalp in order to play with it while she is engaged in the act of sucking.

The seven-year-old son of a waiter puts a piece of bread under his pillow before he goes to sleep. He takes a little piece of bread, sticks it on his palate like a bread sucker, and starts to click with his tongue. Later he takes it out of his mouth, puts it in one nostril, and starts anew with another piece of bread. This goes on until the nose and both ears are stuffed with bread that is drenched with saliva. Only then is he able to sleep peacefully.

The 11-year-old son of a cashier was a lip sucker. Several years ago he had had an inflammation of the eye which was accompanied by photophobia for a long period of time. Because of it, he used a very small headpillow in order to shield his eyes. After the inflammation was cured, he did not give up that funny shield and used it as an active help. I classified him as an exalted sucker, only because he derived particular pleasure when the pillow was not covered by a pillowcase.

I conducted a study comprising 117 families and 500 children. Of these, 69 children, or 13.8%, were suckers. This practice occurred in 54 families under investigation, that is, almost half of the families. Of these 69 suckers, 33 were boys and 36 were girls.

With respect to the types of suckers, 26 thumb suckers, 19 simple, ordinary suckers, and 7 combination suckers were noted. Among these were one occasional sucker, one exalted sucker, one who switched from one type of sucking to another, and one who switched the spot of sensitivity. There were 20 lip suckers, 9 simple ones, and 11 with combination. Among those were one occasional sucker, one excited sucker, several who changed their type of sucking, one who changed the active helping hand, and two who shifted to a different spot of sensitivity. There were

10 tongue suckers, 4 simple ones and 6 with combination. These included one excited sucker and one with mask. Six finger suckers were noted, five simple ones and one with combination. There was one excited sucker in this group. Finally, there were one sucker of the back of the hand and one sucker of the arm.

The oldest thumb sucker was 13 years; the oldest lip sucker was 30 years; the oldest tongue sucker was 40 years; the oldest finger sucker was 12 years. The oldest child who sucked an object was 7 years old; the oldest who sucked the back of his hand was 12. The oldest girl who sucked her arm was 10 years old.

In one family I noted four girls who sucked. They all belonged to main types.

An educated tailor of women's clothes who traveled to the bigger cities of Austria and Hungary in order to instruct girls in his art, told me that nowhere did he meet as many suckers as in Corinthia and Kraiu. In these places all of his students were suckers. The women of these countries, mostly businesswomen, engaged "Lockerinneu" (nannies) especially for the purpose of preparing "Lutchbeutel" for their children. ("Lutchbeutel" is a kind of pacifier prepared in the following way. Crumbs or sugar are placed on a piece of old lint cake. The lint is then tied in such a way that a little bag is formed. The bag is moistened and placed into the infant's or child's mouth and he sucks on it.) At first glance it might seem that the pacifier is the *causa proxima,* the cause for the sucker; but I cannot wholly agree with this. Among my 69 suckers, I noted only 3 children who used such a pacifier. On the contrary, I found that in those 63 families who had no sucker among them, the pacifier was used nine times as much. Furthermore, one would think that those children who were nursed, really stuffed, would suck. I have only met four such children; only two of them sucked. Similarly, the bottle cannot be blamed for sucking. In the families where no suckers can be found, the bottle was used nine times as much, while among the suckers, one could find the bottle used only four times as much. In the case of finger sucking, the mothers hold the nursemaids responsible for the acquisition of this habit.

The mothers believe that the nannies put the fingers into the infants' mouths in order to have peace, and in this way they taught them the habit. This is quite true: 49 suckers were tended by nursemaids. Two children were not breast-fed at all.

It is also an incorrect assumption that only poor and unintelligent children suck; I have met suckers in the best circles. Because of my experience, I also have to defend those children who are usually accused of being suckers because they are spoiled, being first-borns. Attention is also given to the duration of breast-feeding. Some believe that if the children are breast-fed for too long or too short a period, this is responsible for sucking. Among the suckers, I found only five children who were nursed for less than six months, and six who were nursed for one year. The majority were breast-fed for at least eight months, mostly 9-11 months. Among those who did not suck, there were two children who were breast-fed for three months, three who were breast-fed for 15 months, and one child who was breast-fed for more than two years.

Since the above-mentioned reasons cannot be regarded with too much confidence, we have to assume that every child has an inherent disposition toward sucking, which under given circumstances can lead to sucking for pleasure. And indeed, infants take everything which is put in their hands to their lips in order to examine it, because in the first months the lips are more sensitive than the hands. The examining of these objects can, in time, become the cause for sucking on objects, and if such objects are lacking, it can become the reason for finger, arm, or back-of-the-hand sucking. If these are not available either, then the infants simply suck without them.

Let's spend a moment with a child while it sucks. Except for those bread suckers who click their tongue and stick the bread to the hard palate, the others suck quietly and one can see rather than hear them suck. However, at times they are annoying to the listener, when they click their tongue or their lips in their sleep or when they are in a state of extreme pleasure. In such a state, the sucking movements are more forceful and the sucked object is moved and thereby pushed deeper into the mouth, e.g., the whole length of the thumb. Furthermore, if there is rubbing on a sensitive spot, it becomes more intense. Indeed, it is not rare that the suckers get into a state of ecstasy; they move their head downwards, they bend the vertebra, they stamp with their feet, or, if they are lying down, they kick with their legs. This is the state during which excited suckers bleed, pull their hair, or stuff up their noses and ears. If one asks a question of these suckers while they are in that state of ecstasy, they only motion with their head, yes or no. If one attempts to disturb them, they become very angry and run away to a safe place; however, they do not stop sucking, not even for a moment. Sometimes they are so engrossed in sucking that they don't notice any threats and are deaf to nice words.

If the children are in bed after the state of ecstasy, they fall asleep with the sucking object in their mouth; however, the auxiliary helping hand, if it is not bent across the head, returns to its ordinary position.

All suckers, other than occasional suckers, suck wherever they may be and at all times. However, preference is given to this pleasure shortly before they fall asleep, soon after waking up, and after they have taken a bath. The occurrence of an acute or sometimes of a chronic sickness may interrupt the sucking. Conversely, the reawakening of the pleasure for sucking can be taken as a prognostic sign for a speedy recovery. Never did I see my little daughter suck her thumb with such pleasure as after she had diphtheria. My colleagues and I had given her up at that time.

Because children engaged in pleasure sucking are always quiet if they are left alone, and need no rocking or singing to put them to sleep, mothers and nursemaids call these children, out of gratitude, "the religious children." This name may explain why Gandeus Ferrari painted one of his Madonnas with the Christ child sucking his right second finger.

If one showed me a sucker during the time he was not sucking, I could recognize only a thumb or finger sucker. The skin of the finger which is used as the sucking object is wrinkled and sometimes sore, like the skin of the fingers of a laundress. Its nail is cleaner and softer than the nails of the rest of the fingers.

Where Does Sucking Lead?

Laymen believe that children who suck can injure their lungs or their brain. I myself can see two disadvantages: one is from a cosmetic point of view, the other is more serious.

For instance, it does not matter very much if we find a hard spot on the back of a finger of a girl which developed because of the continuous rubbing of the sensitive spot over a long period of time. Similarly, we may see a boy whose hair on the right temple stands upright because he touched it continuously with his left hand. Hyrtl tells us that it is not infrequently that a thumb sucker loses his nail. On the other hand, we have to wonder why the girl who sucks her toe was intellectually quite promising in the beginning, but is now retarded in her school work, despite tutoring. Should we advise those adults who suck their lips and tongues and come to us for help with their compulsion to suck? Do we have to help if we catch someone who masturbates? Do we have to help the anxious mother who shows us the protruding shoulder or the misshapen mouth of her child?

I owe you an explanation for the three aforementioned conditions which often appeared as effects:

On the whole I saw only four children who sucked with active assistance of the genitals. Of these four, only two used this spot as a continuous sensitive spot, while for the other two it was an alternative spot. One might raise the objection that we have here two types of childish play that coexist by chance, but which are independent of each other. However, (1) I have seen suckers who also masturbated, but they did not do it at the same time; (2) the suckers I have seen have stopped sucking the moment they were prevented from active assistance, or they stopped sucking permanently if they were continuously prevented from such assistance. Of course, attempts have been made the other way around, that is, if one disrupted the sucking, the assistance stopped *eo ipso* because there was no reason for assistance any more; (3) I cannot see why a child has to avoid the genitals in his scale of sensitive spots, or if he changes with the helping hand from the nose to the ear, why he should not change to the genitals.

A child whom I have observed for some time spoke for herself. Not quite three years old, lively and healthy in every respect, this girl sucked her thumb, and with the other hand, always played alternately with the nose or the genitals. Once my right hand interfered with her hand which played with her genitals. She then kept my right hand tight in her axilla. Then I did the same with my left hand, with the same result. I freed my hands with the intention to interfere again. Finally the child defended herself with these words, "Leave me alone, otherwise I cannot suck."

There is no doubt about it that, as the years go on, the tickling of the genitals can lead to proper masturbation.

I found a protruding shoulder in the class of the ordinary, simple thumb sucker and in those who suck their lips with the assistance of one hand resting on the head. In the case of a 16-year-old girl, athletically built, who was sucking her lips with the assistance of the right hand on the right ear, the right shoulder protruded. In an 8-year-old girl who sucked her left thumb and who had Pertussis for 18 weeks prior, I found a protrusion of the left shoulder.

From a theoretical point of view, one would look for a primary scoliosis of the thoracic vertebra on the right side of the body. The effect of this would be only a protrusion of one shoulder; this is because thumb suckers choose mostly the right thumb, in the ratio of 20 to 6, because the right hand is more convenient. For the same reason, those who suck their lips or tongue with the assistance of one hand favor the right upper extremity 5 to 1. Based on experience, one is likely to attribute scoliosis on one side to elevation of one shoulder in line with certain occupations, e.g., those who play the harp, or children who open doors for years where the door knob is too high for them. Obviously a secondary scoliosis can be influenced by sucking carried out with the assistance of one hand placed on the head. But as long as both forces which act upon the vertebra keep their balance, a scoliosis of the vertebra to one side can develop. This is why there is no influence on the vertebra if both hands are used alternately or if there are two sensitive spots from which pleasure is derived.

Quite prominent and often permanent is the influence on the beauty of the face because of the recurrent changing position of the mouth; this is in line with every type of sucking. Those who suck their lips are not able to influence willfully the movements of their lips and, therefore, keep their mouth closed; thus, the lips give an appearance of being drawn into one corner. In older suckers, the upper lip usually protrudes and the sucker keeps the mouth half open, as if he wanted to snap at the object of sucking. Often the physiognomy of the face itself can be influenced disadvantageously for life because the sucking can result in a distortion of the mouth, in misformed jaws, and misplaced teeth. In one little girl who was sucking her thumb and in one who was sucking her tongue, I found a protrusion of the upper lip because the upper medium incisors were protruding. In the first case, the teeth were arranged like a fan; in the second case, like tiles on a roof. I call this misshapen mouth consequent to sucking a temporary or permanent "ludel mouth."

You are justified in saying that because two children have a scoliosis or four children masturbate, this does not enable me to consider sucking a cause for masturbation or scoliosis. Many of my cases of suckers came from circles where I did not think it appropriate to inquire more deeply. It is possible, even probable, that without such obstacles I could have found out more. Regarding the "ludel mouth," I am very cautious myself. As long as I am not certain that the permanently misshapen mouth is not of a familiar type, I do not consider it as such.

It is much more difficult to wean children from the sucking object than to wean them from the breast. We can deal more easily with those suckers whom we can deprive of the sucking object than with those who only suck on their mouth. I know of grandparents who are lip and tongue suckers who are still sucking today with assistance of the hands. Even adults who have given up the habit since childhood will engage in this childish play as soon as they get too engrossed in something, no matter how highly educated they might be.

If a mother wants to be sure not to have a finger sucker on her hands, she should observe, during the first months of life, whether the infant tries to put his thumb or his fingers in his mouth or tries to suck the back of his hand. If so, she should hinder these manipulations. In this way, the observant wife of a physician stopped her four children from thumb sucking, which had begun during their first months of life.

If an older child sucks, one should do exactly the same. In addition, one should not put the child to bed too early, one should take the child out of bed as soon as he awakens, and one should not leave the child alone after his bath; these are the times when children particularly enjoy sucking. In cases where suckers use another hand for assistance, remove the hand from the pleasure point; one should do the same if the child uses the hand as a mask while sucking. One should never give a pacifier to a crying child in order to make him stop. In general, one should not offer him the pacifier, because even if the pacifier is not the only cause for sucking, it nevertheless plays a part in it.

If one is faced with an established "sucker," strictness seldom helps. As a rule, neither bandaging nor threats of bandaging will help, and least of all will beatings prove successful. To quote the girl who used to suck her toes, "It is sweeter to suck than to eat."

Benevolence will prove more successful. All parents know the weaknesses of their children. Whoever will make use of them will succeed. If one has to deal with a stubborn "sucker," it is best to enlist the help of a relative whom the child likes, or a friend or educator. The child who was an excited sucker of bread had an aunt who succeeded by making him promise that he would not suck any more. Another girl who used to suck discovered a colored ring on her forehead one morning. Her teacher told her that this was the obvious consequence of her sucking.

If one does not succeed in this way, then one should put salt on the finger, or strong black pepper, or one should paint the finger with a bitter solution, for example quinine solution. If one does not succeed with one of these methods within a few days, it is better to abstain from it, as the child might soon get used to very salty and spicy food. Placing a glove or stocking on the child's hand overnight is not always successful. I have observed children who have bitten a hole in the glove, even if it was made from very coarse leather; then they continued to suck the thumb which appeared in the hole. Furthermore, most of the children keep on crying until one removes the glove or the stocking. I recommend the following procedure which I used with a girl of 2¾ years, with her consent:

Put a pair of clean children's stockings which go up to the elbow over both hands (because otherwise one can suck the other thumb). Over these put another pair of clean stockings which belong to the mother. These will reach as far as the upper arm, so that the foot part of the stocking will hang down. With this part make a relatively tight bandage over the hand, so that the thumb is placed in the palm of the hand between the second and third finger and thus cannot be used as a sucking object. The stocking is tied with a wide ribbon on the upper arm and near the wrist of the hand.

The next day the girl stopped sucking, but she also stopped with her afternoon nap. In order that she should not forget, it was necessary to have the bandage on her hands for three months. Nevertheless, we still have to remind her, even today, to keep her mouth shut and she really tries hard.

It is not uncommon for those who suck their fingers to stop spontaneously; either their fingers become very sore from sucking, or they no longer derive any pleasure from sucking. It is easy to "wean" the lip and tongue suckers from the hand which is used as an assistance; the rest one has to leave to psychological training or to the child's own will.

It seems to be a fact that the pleasure points of the "fromme children" (quiet suckers who need no rocking or singing to be put to sleep) are almost equalized to the pleasure points (*puta libidiuosa*) in the erotic sexual life. The difference is only that in sexual life "the active assistance" is directed as a rule towards another heterosexual individual and only as an exception, through a deviation, toward oneself (masturbation) or toward another person of the same sex (homosexual or lesbian love). Another point of difference is that the playing around with these pleasure points have more the meaning of a forerunner than of an accompanying runner.

10

Sex Therapy: An Overview

HELEN SINGER KAPLAN, M.D., PH.D.

THE OBJECTIVE OF THIS PAPER is to present an overview of the new techniques for the rapid treatment of sexual disorders, which have been termed "sex therapy." The discussion will be organized around three questions:

1. *What is sex therapy?* What are its distinguishing features? How does it differ from psychoanalysis and in what ways, if any, is it similar?

2. *How effective is sex therapy?* What is the current evidence? Is sex therapy a passing fad or will it stand the test of time and prove to represent a significant advance?

3. *Does the success of sex therapy invalidate psychoanalysis?* This last question entails a comparison of the presumed mechanisms of actions of psychoanalysis and of sex therapy.

WHAT IS SEX THERAPY?

The new approach to the treatment of sexual disorders differs from other forms of therapy in two respects: first, *its goals are limited* essentially to the relief of the patient's sexual symptom; second, it represents a departure from traditional techniques in that it employs a combination of prescribed *sexual experiences* and psychotherapy to achieve its primary objective.

Limited Goals

Sex therapists differ somewhat in the way they define their therapeutic goals. All workers in this field focus on fostering better sexual functioning, but some espouse broader objectives, including improvement in the couple's mode of communication and their relationship in general, as well as resolution of intrapsychic conflicts which may underlie their sexual problems. However, the overriding objective of the new treatment of sexual disorders is to cure the patient's sexual symptom. All therapeutic interventions—psychotherapy, couples therapy, etc.—are ultimately in the service of this goal.

It is this admittedly limited objective which distinguishes the new sex therapy from other treatment modalities, such as psychoanalysis and marital therapy. Although the patient's problem may appear to be limited to his inability to function adequately in the sexual sphere, psychoanalysts tend to regard the presence of a sexual dysfunction as a manifestation of psychological illness. Proponents of this position contend that all sexual disorders, regardless of their nature and severity, are expressions of unresolved intrapsychic conflicts and/or destructive interpersonal interactions. The patient's conflicts and his interpersonal difficulties invariably exert their noxious influence on other aspects of his behavior as well. The aim of treatment, therefore, necessarily extends beyond alleviation of the patient's sexual difficulty; rather, its main objective is the resolution of the patient's deeper intrapsychic and interpersonal problems, and the concomitant reconstruction of his neurotic personality.

Psychoanalytic treatment techniques reflect this theoretical orientation. First, sexual problems are never treated in isolation from the patient's other problems. Second, the sexual symptom is not treated directly, that is, no attempt is made to modify the immediately operating, "here and now" causes of the patient's sexual dysfunction. Instead, the psychotherapist proceeds on the assumption that the intrapsychic and/or interpersonal causes of the patient's sexual dysfunction are invariably embedded in the developmental matrix of the past. Third, since, as noted above, the patient's sexual disorder is regarded as a manifestation of his deeper psychological problems, any symptomatic improvement which may occur in the course of treatment is considered a "by-product" of the resolution of his more basic personality problems and/or the modification of his pathological pattern of interpersonal relationships. Therefore, when the impotent man becomes able to have intercourse, or the inorgastic woman has an orgasm, treatment is not terminated. Therapy ends only when the psychotherapist feels that the basic oedipal conflicts and/or the marital power struggles which have presumably given rise to the patient's sexual problems have been resolved.

Sex therapists, when they are dynamically oriented, do not dispute the fact that some sexual symptoms can be traced to intrapsychic conflicts and destructive interpersonal relationships, and can best be understood in terms of the patient's childhood experiences. However, the sex therapist is concerned, first and foremost, with the immediate causes of the patient's sexual problem and the specific defenses he has erected against sexuality. In contrast to the treatment modalities described above, the remote determinants of the problem are dealt with in sex therapy only to the extent necessary to cure the sexual target symptom and prevent a recurrence of the disability. Psychodynamic and transactional factors are interpreted, and neurotic behavior modified, only if these are directly operative in impairing the patient's sexual functioning, or if they obstruct the progress of treatment. Therefore sex therapy is concluded when the patient's sexual functioning has been restored. This is not to say, of course, that treatment is terminated precipitately, as soon as the impotent patient, for example, manages to have intercourse on one or two occasions. Treatment is terminated, however, when in addition to alleviation of the sexual dysfunction, the factors which were immediately responsible for its onset have been identified and sufficiently resolved to warrant the assumption that sexual functioning is now reasonably permanent and stable.

The following case is presented to illustrate the influence on therapy of the limited objective of relieving the sexual symptom, and the manner in which psychodynamically oriented sex therapists generally handle related intrapsychic and marital problems. In addition, the ways in which clinicians of other orientations might be expected to manage certain aspects of this case will be discussed briefly in order to underscore the unique features of sex therapy.

> Mr. and Mrs. A., both of whom were in their early twenties, came to the clinic to seek help for Mr. A., who suffered from severe premature ejaculation.
>
> *Formulation.* It became apparent in the course of the initial interview that Mr. A. harbored a good deal of unconscious hostility toward his wife. At the same time, however, he seemed to be quite dependent on her. Although he was not aware of these feelings, it was the therapist's impression that Mr. A. was afraid that he would be abandoned by his wife if he did not "perform."
>
> In all probability, Mr. A.'s conflicts had their roots in disturbances in his interactions with crucial members of his family in early childhood. It is also possible that these conflicts played a role in the genesis of his sexual problems. Certainly, it is safe to assume that a psychoanalyst confronted with this case would proceed on this premise. Accordingly, he would attempt to help the patient resolve his residual oedipal conflicts and gain insight into the unconscious sources of his anger at women and his fear of abandonment by maternal figures, with the expectation that he would thereby gain ejaculatory competence. The marital therapist, on the other hand, would try to identify and resolve the transactional causes of Mr. A.'s problem, i.e., the hostilities between the couple, which very possibly might be reinforcing the husband's prematurity. And this approach would be no less valid, for it was obvious that this couple had serious marital problems. As mentioned above, the quality of their relationship reflected Mr. A.'s ambivalent feelings toward his wife. Moreover, Mrs. A.'s fears, on some level of awareness, that if the husband were to function well sexually he would abandon her for a more attractive woman, had also had an adverse effect on their relationship. The interpersonally-oriented therapist would, therefore, consider the resolution of this

couple's destructive marital interactions as his first order of business.

As noted above, in contrast to these approaches, the sex therapist's initial objective is to attempt to modify the immediate cause of prematurity, which, presumably, is the patient's lack of awareness of his erotic sensations prior to orgasm. Thus, in such cases, during the first therapeutic session, the patient and his wife are instructed in the Semans procedure, which enables the achievement of ejaculatory control without producing insight into the intrapsychic or interpersonal dynamics which may play a role in the genesis and perpetuation of that dysfunction. Essentially, the therapist instructs the wife to stimulate her husband's penis, and instructs the patient to focus his attention on the premonitory cues to orgasm. This is not to imply that therapeutic interventions are limited to the prescription of such behavioral tasks. On the contrary, the psychodynamically oriented sex therapist must be an extremely skilled psychotherapist and couples therapist. However, those skills are employed in order to implement the top priority objective, namely, the relief of the sexual target symptom. Once again, psychodynamic and/or transactional material, i.e., the remote causes of the sexual symptom, are dealt with skillfully and effectively, but only insofar as these variables present immediate obstacles to the couple's sexual adequacy and/or give rise to resistances which interfere with the implementation of the essential therapeutic tasks.

Treatment. In this case, such obstacles to treatment did not arise initially, with the result that after four sessions Mr. A. was able to exert good ejaculatory control in the female superior position. However, at this point treatment reached an impasse. The couple managed to avoid the sexual tasks for a whole week. Mr. A. rationalized his behavior on the grounds that he was extremely involved with business and could not find the time to devote to the exercises. His wife felt irritable and tired, and did not pursue the issue. It was apparent, of course, that this avoidance of the sexually therapeutic tasks was a manifestation of resistances which had been mobilized by treatment. Therefore the therapist's efforts now focused on the clarification and resolution of these resistances. Specifically, therapeutic emphasis was shifted to the husband's hostility toward his wife, and the wife's anxieties which seemed to have been mobilized by his improvement. Inasmuch as treatment of the husband's dysfunction could not proceed in the face of the resistances created by these problems, this shift in therapeutic emphasis was mandatory at this point. But apart from the fact that it would ultimately serve to foster ejaculatory control, it also afforded the therapist an opportunity to identify and explore important marital and intrapsychic problems. In this case the therapist was able in the next four sessions to foster sufficient resolution of these resistances—by confronting the couple with their avoidance of sex and by active interpretation of the unconscious problems which had given rise to their resistances to treatment—to enable the husband to achieve excellent ejaculatory control.

Treatment was terminated when the husband's ejaculatory competence appeared to be stable, although, of course, many of the couple's marital and intrapsychic problems remained unsolved.

Relief of the sexual dysfunction is the crucial criterion for the termination of sex therapy, unless it becomes apparent that severe marital difficulties or neurotic conflicts preclude satisfactory sexual functioning—even though the patient's symptom no longer presents an impediment to the achievement of this goal—or unless the couple want further treatment for other problems which have come to light in the course of sex therapy.

Sexual Tasks Combined with Psychotherapy

The case also points up the crucial technical difference between the new sex therapy and traditional treatment modalities, namely, the synergy of sexual tasks and the psychotherapeutic procedure. In other forms of psychotherapy the events which occur in the therapist's office provide the setting for the therapeutic process. Thus, in traditional treatment based on the psychoanalytic model, the analyst does not intervene directly in the patient's life, except perhaps to admonish him against the self-destructive "acting out" of his conflicts and resistances. He generally refrains from making specific suggestions, and certainly he never instructs him to engage in specific experiences outside the clinical setting. Such behavioral prescriptions would be interpreted as an attempt on the part of the therapist to "manipulate" the patient, which is considered by many authorities to be contraindicated in psychoanalytically-oriented psychotherapy. Instead, the psychoanalyst relies exclusively on the events which transpire during the therapeutic sessions—and particularly on the patient-analyst relationship—to achieve his results.

The marital therapist, who generally employs conjoint sessions in which husband and wife, as well as the therapist, participate to resolve marital discord, also considers the couple's experiences during these sessions to constitute the primary cure-producing agent. Similarly, the various techniques employed by behavior therapists to extinguish the fears and inhibitions which impair the patient's sexual response are generally administered in the therapist's office under his direct guidance. For the most part behavioral therapists also do not exploit the therapeutic potential of extra-office experiences.

This exclusive reliance on the office session is in sharp contrast to the approach of sex therapy. Sex therapists consider specific experiences suggested by the therapist, but conducted by the patient and his partner while they are alone together, to be a crucial feature of the therapeutic process; indeed, these prescribed tasks are regarded as essential change-producing agents. The rational use of these therapeutic experiences enhances the effectiveness of psychotherapy enormously.

However, if it is psychodynamically oriented, the new therapy does not rely exclusively on prescribed sexual interactions. Rather, it employs an integrated combination of sexual experiences and psychotherapy. This combination constitutes its main innovation and is probably largely responsible for its impressive success. Psychotherapeutic intervention, in itself, whether it is conducted on an individual basis or addresses itself to the joint treatment of husband and wife, alleviates sexual problems to some extent. It is also safe to assume that highly stimulating and concomitantly reassuring sexual experiences have enabled some persons to overcome their sexual difficulites. However, the judicious combination of prescribed sexual interactions, which are systematically structured to relieve specific sexual difficulties, and psychotherapeutic sessions, which are designed to modify the intrapsychic and transactional impediments to adequate sexual functioning, is the most effective and far-reaching approach to the treatment of sexual difficulties devised to date. As such, the new sex therapy may be considered to constitute a major advance in the behavioral sciences.

The therapeutic sessions and prescribed sexual experiences act in synergism to reveal and resolve the personal and marital problems which impede the couple's free and healthy sexual expression. Thus, on the basis of his initial evaluation of the couple, the therapist formulates a provisional concept of their sexual problem, and of its psychodynamics. In prescribing the initial sexual tasks he is guided by this formulation. The couple's response to these tasks further clarifies the dynamics of their difficulty. For example, the case presented earlier was formulated as follows: The presenting problem was the husband's ejaculatory incontinence. The immediate cause of the problem was his apparent inability to experience the high surges of erotic sensation prior to orgasm. On a deeper level, his problem presumably had its roots in his unconscious hostility toward women in general, and his wife in particular, which made him ambivalent about giving her pleasure. A contributory factor, which created a pressured sexual system between the couple and reinforced the patient's premature ejaculation pattern, was his wife's fear that a sexually adequate man would abandon her for another, more desirable woman. The strategy adopted in this case, on the basis of this provisional formulation, was to attempt to modify the immediate cause of the husband's dysfunction and to circumvent the conflicts which had given rise to his problem to the extent that this was possible. Thus the initial sig. was the Semans exercise, and the couple was instructed in the implementation of this procedure. After they had conducted the prescribed experiences at home, they returned to the clinic to discuss their reactions in detail with the therapist. Usually, a wealth of psychodynamic material is evoked by these experiences. With these data the therapist can correct and refine the concept of the deeper structure of the couple's problem, and devise and prescribe additional relevant sexual tasks. Concomitantly, this psychodynamic material becomes available for psychotherapeutic intervention during the therapeutic sessions. Thus, in actual practice, although relief of the sexual problem is the prime objective of the new sex therapy, the dynamically oriented therapist invariably works with the couple on related intrapsychic and dyadic difficulties, to varying degrees.

Specifically, in the case cited above the wife's dormant anxiety, which centered on her fears of being abandoned, was mobilized by her husband's rapidly growing control over his ejaculatory reflex. She manifested this anxiety by being generally unpleasant and by her resistance to treatment, i.e., her reluctance to carry out the assigned sexual tasks. Although these resistances impeded treatment temporarily, they also provided the therapist with an opportunity to deal with this significant material during the therapeutic sessions. The wife's fears of abandonment had to be dispelled before the couple could achieve satisfactory functioning. But apart from fostering ejaculatory control, the resolution of this long-standing problem also had an extremely beneficial effect on the wife's general psychological functioning.

The Treatment Format

The treatment formats used by various sex therapy clinics and therapists have one feature in common—they all provide for the combined use of prescribed sexual experiences and psychotherapeutic sessions. Within this general framework, however, workers in this field differ considerably with respect to the specific format they employ.

Therapists who follow the Masters and Johnson format see patients daily for a period of two weeks. Other programs, including our own, see couples one to three times per week for as long as is necessary to restore and stabilize sexual functioning. Some sex therapists follow Masters and Johnson in employing mixed gender co-therapy teams. Others, including ourselves, have found this unnecessary and get very good results with well trained solo therapists of either gender. Some programs insist that one member of the therapy team be a physician, others have no such requirements. Programs also differ as to the specific tasks which they employ in treatment. However, the most significant differences among sex therapy programs arise from differences in the conceptualization of the therapeutic process, which are ultimately reflected in the conduct of the psychotherapeutic aspect of sexual treatment. Some of the clinicians who practice sex therapy have had no prior instruction in the theory of psychopathology; nor have they had clinical training in psychotherapy. They lack the theoretical conceptualization of the therapeutic process which is an essential prerequisite of clinical competence; consequently, they are forced to work empirically and to deal only with surface causes. They rely exclusively on sex education and counseling and the prescription of erotic tasks to achieve their therapeutic objectives. In sharp contrast, our own program, as well as some others, places heavy emphasis on psychotherapy. Although the sexual experiences are crucial to the success of treatment, they constitute only one aspect of the total therapeutic process. They are of value primarily when they are integrated with the psychotherapeutic sessions.

Our own program is conducted strictly within a psychodynamic conceptual framework. An attempt is made to understand the causes of the patient's problem, and to relate treatment to this formulation. Both the immediate and the deeper causes are considered, and each task and each therapeutic maneuver is based on a rational consideration of its impact on the couple's psychopathological structure. Resistances, unconscious motivations, and the pathological dynamics of the couple's relationship—all these factors are considered and dealt with in therapeutic process.

The counterpoint between the prescribed sexual interactions and the psychotherapeutic experience is exploited fully. The sexual tasks reveal individual conflicts and marital pathology far more rapidly and dramatically than do mere discussions, and this material is worked with extensively and intensively in the psychotherapeutic sessions.

Essentially, we view sex therapy as a task-centered form of crisis intervention which presents an opportunity for rapid conflict resolution. Toward this end we employ the various sexual tasks, as well as the methods of insight therapy, supportive therapy, marital therapy, and other psychiatric techniques as indicated.

We believe that the treatment format must be flexible and rational and psychodynamically oriented if it is to meet the specific needs of the diverse patient population who suffer from sexual dysfunctions. At the same time, however, it must retain the essential ingredients of sex therapy, i.e., the combined and integrated use of prescribed sexual experiences and psychotherapeutic intervention within a basic psychotherapeutic context.

This brief overview raises certain crucial questions: Can sexual dysfunctions really be alleviated with any degree of permanence by such direct intervention which, essentially, is limited to modifying their surface causes without resolving the conflicts which underlie such disorders? Can sexual symptoms be treated in relative isolation from other neurotic symptoms? Can the intrapsychic conflicts which give rise to sexual symptoms be circumvented in the treatment of such symptoms? Not surprisingly, those who subscribe to traditional psychoanalytic theories predicted early on that an approach to the treatment of sexual disorders which incorporated such premises would not be effective. These questions raise the second major issue to be considered in this paper: What is the evidence for the efficacy of sex therapy?

HOW EFFECTIVE IS SEX THERAPY?

Sex therapy promises rapid and permanent relief of distressing sexual symptoms which have heretofore been regarded with therepeutic pessimism. However, many of the claims and optimistic preliminary impressions have not yet been scientifically substantiated.

The efficacy of any therapeutic modality, be it psychotherapy, drug therapy, behavior therapy, or the new approach to the treatment of sexual dysfunctions, can be established with confidence only if that modality has been tested under controlled conditions. The well designed evaluation study provides an opportunity for comparison of the outcome of a given therapeutic approach with the effects of various other treatment techniques which have some demonstrated value. It will be designed to guard against the possibility that the findings derived therefrom will be contaminated by experimenter bias, and such common error as attribution of "false positives," i.e., cures which result from the therapist's enthusiasm for, and the patient's suggestibility to, the treatment procedure under investigation. Inasmuch as studies of sex therapy conducted to date have not provided controls against such errors, our current enthusiasm for this approach is unfortunately not based on solid evidence of its effectiveness. Instead this enthusiasm stems, for the most part, from admittedly impressive findings which, however, derive from uncontrolled outcome studies.

The new therapy is not unique in this respect. None of the other methods, including psychotherapy and psychoanalysis, currently used in the treatment of sexual disorders have been adequately evaluated under controlled conditions. Consequently, claims regarding their efficacy also await scientific validation. Thus, the results of sex therapy will be discussed on the basis of preliminary impressions and the reports of uncontrolled studies, with the understanding that these may have to be revised in future, when the definitive data yielded by controlled outcome studies are published.

The discussion of outcome will consist, first, of a report of the effects of the new treatment on the sexual target symptom, and these data will be compared as far as possible with the results reportedly achieved by psychoanalysis.

The Effects of Treatment on the Sexual Target Symptom

Masters and Johnson carefully evaluated the effects of their two-week-long intensive sex therapy on the sexual symptoms of the couples they treated over a ten-year-period. The results were excellent. In addition, the scientific committee was impressed by their meticulous five-year follow-up which revealed a small relapse rate. Masters and Johnson's reported that with a total of 510 dysfunctional couples they attained an 80% success rate, with a relapse rate after five years of 5%.

The different dysfunctional syndromes differ to some extent with regard to their prognosis. The following are the Masters and Johnson outcome figures as reported in their book, *Human Sexual Inadequacy* (1):

Male Dysfunctions:
- Primary impotence–60% cured
- Secondary impotence–74% cured
- Premature ejaculation–98% cured
- Ejaculatory incompetence (retarded ejaculation)–78% cured
- Total: 80% cure

Female Dysfunctions:
- Vaginismus–100% cure
- Primary orgastic dysfunction–83% cure or improvement
- Absolute orgastic dysfunction–78% cure or improvement
- Total: The sexual symptoms of 80% of patients were cured or improved after two weeks of sex therapy.

While Masters and Johnson did not conduct their studies according to a controlled model, the work is unique in the size of their sample, and in the fact that they conducted five-year follow-ups. It is difficult to find comparable data on the effects of other treatment modalities, notably psychoanalysis, on sexual dysfunctions. The best outcome study in this area to date is that of John O'Connor, who studied the effects of psychoanalytically oriented psychotherapy and psychoanalysis on the sexual symptoms of patients seen at the Columbia Psychoanalytic Clinic during a period of two years. The data represent the opinions of the treating doctor regarding his patients' symptoms. With 96 patients included in the survey, the results were as follows:

Male Dysfunctions: 57% cured, 17% improved

Female Dysfunctions: 25% cured, 36% improved

Total: The sexual symptoms of 66% of patients were improved or cured after two years of psychotherapy or psychoanalysis.

The two populations, that studied by Masters and Johnson and that studied by O'Connor, are not comparable on several grounds. For one, the patients seen at the psychoanalytic clinic were suffering from various personality and neurotic disorders, while the Masters and Johnson population presumably contained many couples who were healthy in all other respects except for their sexual symptom. Nevertheless, one can not fail to be impressed by the 80% cure rate (with only 5% relapses after five years) obtained by two weeks of treatment, versus the 66% cure rate obtained after two years of intensive insight therapy.

Our own experience at the Cornell Sex Therapy and Education Program, while by no means definitive, tends to support Masters and Johnson's contention that one can expect approximately 80% cure rate with brief, intensive, experientially oriented treatment which involves the active participation of both sexual partners. Again, however, it is too early for any definitive claims to this effect.

Effects of the Rapid Relief of Sexual Dysfunction on the Psychological Status of Patient and Partner

Apart from improvement of the sexual disability, the new techniques afford us an opportunity to observe the effects of the rapid relief of long-standing sexual disabilities on the general psychological and emotional status of the symptomatic patient and his partner, and on the quality of their relationship.

Two major conceptual models of human behavior predict that rapid symptom-focused therapy will have diametrically opposite results. On the one hand, psychoanalytic theory predicts that direct removal of a symptom, when not accompanied by concomitant resolution of the conflict which underlies that symptom, will result in the psychological deterioration of the patient and/or the formation of substitute symptoms which serve the psychological needs hitherto served by the "cured" symptom.

In contrast, learning theory considers the symptom to *be* the disorder, and discounts the possibility that its removal will engender the formation of substitute symptoms. On the contrary, it is predicted that the patient's consequent sense of mastery will result in enhanced self-esteem and a decrease in anxiety. This generalization of improvement to other aspects of the patient's functioning has been described as the "ripple effect."

In our own clinical experience we have observed that the rapid treatment of sexual problems may affect the patient's overall functioning in one of three ways: there may be no change in his psychic status; there may be a positive change; or negative changes in his psychic status may occur as a result of treatment. In the great majority of cases, no permanent significant changes in the patient's psychic status seem to occur as a result of the successful rapid treatment of his sexual dysfunction. In rare instances, however, profound positive changes, as well as profound negative changes are seen.

While most patients tend to respond to the rapid treatment of sexual symptoms as predicted by learning theory, i.e., without the development of substitute symptoms, clinical experience has also yielded evidence in support of the psychoanalytic position which states that sexual dysfunctions have their genesis in the patient's unconscious unresolved conflicts, and further hypothesizes that sexual symptoms have a symbolic meaning and serve a defensive function. The mobilization of anticipatory anxiety prior to symptomatic improvement, which is a very common phenomenon, and the adverse reactions to treatment which are observed at this stage, albeit in rare instances, provide compelling evidence in support of the validity (but not the universality) of this theoretical formulation.

Almost invariably, patients manifest a good deal of anxiety and resistance just before their symptom yields to treatment. In fact, this reaction is so predictable that the trainees at our clinic anticipate the third and fourth treatment sessions, at which point the anxiety-resistance phenomenon usually occurs, with some trepidation. These feelings of trepidation are not without justification. In fact, the way in which the anxiety aroused by the prospect of relinquishing sexual dysfunction is handled largely determines the outcome of treatment. Clinical competence at this crucial stage can make the difference between a favorable outcome and treatment which is interrupted prematurely and/or reaches a stalemate.

According to psychoanalytic theory, relinquishing a painful neurotic symptom arouses anticipatory anxiety because that symptom once served as an important defense against the emergence of dangerous impulses and wishes, which were adaptive during the patient's childhood. This material now lies outside the patient's conscious awareness. Nevertheless, acute anxiety is experienced when the loss of the old defense, i.e., the symptom, appears to be imminent, to the degree that some transient substitute symptoms may develop during this period.

Psychoanalysis and psychoanalytically-oriented treatment modalities seek, first and foremost, to clarify the nature of the patient's conflict, for only then can the defensive function of the symptom be fully understood. To illustrate, if it becomes apparent in the course of treatment that the patient's impotence is based on the persistence of an unconscious sexual attachment to his mother, and the concomitant existence of the unconscious belief that such feelings are extremely dangerous, the meaning of his symptom becomes self-evident. Specifically, in such cases impotence serves as a defense against the emergence into consciousnes of "dangerous" incestuous wishes. Once the patient senses that the cure of his impotence is imminent, that he will soon be capable of normal sexual functioning, the infantile sexual aims which had been warded off are reactivated, and there is a concomitant mobilization of the fears which were once associated with these infantile sexual aims. In short, unconsciously, the patient believes that sexual intercourse is connected with an intense danger which, according to classical analytic theory, is believed to take the form of castration. In essence, this is the source of his anticipatory anxiety. In psychoanalysis this type of material is discussed, and an attempt is made to resolve the patient's basic oedipal conflict.

In sex therapy the therapist does not usually make such interpretations, but may point out to the patient that he is behaving as though he anticipated some punishment if he should have intercourse. In some instances the childhood roots of such fears and the former importance to the patient of his defenses are also discussed. However, the therapist does not rely solely on interpretation of unconscious material but usually attempts to deal with this kind of anxiety by actively confronting the patient with the irrational nature of his fears, and reassuring him that his ability to have intercourse will not result in injury. These rather simple and direct tactics are frequently effective in helping the patient rapidly to resolve the anxiety engendered by his improvement and imminent cure. At times, however, these simple supportive strategies are not sufficiently effective to permit treatment to proceed in the face of the patient's anticipatory anxiety. In that event, the therapist may attempt to resolve the deeper issues which underlie the patient's response by identifying and clarifying the genetic roots of his unconsious fears and the defenses he has employed against the emergence of feared impulses into conscious awareness in accordance with the principles of psychoanalytic treatment.

As mentioned above, usually, as soon as the symptom is cured and the patient finds that the anticipated injury does not occur, his anxiety tends to disappear rapidly and permanently. However, in the psychologically fragile patient, anticipatory anxiety represents a more serious hazard in that it poses a potential threat to his ability to maintain his psychic integrity. Consequently, it is at this point, immediately prior to the achievement of symptomatic relief, that adverse reactions to treatment are most likely to occur.

Thus, as a general rule, the patient manifests adverse reactions to treatment before his symptom has been cured. Occasionally, however, adverse reactions emerge after relief of the symptom enables the patient to function well sexually, often for the first time in his life. For example, this is not uncommon among premature ejaculators, who may experience transient episodes of impotence following the rapid attainment of ejaculatory control.

Effects of the Rapid Relief of Sexual Dysfunction on the Marital Relationship

The sudden attainment of sexual adequacy seldom leaves the partner unaffected. The effects of sex therapy on the psychologic status of the partner of the symptomatic spouse also range from highly beneficial to dangerously disruptive. It is most beneficial where treatment affords an opportunity for effective psychotherapeutic intervention in the problems of both spouses.

As is true of the symptomatic patient and his spouse, the brief treatment of sexual problems may have no discernible effect on the marital relationship; it may have a positive effect; or it may affect the relationship adversely.

There is a difference, however, in the frequency with which these specific effects occur. As stated earlier, as a general rule, rapid relief of sexual dysfunctions has little discernible permanent effects on the psychological status of the individual patient or his partner. In contrast, successful sex therapy usually has a decidedly beneficial effect on the marital relationship.

Sex therapy usually entails changing the insecure, guilt-provoking, and constrictive sexual system which the couple has created for themselves. They must learn to be open, to trust, to communicate on a more authentic level, at least in their sexual transactions, if they are to be able to abandon themselves to their sexual feelings when they are with each other. The benefits of this new openness often generalize outside of the bedroom, with a salutary effect on the relationship as a whole. Unfortunately, this is not always the case, and a couple may find that, although they now enjoy an excellent sexual relationship, their other difficulties and hostilities continue to plague them.

Sometimes the changes entailed in the sex therapy process are threatening to the relationship. In most cases the crisis is temporary and ultimately salutary. In rare cases, sex therapy reveals serious marital difficulties which cannot easily be resolved.

Adverse Reaction to the Rapid Treatment of Sexual Disorders

Psychiatric crises occur when the individual is overwhelmed by anxiety or rage and concomitant feelings of low self-esteem, helplessness, and despair. The rapid treatment of sexual disorders may, in rare instances, precipitate such psychiatric casualties.

Sometimes these adverse reactions occur in the symptomatic patient; at other times, the partner is the victim. When the sexual dysfunction serves an important defensive function in a psychologically fragile patient, the anticipatory anxiety which often occurs prior to symptomatic improvement presents a hazard to the maintenance of psychological integrity. When the sexual symptom serves as a defense for the partner, then he or she may react with panic to the patient's rapid improvement.

Adverse reactions may result not only from the threat of the removal of a defensive sexual symptom, but from the anxiety which may be evoked by the very process of sexual therapy. During the course of treatment, couples must discuss previously hidden feelings and wishes which were never disclosed before; they must touch each other in intimate ways which had always been forbidden; and they must allow themselves to experience sensuous, sexual, and intimate feelings which they have avoided all their lives. Old defenses against emotion and openness must be relinquished. Such new and previously avoided experiences are apt to engender severe anxiety and anticipation of humiliation and rejection. It is incumbent upon the therapist to remain alert to the potentially disruptive emotions evoked by his or her directions and suggestions, and to deal with these actively and supportively. However, in the extremely fragile patient, even the most skillful and sensitive psychotherapeutic management cannot prevent an occasional adversive reaction to these threatening new experiences.

In summary, on the basis of pilot studies and the clinical data accumulated to date at various clinics, it can be stated that the new rapid treatment of sexual dysfunction seems to produce excellent results in terms of relieving the specific sexual symptoms of the great majority of patients. Certainly this approach merits the attention of the investigator. Furthermore, on the basis of comparing the outcome statistics of alternative treatment methods, one may even venture to claim, until evidence to the contrary is published, that sex therapy constitutes the treatment of choice for the sexually dysfunctional patient who is free of major psychopathology and who is involved in a stable and affectionate relationship with his sexual partner. Successful treatment of the patient's sexual dysfunction does not necessarily mean that a concomitant improvement in his psychological and emotional status will occur. Although the effects of the new treatment seem to be impressive for the most part, its benefits are limited to the patient's sexual functioning. There are exceptions. For example, when sexual conflicts are central to the patient's psychic economy, the alleviation of the sexual disorder may result in a dramatic improvement in overall functioning. And, similarly, although sex therapy usually improves a couple's communication and intimacy to some degree, the quality of their marital relationship may be greatly enhanced as a result of treatment if the couple's sexual difficulties have been the sole cause of marital discord. In brief, the new sex therapy seems to constitute a major advance in our understanding and treatment of the difficulties which impair sexual functioning. It is not a panacea; it cannot cure a neurosis, or a sick marriage, or improve the quality of life.

DOES THE APPARENT SUCCESS OF SEX THERAPY INVALIDATE PSYCHOANALYSIS?

Yes. But only if one adheres strictly to a monocausal view of psychopathology. If the psychoanalytic position maintains that unconscious conflicts which derive from childhood maladaptations are the *only* cause of sexual disorders, it is seriously undermined by a treatment method which is successful in relieving sexual symptoms without resolving deep unconscious conflicts. If psychoanalysis insists on the view that *only* insight into and resolution of unconscious conflict can lead to the permanent remission of psychopathologic symptoms, then the success of the symptom-focused sex therapy would threaten to invalidate psychoanalysis.

Fortunately, however, psychoanalysis rests on firmer or more flexible ground. The survival of psychoanalysis depends on its accommodation to a multidetermined model of pathogenisis. Deep unconscious conflicts which derive from childhood are of course very important causes of sexual symptoms and of other disorders as well. However, they are not the only causes. More immediate anxieties and learned reactions may also produce sexual and other symptoms. In addition, making conscious the previously unconscious, which is the major strategy of psychoanalysis, is an important but *not* unique way of modifying human behavior. Experiential methods, behavioral therapy, and transactional techniques are also highly effective in bringing about therapeutic changes. However, the symptom-focused methods seem more useful for changing isolated symptoms, while insight methods seem more suitable when broader therapeutic changes are indicated.

Analysis and sex therapy are not in opposition. They intervene at different levels and are indicated for different problems. Sexual dysfunctions can be the product not only of deep unconscious conflict and profoundly rooted disturbances in the marital relationship, but also of surface anxieties such as the simple fear of failure to perform. Psychoanalysis has addressed itself solely to the former, and has ignored the latter. On the other hand sex therapy, when it is not practiced within a psychodynamic context, runs the danger of ignoring the deeper roots of a couple's sexual problem and becoming mechanical by focusing only on the surface or immediate antecedents. Optimally, sex therapy works both dynamically and experientially in counterpoint. The two approaches do not represent a dichotomy. The prescribed sexual experiences evoke sensitive material, which is then dealt with in an analytic manner during the sessions. The couple's experience of previously avoided feelings and actions evokes insights and conversely, the insights gained during the sessions foster the experiencing of new and freer modes of sexual expression. Thus sex therapy without analytic orientation is limited and sterile, and a psychodynamic viewpoint enriches it and extends its scope. And perhaps analysis can also gain from sex therapy. New experiences and improved communications can be a powerful stimulus to promote insight into previously unconscious and repressed material. Resistances tend to melt in the face of rationally prescribed transactions. Also, analysis might profitably free itself from its exclusive concern with great depth. The roots of problems do not always run so deep and the optimal focus of intervention does not always involve probing into the foundations of the patient's psyche. Immediately operating factors are also potent psychopathogenic elements in many disorders. These are frequently overlooked in psychoanalytic treatment.

The behavioral and experiental methods of sex therapy do not displace psychoanalysis. Rather they place at our disposal additional and alternative strategies which can extend our therapeutic spectrum.

References

1. Masters, W. H., and Johnson, V. E. *Human Sexual Inadequacy*. Boston: Little, Brown, 1970.
2. Kaplan, H. S. *The New Sex Therapy*. New York: Brunner/Mazel, 1974.
3. O'Connor, J., and Stern, L. O. Results of treatment in functioning sexual disorders. *N.Y. State J. Med.*, 72:15, 1927-1934, August 1972.

Discussion

Ian Alger, M.D.

In attempting to clarify the nature of sex therapy, Dr. Kaplan compares it to other forms of therapy. Because the definition of these other forms, and an adequate understanding of why they sometimes "work," is not generally agreed upon by therapists and theorists, the clear delineation she wishes to make seems to me blurred in the comparison. Perhaps this discussion can serve as another overview of the broader concept of therapy itself, and in this context sex therapy can be seen in its relationship to other therapeutic strategies (2).

In any form of therapy, the patient, client, supplicant comes to the doctor, therapist, counselor with a complaint, or suffering, wishing that something about his or her existence be changed. The therapist (from here the words patient and therapist will be used), has a position "meta" to the patient; that is, the therapist is related to the patient as a person, but also is related as a specialist, with *special* knowledge and understanding and, therefore, with *special* power to help the patient in his suffering. Explicitly and/or implicitly the therapist defines the situation for the patient, and also indicates the kind of therapeutic endeavor which can be expected to be helpful.

In the clinical examples we have under discussion, the "patient" is a couple who want to be helped with a difficulty in their sexual functioning together, and this latter usually has a focus on the activity of one or the other partner, such as premature ejaculation or lack of orgasmic response. The therapeutic strategies may be seen as direct or indirect. The classical psychoanalytic approach is indirect, in that the "problem" is redefined as being intrapsychic in nature, and the symptom is then classified as being of lesser importance, and only an indicator of something else which is "deeper." The same basic maneuver operates in other indirect therapies when the essential "problem" is defined as one having to do with the relationship between partners, with the sexual behavior seen as a manifestation of some interpersonal difficulty. The direct therapies focus on the symptom itself, and classify other behaviors, both intrapersonal and interpersonal, as having no special relevance to the problem at hand.

In comprehending both the direct and the indirect approaches, one can see that the aim of both is essentially the same; that is, to make an intervention in an ongoing system which will result in behavioral change. But the focus of the sex therapist, as Dr. Kaplan emphasizes, is on the behavior of which the couple complains, the specific sexual dysfunction. In its direct approach to the symptomatic (complained of) behavior, sex therapy is behavior therapy (1). The therapist prescribes detailed procedures for the patients to follow, and instructions are given for the couple to practice at home, and to report back on the results. The procedure can be understood as a desensitizing and reconditioning approach, which has clearly defined and delimited goals. The results reported by workers such as Masters and Johnson, and confirmed by other workers, including Dr. Kaplan, are impressive. However, as noted by Dr. Kaplan, they, like other results in psychotherapy, are not confirmed by well-controlled and fully convincing scientific validation.

Dr. Kaplan describes a second approach in her therapy which utilizes a more indirect strategy. This is utilized when the couple does not follow instructions, but rather shows "resistance" (which actually in all therapy may be simply understood as the patient not following the therapist's orders, whether the latter be direct or indirect). This need to utilize other therapeutic strategies to continue to engage the patient in the procedure which he himself originally sought is also being acknowledged in other forms of behavior therapy, and the "problem of resistance" which Freud so early came to identify as central in the psychoanalytic therapeutic model has now been given its due recognition in the newer therapies as well.

But the emergence of the concept of "resistance" signals the presentation of various explanatory theories and, based on them, various therapeutic approaches. In the psychoanalytic model, Dr. Kaplan has briefly outlined some of the possible intrapsychic postulates. In other words, intrapsychic dynamics are used to explain disruption of personal equilibrium, which then results in various symptomatic behaviors utilized in a defensive way for the preservation of functioning and integrity.

Systems theory places the explanation in a very different plane, and sees all behavior of members of a system as related to the contexts and interrelatedness of the members of the system, among themselves and with other systems. Therapy is then seen as an intervention into an ongoing system, resulting in the development of a new system which disrupts old patterns and agreements and creates new possibilities and necessities for different behavior.

Regardless of the various theories, certain experience is clear. The patients who do well with sex therapy come to therapy with a definite and limited goal of changing their sexual behavior together. This specific goal is reinforced by the therapist. Furthermore, the couple comes with a mutually cooperative attitude, and with an agreed goal. In other words, people in a small social system are seeking help with a very specific and defined behavior. In addition, when the goal is blurred, or the cooperativeness lost, the therapist undertakes an intervention, depending on other theoretical orientations (psychoanalytic, interpersonal, systems theory) designed to focus the therapy back on the original goal of changing the sexual functioning. When this latter goal is achieved, and there is some evidence of a new and sustained pattern having been developed, the therapy is over.

This limitation of goal has the merit of responding to the original request of the patients. This is not to say that if during the experience of sex therapy a couple decides that they would like to explore other changes in their behavior together, and even to explore their whole life outlook and value system, they cannot then continue in a therapy which would respond to these new goals. What it does imply, however, is that the therapist will not unilaterally decide that these other goals should be the *real* goals of the therapy, and attempt to engage the couple in a prolonged and involved therapy they might not otherwise choose.

In addition to the advantage just mentioned, sex therapy has a special distinction among behavior therapies, and this stems from the nature of the symptoms dealt with. The fact that therapists now deal openly and directly with the sexual behavior of a couple is a truly new development. The format of giving direct sexual instructions to a couple, whether by a single therapist or a therapist couple, reflects a new and important direction. This can be understood in part as a reflection of a greater openness in our society, where sexual knowledge is more widely available through books and magazines, and especially in films and on television. Furthermore, sexual mores have changed so that premarital sexual activity is often actually encouraged, and new birth control methods make wider choices of sexual behavior more available for those who are single as well as those who are married.

But most of the credit for the introduction of this new freedom into the arena of therapy must go to the sex therapists. In leading this pioneer direction, they not only have shown the applicability of direct methods of therapy to problems in human sexual behavior, but they have also stimulated a new awareness of the importance of reexamining our older theories and working methods. In this sense, then, our therapeutic system has been forced to change by the intervention of newer and different models of therapist behavior, and for this new opportunity we can all be grateful. The issue is not whether psychoanalytic theory or interpersonal theory have been invalidated, but rather that new clinical findings challenge all of us to create a broader and more accurate theory of human behavior and the factors which influence it.

The particular emphasis Dr. Kaplan has placed on using psychotherapy to work with "resistances" and other behavioral consequences developed during the more direct interventions further stimulates us to examine our own theoretical positions, and may also lead us to temper enthusiasm with humility as we recognize anew how complex the problem of therapeutic intervention really is.

References

1. Franks, C., and Wilson, G. T. (Eds.) *Annual Review of Behavior Therapy: Theory and Practice.* New York: Brunner/Mazel, 1973.
2. Haley, J. Marriage Therapy. *Arch. Gen. Psychiat., 8,* 213-234, 1963.

11

Sex After Fifty

EWALD W. BUSSE, M.D., SC.D.

The Sex Taboo in Old Age

SOCIAL AND BEHAVIORIAL SCIENTISTS who have studied the question of sex in old age agree that in our society a taboo against sex is imposed upon the elderly. This widespread, socially determined sanction reduces, by suppression and repression, sexual feelings, thoughts, and behavior.

I do not pretend that I comprehend the origin or the perpetuation of this taboo. There are some who believe that it is merely a hangover from the Victorian age and that it is gradually dissipating. However, the fact that it persists makes it seem likely that major forces perpetuating this taboo continue to be present (1).

There is little doubt that our society is currently engaged in a major change in regard to the value and place of sexual activity in the young adult and middle-aged adult. Our society is moving from a position that sex is primarily for procreative purposes to one that it is a highly valued recreative pursuit. Sexual permissiveness is permeating the adolescent population, but clearly observable changes are as yet not evident in our elderly population. Our experience indicates that children at all ages develop anxiety when observing or imagining their parents or parent engaged in sexual activity. The adult offspring observing an elderly parent is often upset by observing the flirtatious behavior of this aged par-

The research on which this paper is based was supported in part by Grant HD-00668, National Institute of Child Health and Human Development, USPHS.

ent. Many elderly persons are aware that this bothers their adult children and deliberately avoid such anxiety-producing behavior when in their presence. It is also possible that the taboo against sex in old age serves the selfish interests of the middle and younger generation. The stereotype of the elderly as an asexual group, or as a group incapable of competing with them in many aspects of living, is fostered by younger people.

Granted that a taboo does exist, it also must be recognized that substantial differences in all types of behavior and capabilities including sexual activity exist in males and females at all ages. Furthermore, with the passage of time at least until advanced age, men and women become increasingly physiologically different. Hence, considerable variation must be expected.

A recent article (2) quite accurately reports many of the adversities and discriminations suffered by elderly women. This article expresses the belief that these women are being neglected by women's lib. Furthermore, the authors believe that society is not actually considering the sexual needs and rights of elderly women. They contend that sexual activity of an elderly male is sanctioned, and it is permissible for him to marry a younger woman. In contrast, women who show an interest in sexuality are seen as depraved or "grasping for lost youth." Sexual interest by an older female involving a younger male is not socially condoned. These observations are substantially accurate, but no effort is made to understand the resisting forces that prevent the sexual liberation of the elderly woman. One factor may be that from early adulthood on, that is, from age 20, there is an imbalance between men and women in our population. At age 20 there are 105 females for every 100 males. This imbalance in our population increases so that by the age of 65 there are 138.5 females to 100 males. Under these circumstances the surviving male expands his sexual horizons, while the elderly woman is being restricted by the reality of male-female imbalance.

Other reality factors are physiological determinants. The postmenopausal woman cannot contribute to the primitive drive to reproduce and ensure survival of the group. Hence her continuation of sexual activity has no obvious social value. The premenopausal woman in the fourth decade of life who becomes pregnant is not only jeopardizing her own health but significantly increases the risk of bearing a genetically defective child. However, the elderly male who marries a young woman is capable of producing healthy offspring.

On a number of occasions responsible physicians and social scientists have advocated that polygamy be permitted after the age of 60. In fact, one author (3) believes that a man should have the right to marry two to five women in the same age group. According to these advocates of polygamy, plural marriages have many advantages which include a reestablishment of a family constellation, a method of insuring a better diet, improving the economic status of the participants, reducing illness, providing better care while ill, sharing housework, and avoiding depression and loneliness. It also is believed that the aging male will respond to the extra stimulation and function appropriately.

The Aging Male and Female—Anatomic and Physiological Changes

The majority of the information presented in the next portion of this paper is derived from the work of Masters and Johnson (4). The data utilized by these two investigators can be divided into two categories. The first category consists of laboratory observations related to the anatomic and physiological changes in old age, and the second category is composed of data derived from interviews with a larger but self-selected group of aged subjects. Laboratory observations were conducted on 35 men whose ages ranged from 51 to 89 years. Sociosexual interviews were carried out with 212 men beyond the age of 50 years. As to the study of females, 61 menopausal and postmenopausal subjects were utilized. In this grouping the youngest was 41, and the oldest 78. Thirty-four of the participants were considered to be postmenopausal. Masters and Johnson cautioned that in many instances the number of women was insufficient to provide biological data of statistical significance.

In aging men with the passage of time the usual nipple erection that accompanies the act of ejaculation declines so that the majority if not all of males after the age of 60 do not demonstrate nipple erection at the time of ejaculation. Under the age of 60, the correlation of these two events is expected. It is evident that most if not all physiological processes are slowed with the passing of time. Consequently it takes the aging male a longer period of time to achieve erection. For the male 60 or over full penile erection is frequently not attained until just before ejaculatory experience. However, the maintenance of penile erection over long periods of time without ejaculation is an achievement of old age. Masters and Johnson point out that a slowing process is inevitable, and this slowing should be recognized as normal by both the male and his female partner. Probably the most important change in the male sexual function associated with the aging process is the reduction in the frequency of ejaculation and the need to ejaculate (5). A male in his middle and late 60's often finds that his demand for ejaculatory release of sexual tension levels out to about once a week, while he may enjoy sexual intercourse twice a week or more. Again, the reduced demand for ejaculatory release should be accepted without reservation by both husband and wife.

The aging process also has obvious physiological influences on the sexual response cycle of the female. Production of vaginal lubrication is the exact physiological counterpart of the male erection. Consequently, vaginal lubrication may be delayed in onset and in full development. These changes develop relatively rapidly in the postmenopausal woman. In addition to the delay in the response, there is also a reduction in the amount of lubrication. Not infrequently, the postmenopausal woman reports that she is more easily distracted from the sexual response cycle, and the lubricating process may be slowed or even terminated in situations where previously stimuli may not have interfered with the response.

After the menopause the mucosal lining of the vagina usually becomes very thin and atrophic; hence the vaginal wall is vulnerable to the trauma associated with the sexual act. Local irritation and bleeding may occur. Aging usually brings a loss of some of the fatty integument of the external genitalia with constriction of the vaginal outlet. Hence, there are other factors that may contribute to distress or pain during intercourse.

Few postmenopausal women experience painful tonic contractions of the uterus accompanying orgasm. In younger women the uterus contracts rhythmically with orgasm. This pattern is not dissimilar to the contractions observed during the first stage of labor. However, in advanced years the rhythm of the contractions may be lost and a spasm can occur which is experienced as a severe lower abdominal pain. This type of spastic uterus response accompanying orgasm reflects a state of sex steroid starvation. Consequently sex steroid replacement is particularly useful in such cases.

Sex Endocrine Changes and Replacement

At the time of the menopause there is a loss of primordial germ cells, that is, undeveloped ova from the ovary. Consequently, the reproductive capacity of the ovary ceases, and two of the three compartments that produce steroids in the ovary cease to function. These two so-called compartments are the follicle and corpus luteum. The third ovarian compartment for steroid synthesis, that is, the stroma, may continue to be active. There is considerable variation in women in regard to the continuation of steroidogenesis. In some women extra gonadal sources of estrogens play a major role. Although most women show signs and symptoms of the menopause, such as autonomic nervous system imbalance, metabolic disorders, and the exacerbation of psychoneurotic symptomatology, there are some who manifest little or no evidence of estrogen starvation (6). Although estrogen replacement therapy has been advocated by many individuals, there are some who condemn its use because of the fear of stimulating cancer development. Generally speaking, most experienced clinicians feel that when signs and symptoms of estrogen deficiency occur, they should be treated adequately for as long a period as is reasonable and desirable. However, in some individuals if the replacement of estrogen is maintained for long periods of time, androgens (testosterone) will sometimes have to be added to prevent overstimulation of the breast and progestogen given periodically so that endometrium is shed. In this way one can avoid annoying periodic bleeding.

The existence or absence of the male climacteric continues to be a subject of debate. If it occurs it is, in my opinion, quite rare and difficult to distinguish from a depression. The testes of the aging male show little change in normal structure. If the clinician elects a trial on hormone replacement for the elderly male, one must exercise considerable caution, as prostatic hypertrophy is common in elderly men, and testosterone frequently accentuates this condition. Furthermore, testosterone is definitely counterindicated if a neoplasm of the prostate is suspected, as this hormone speeds up the development of a carcinoma. Another complication in males is the possible development of polycythemia. Therefore, if testosterone is given to a male, regular hemoglobin and red cell determinations are important and attention must be given to the possibility of prostatic changes.

Duke University Center for the Study of Aging and Human Development

The Duke University longitudinal study of aging was initiated in 1954. This study is a complex interdisciplinary project that has resulted in many scientific publications and several books. Since that time, a second longitudinal study has been initiated. Both are concerned with so-called "normal" aging. No attempt will be made to review the objectives or hypotheses of these studies, the sample, the methodology, or the many physiologic, psychologic, and social studies that are connected with these projects. However, many reports related to sexual behavior and attitudes based upon data derived from these studies have appeared in scientific journals. The reports concerned with the frequency of sexual activity have remained relatively consistent over the past 19 years. However, the sexual changes that do occur are probably accurate but reflect cohort differences rather than age changes. A publication in 1954, which was actually based upon a cross-sectional analysis, reported that the amount of sexual activity was correlated with socioeconomic status; that is, the better the socioeconomic status of the subjects the more likely was the continuation of sexual activity. Since that time it is evident that the important variable of physical health must be given primary attention, as physical health is an important determinant regardless of socioeconomic status. Individuals who live in poverty or near poverty are not as likely to be in good health as those who are better off. Consequently, there are several factors that interact which influence the continuation or termination of sexual activity.

Sexual activity between marital partners tends to be maintained until after the age of 75. Approximately 60% of married couples between the ages of 60 to 74 years of age remain sexually active. After the age of 75 coitus declines to less than 30% of married couples. The continuation of sexual activity is dependent upon several interrelated factors, including the availability of a sexual partner. Among the married, the physical and mental health of the partner is important as are the patterns of sexual interest and activity that have been established in early adulthood. Only 7% of the elderly subjects without a wife or husband continued to have sexual relations in old age. This small percentage drops rapidly with advancing age. A larger number of men, four of five in good health, express a continuing interest in sexual activity (7). Verbalized interest in sex is found in about a third of elderly women—this loss of interest by the female may be a direct result of the lack of stimuli, since the older woman lives in a predominantly women's world.

Marriage in Late Life

Two-thirds of men 65 years and over live with wives, but only one-third of women over 65 have husbands. Most older men are married, while most older women are widows. There are almost four times as many widows as widowers. It should be noted that about two-fifths of the older married men have wives under 65 years of age. There are at least 35,000 marriages a year in which the groom and/or the bride is 65 years of age or over. The number of marriages among elderly people has been steadily increasing.

The marital status of the aged group—that is, 75-plus years—reflects the social tradition for men to marry younger women. Twice as many aged men as women are married, and only one-third of the men have wives over 75. About one-half have wives between 65 and 74 years of age, and a fifth have wives under 65 years of age.

Of men 75 years or older, 33.9% are living with their wives. In contrast, of 75-plus women only 17.8% are living with their husbands. Of these women who are 75 years or older, 3% have husbands under 65 years of age; roughly 20% have younger husbands between the ages of 65 and 74; and the remainder have husbands their own age or older. Each year approximately 2,000 women age 75 or older marry, and 6,000 men 75 years or older go to the altar. Both of these groups are usually moving out of widowhood. Of these 8,000 marriages, over 4,000 are involved with partners under age 75.

The difference in married and unmarried status for older patients is of significance to the physician, as it has been reported that the hospital admission rates and stays of the unmarried exceed those of the married (8).

The Single Woman—Widowed or Divorced

The single woman who is seeking to marry finds that the probability of her achieving a state of marriage is very much influenced by her previous marital status. At age 35, a never-married female has a 50% chance of marrying; a widow, a 67% chance; and a divorcee, a 94% chance. At age 40, the single never-married has a 20% chance of marrying; a widow, 50%; and a divorcee, 84%. Five years later, that is, at age 45, a single woman has a 12% chance of marrying; the widow, 34%; and the divorcee, 69%. No national figures are available regarding the marrying possibilities of the never-married single, the widow, or divorced elderly person. However, it is my impression that regardless of the age, the divorcee has the best chance of being remarried. One would doubt that this was based upon the desirability of the woman as determined by such things as appearance and economic status, but may merely be the result of the car rental slogan, "we try harder" (9).

Many women, particularly those in late middle-age, realize that they in all likelihood will outlive their husbands. Many such women begin to indulge in fantasy and behavior that Neugarten labels "rehearsal for widowhood" (10). This preparation for widowhood, when approached sensibly and realistically, can be of considerable benefit but, when the relationship is far from congenial, the wife may begin to develop plans and behavior which are quite divergent from the interest and even well-being of her husband.

In a seminar at Duke University (February 26, 1973), Dorothy Heyman and Daniel Gianturco presented some preliminary observations regarding the reaction of elderly female subjects to widowhood and their attitude towards remarriage. It was reported that several widows found it extremely difficult to nurse a very sick husband until his eventual demise. Their attitude now is that under no circumstances do they want to remarry because they are fearful of marrying an elderly man who is merely looking for someone to take care of him. These investigators realize that these comments deserve further exploration, as it is very possible that these women would be quite content to marry a man who obviously was in good health and offered financial security. Furthermore, in the discussion it was pointed out that retirement is not unlike widowhood and that both events cannot be seen as an occurrence that has the same specific impact upon all individuals.

Assuming that the health of the elderly will continue to improve, and assuming that neurotic sexual conflicts will be less prevalant, it is my opinion that sexual activity among the elderly in the years ahead will show a definite increase (11), (12), (13), (14).

References

1. Pfeiffer, E. Sexual behavior. In E. W. Busse and E. Pfeiffer (Eds.), *Behavior and Adaptation in Late Life*. Boston: Little, Brown, 1969. Pp. 151-162.

2. LEWIS, M., and BUTLER, R. N. Neglected by women's lib. *The National Observer,* Dow-Jones & Co., July 29, 1972, p. 20.
3. KASSELL, V. Polygyny for aged could add spice to life. *Geriatric Focus,* 5:1, June 1966.
4. MASTERS, W. H., and JOHNSON, V. E. *Human Sexual Response.* Boston: Little, Brown, 1966.
5. MASTERS, W. H., and JOHNSON, V. E. Sex over sixty. *Geriatrics,* Medical World News, pp. 74-76, 1971.
6. STAHL, N. L., and GREENBLATT, R. B. Endocrinology in geriatric practice. In *Theory and Therapeutics of Aging.* New York: Medcom, 1973.
7. PFEIFFER, E. Geriatric sex behavior. *Med. Aspects of Human Sexual., 3,* 19-28, July 1969.
8. BROTMAN, H. B. "Who Are the Aged, A Demographic View." Read before the 21st Annual University of Michigan Conference on Aging, Ann Arbor, August 5, 1968.
9. KLEMER, R. H. Problems of widowed, divorced and unmarried women. *Med. Aspects of Human Sexual., 3,* 26-34, April 1969.
10. NEUGARTEN, B. Personal communication re two studies: (1) One Hundred Middle-Aged Women; and (2) One Hundred Middle-Aged Men and Women, Fifty Each.
11. BUSSE, E. W., BARNES, R. H., SILVERMAN, A. J., THALER, M. B., and FROST, L. L. Studies in the processes of aging: IV. Factors that influence the psyche of elderly persons. *Amer. J. Psychiat., 110,* 897-903, 1954.
12. NEWMAN, G., and NICHOLS, C. R. Sexual activities and attitudes in older persons. *JAMA, 173,* 33-35, 1960.
13. VERWOERDT, A., PFEIFFER, E., and WANG, H. S. Sexual behavior in senescence. *Geriatrics, 23,* 137-154, 1969.
14. PFEIFFER, E., VERWOERDT, A., and WANG, H. S. Sexual behavior in aged men and women. *Arch Gen. Psychiat., 19,* 756-758, 1968.

Discussion

ALVIN I. GOLDFARB, M.D.

It is a pleasure to hear such a clear and scholarly exposition of what we know about sexual behavior and interests in the older age group. I welcome this opportunity to comment on the topic and to add to, reinforce, or extend Dr. Busse's discussion on the basis of my experience with a very large number of elderly patients.

Sexual activity and interest have long been associated with longevity in the evolution of medicine, i.e., sexual activity adds "life to years" and, if pleasure is prolonged, years to life as well.

You may remember that one of the great pioneers in endocrinology was Brown-Séquard, the French neurologist, who attempted, on himself, to improve sexual behavior and increase longevity by the implantation of monkey glands—testes. Brown-Séquard's original method was poor, but his concept was good in that it led to the purification of hormones and provided great impetus to the science of endocrinology. More recently, Niehans has recommended injections of pulverized sheep embryo glands and Aslan procaine as sexual energizers as well as to enhance health and prolong life. These claims are based on doubtful evidence, at best.

Dr. Busse dwelt briefly on polygyny. It has been advocated that there be successive age difference in marriages. It has been suggested, since men die before women do, being biologically more vulnerable to death at every age, that older women should marry young men and educate them sexually; these men, when their wives die, would marry much younger women who would in turn be educated by them, outlive them, and pass the information on to the younger men they would then marry.

The sexual attitudes of chronologically old persons appear to be an outgrowth of those acquired early. Prudery in youth may be modified with growth and development but, more often, it still shows as prudery in old age. Puritanical attitudes that delay sexual performance appear to lead to early decline of sexual activity. Late starts, whether they be in sexual self-manipulation or in homosexual or heterosexual activity, result in early decline, whereas early starts appear to be associated with late decline in both interest and performance. In this, the evolution of sexual behavior is like that of intellectual ability and physical competence. Is this a reflection of more sexual vigor to begin with, or does early exercise mean more vigorous development? Is this a problem of nature or nurture? As with most development, it is probably a combination of both; without the proper nurture natural potentials will not emerge fully.

Sexual interest and behavior appear to resemble both intellectual interest and ability and performance of athletic-physical nature: that which decreases use or exercise results in decline in ability—atrophy; that which encourages interest and exercise results in strength, vigor, and continued ability. At any age, but especially in the late years, a decrease in exercise appears to lead to decline in physical ability. Is the cart before the horse? Does decline in ability actually lead to the decline in interest and performance, and, finally, to incapacity to perform? It is true that with advancing years biological changes do, of themselves, occur which are added to by abstinence should it be voluntarily or involuntarily imposed on oneself or by the action of others. Temporary or prolonged abstinence or decrease in frequency of performance may affect interest or ability for short or prolonged periods. That is to say, decline in ability after abstinence may be corrected by return to activity if there is understanding, tolerance, and patience on the part of the person with himself and on the part of the partner. Long abstinence or relative abstinence in later years may result in irremediable loss of ability. This is hard to prove for reasons made clear by Dr. Busse's statistics. The loss of available partners, social attitudes, and the loss of opportunities because of change in self do not favor our seeing the experiment of nature in which a sexually disinterested and nonperforming old person is highly motivated and helped toward "sexual rehabilitation." For such efforts I think we should turn to the techniques of Masters and Johnson referred to by Dr. Kaplan. These inactive persons must be taught, or retaught; they must be physically and mentally reconditioned.

Among the causes of sexual deprivation are changes in the availability of a partner. To the loss of a partner by illness or death can be added loss because of the partner's refusal on the basis of age. This can be the late expression of early prudery in the words, "I am (or you are) too old for that now." This is commonly used by women who have themselves been late starters, passive, uninterested, and cold partners, possibly, but not usually, dissemblers of enjoyment. This sexual removal from the other may be expressed in action instead of, or in addition to, words.

The person may permit himself or herself to "grow old," look old, dress old, act old, so as to become undesirable or even repulsive in dress, appearance, demeanor, behavior. Obesity and lack of care to hair, skin, nails, teeth, and the natural orifices are among the ways chronologically aging persons may "put others off." In words or action, by the use of illness, either physical or emotional, a partner may be discouraged and pushed into abstinence. This may lead, according to some observers, to self-manipulation on the part of the rejected one as a continued mode of sexual behavior, rather than to its disappearance. This I have seen occur only rarely. It also seems less common than is supposed, at least as reflected by my psychiatric practice, that rejection of this type leads the rejected partner to look outside the marriage, although it is certainly not unknown. Rather there may be, after a stormy period, an acceptance of the expressed decision to abandon sexual relations. At times this may be followed by expressions of interest in resuming sexual relations by the originator of its abandonment, to the chagrin of the now "impotent" or "frigid" partner. This may have many psychological determinants such as anger or the projection of feelings of responsibility for the changed relationship.

Decline in sexual ability is often related to the use of alcohol. This drug tends to decrease ability first, and later to eliminate interest. The joys of drinking appear to become more desirable than the pleasures of sex. Many drugs such as the barbiturates act first to break down sexual fears—inhibitions—and thus lead to ability to perform, but finally lead to their complete replacement of the sexual act and of even the sexual, or any type of, company. Drugs may contribute to loss of sexual interest and ability to function in other ways. Analgesics—aspirin is the best known but least recognized by patient, doctor, and unsuspecting self-treater—because they reduce genital sensation, result in poor performance, lack of pleasure, and thus, by slow degrees, to attrition in sexual relationships. Antihypertensive drugs, antidepressive drugs, phenothiazines, and thiorodizine appear to affect the ability to maintain penile or clitoral erection or to achieve orgasm or climax.

Dependency striving in the development of personality is usually sexualized. This can make for differences in the way sexual activity is sought for, performed, continued, or even sold. Also, we must not forget that with chronologic aging and accompanying diseases there may be changes in the brain. With some organic mental states there is hypersexuality. We may not always recognize this in the person with organic brain syndrome who becomes desirous of being held, caressed, or cuddled: Kluver and Bucy tamed monkeys but altered their orality and sexual interest by damaging their temporal lobes. In Alzheimer's Disease, and in certain types of developing brain syndromes in which the temporal lobes may be affected, we sometimes see behavior which can be interpreted as increased sexuality or sexual drive. An example would be an old man with circulatory problems, heart attacks, dizziness, and transitory visual hallucinations suggestive of temporal lobe disorder. He fails to recognize his daughter, whom he touches and invites into bed. If the daughter thinks of this only in psychodynamic terms, she is in trouble. If she can be helped to understand that this behavior is related to brain damage, she can deal with it more easily.

Sexual interest may appear to increase in the male because of prostatitis. This spurious sexual need from local irritation may lead to demands in a marriage already troubled by lack of mutual sexual interest.

Women, frightened by their aging, may become sexually demanding for reassurance. This can become a vengeful assault of the seemingly deprived upon the physically unable. Just as young people who have great sexual drive which is discordant with their enculturated values may become angry with the tempters around them and want to kill them, old people can become angry with mates who are tempting but rejecting. Murderous ideas toward the rejecting spouse can possibly be dealt with in ways which do not seek for remote causes. How can sexual compatibility be established or reestablished in an old couple? When he has a rejecting wife, a man may become paranoid and angry with her; can this best be dealt with by treatment of the wife or the husband?

Cicero long ago suggested that the needs of males decline with growing old in years, and that this is a great boon. The man, relieved of his perennial tension, relieved of his disturbing, distracting, goal-selecting, time-consuming—where courtship, support, and tokens of gratitude are required—pressures, now has time for other things: his work, his play, his thoughts, creativity of a nonprocreative nature. But there is obviously more. With the decrease in need there can be great changes in man-woman relationships. As the man becomes disinterested and sexually less demanding he perhaps can develop a better relationship with his wife. Or, the relationship may become very much worse because, no longer caring whether or not he has any relationship at night, he does not care any more whether he quarrels by day. This of course is also true for women.

12

Developmental Readiness and Dependency in Adolescent Sexuality

SHEILA KLEBANOW, M.D.

AS THE PREACHER NOTED TWO MILLENNIA AGO, "To everything there is a season and a time to every purpose under the heaven. A time to be born and a time to die; a time to plant, and a time to laugh . . . a time to love and a time to hate. . . ." It is now our time to look at adolescent sexuality in three basic themes:

1. What changes, if any, have come about in adolescent sexuality as an aftermath of the sexual revolution in the past generation?
2. What effects, if any, are observable in the psychoanalytic treatment of adolescents in terms of identity formation and sexual identification?
3. How have these changes, if any, affected the development of object relations during adolescence?

Adolescence is the time to consolidate a stable sense of identity and to establish a secure sexual identification, to make vocational choices, and, finally, to develop the capacity for mature object relations.

Most of our professional dealings as psychoanalysts are with adolescents with varying degrees of maladaptation and malfunction. To the impressions we derive from our patients, we add observations of our adolescent offspring, their friends, and our friends' youngsters. What conclusions can we draw?

Recent statistical studies would indicate that a sexual revolution has taken place within the past generation—if we define revolution as the increased incidence of sexual intercourse in our adolescent population. Concomitant with this are greater societal, peer group, and (often) parental sanctioning of earlier sexual experience.

In his studies on male and female sexuality, Kinsey (6, 7) reported the incidence of premarital coitus as follows:

	Female	*Male*
Onset of adolescence to 15	3%	40%
Age 16 to 20	20%	71%

By contrast, a 1972 study by Kantner and Zelnik (Report to the Presidential Commission on Population Growth and the American Future) (3), indicated that by age 19, 46.1% of all unmarried women have had intercourse.

	Female
At age 15	13.8%
16	21.2%
17	26.6%
18	37.1%
19	46.1%

There is an overall incidence of 27.6% in the entire group. About 60% of these girls had intercourse with only one partner while more than 75% had not used contraceptives or had used them only sparingly. In all age categories, about twice as many black girls had intercourse than had white girls while both groups frequently lacked adequate contraceptive means and had a high risk of unwanted pregnancy. The authors suggest that not all of the virgin girls were virgins by choice since "not all intentions are shared or fulfilled" (5).

I offer some of my own impressions based largely upon observations of adolescents seen in my private practice and in the Adolescent Psychiatric Clinic of the Mount Sinai Hospital. These are primarily white, lower-middle- and upper-middle-class youngsters, with girls predominating.

By age 16½ or during the last year of high school (whichever event occurs first) more than one half of girls have had their first coitus. Although there is greater freedom to experiment, anxiety and guilt about intercourse and masturbation are constant but with varying degrees of repression and denial. That there is a new sexual freedom with earlier and more frequent genital contact does not suggest widespread promiscuity. Invariably, the adolescent girl who goes casually or frantically from one sexual encounter to the next tends to be psychotic or borderline and is desperately seeking through sexual union the sense of wholeness which she lacks. In many more situations, a young couple attempt to make a deep commitment to each other. This commitment may have many vicissitudes.

The first sexual relationship may serve a variety of functions. When it represents an orderly progression of sexual intimacy in a young couple who gradually have gotten to know each other, it is ego-syntonic and has little, if any, psychic trauma. For both a boy and girl involved in a new sexual relatedness, it denotes at least the beginning ability to relinquish old bonds to the parents and to form new, age-appropriate object ties.

Where the first coitus takes on a distorted meaning is in situations where it represents either a defense against oedipal wishes or an overt acting out of these wishes. A girl, impelled by the force of her sexual impulses, by peer pressure, and by her wishes to rid herself of her old, incestuous ties to her parents, may select as a first sexual partner a boy who is patently unsuitable for her. Such a boy does not remain a constant partner, generally by the girl's choice rather than by his. In one situation, a 15-year-old white girl impulsively had her first coitus with a black classmate. When the connection to father was explored (her reaction formation to the wish for father), she quickly gave up this boyfriend. Another girl of 18 acted out her oedipal fantasy by having her first intercourse with a middle-aged man. She, too, recognized the transparent quality of this relationship and terminated it after she grasped its unconscious meaning. After the oedipal wishes were explored, both girls felt less urgency about an immediate sexual involvement. Each went out with her subsequent (and more appropriate) boyfriend for a considerable time before proceeding to intercourse. This acknowledgment of emotional unreadiness for mature heterosexual relatedness in both girls involved a healthier awareness of their adolescent developmental tasks than had their first impulsive sexual encounters.

Sexual relationships in young and middle adolescents frequently have a pseudo-sexual quality, with sexuality used to secure nurturance in a quid pro quo from one's partner. The acceleration of age of onset of major sexual experimentation and proceeding to intercourse is no guarantee that emotional maturity similarly will be hastened. A boy and girl may "go together" for a period ranging from several months to a year or longer, with increasing sexual intimacy and sexual fun, and still be looking for something which is not sexual. The wish to be taken care of, to be tended by a parent, is entwined and confused with sexuality. A youngster who consciously may be repelled by the thought that he needs his parents and their care, still wants someone to minister to him. Sexual intimacy is used as an exchange as each partner looks to the other for parenting as well as for sexual gratification.

The adolescent boys whom I have seen present a different picture, with many older boys (16 and older) who are sexually inhibited or suffer from severe competitive anxiety. In several instances, they have sought help on account of impotence with their girlfriends or an inability to relate to girls. They rarely describe much sexual fun. The boyfriends of my adolescent girl patients and other boys who enjoy their sexuality rarely enter therapy. Occasional younger adolescent boys who have frequent intercourse appear to use their sexuality either exploitatively, in an attempt to work out their fears of their frightening and overpowering mothers, or to substitute one dependent relationship for another. They do not convey any sense of genitality in the service of object relatedness.

A ubiquitous phenomenon of the current generation is the

prevalance of unisex clothing. Deutsch (4) has postulated that this represents an acting out of unconscious fantasies of double-sexed unity. "The boy's fear of women is conquered by his making the girl into a boy, while . . . homosexuality is ruled out by the actual sex of the love partner." Regeneration is achieved through the bisexual character of the individual who attains immortality through self-propagation. In noting the universal concern in adolescents about death and the wish for immortality, she suggests that the attempt to gain double-sexed unity has as its ultimate goal the achievement of immortality through a bisexual fusion.

Perhaps other intrapsychic factors are involved. In our era of greater sexual permissiveness, of woman's liberation, and rapid societal change, unisex clothing may serve as an effective way of denying and repressing sexual anxiety.

When one's sense of effective masculinity or femininity has not yet solidified, despite an active heterosexual involvement, does it not seem "safer" for boys and girls to look alike? For youngsters whose identities are still unclear, who have come together prematurely out of dependency needs as well as for sexual needs, dressing alike offers considerable security. In looking alike, they attempt to undo their sexual activities by denying the differences between the sexes. I have often been struck by the anxiety, annoyance, and irritation with which a teenage girl greets an occasion when she must wear a dress. This seems to go far beyond the adherence to the mores of her peer culture or a rebellion against adult authority. The foundations of her still shaky femininity appear threatened if she is asked to reveal more of her femaleness. Is this because she has too early taken on an active sexual role for which she is unready?

In discussing parental roles, Russell Baker (1) has noted facetiously, ". . . sex should never be discussed with an adolescent. He believes that sex was not invented until six or seven years ago and he is embarrassed at the possibility that adults may ask him about sex, because he is not sure how much, if anything, they should be told about it at their age." Paradoxically Baker has described the abdication of parental responsibility in the guise of the generation gap. When parents are unsure of or uninterested in their role as parents, are overly competitive with their youngsters, or unable to handle their own sexual feelings for their attractive adolescent offspring, they may tacitly or overtly encourage adolescent sexual activity.

A mother, for example, suggested that her 14-year-old daughter, who rarely dated, go on the Pill for the relief of dysmenorrhea. The girl got the message that her mother expected her to become sexually active and shortly thereafter acted out her mother's unconscious wishes by embarking upon a disastrous sexual relationship. In keeping with Baker's dictum, this girl could never discuss any of her difficulties with her mother. This situation is illustrative of many where parents foster premature sexual behavior.

Blos (2) has defined the sex-adequate task of adolescence as involving an advance to the heterosexual position and the disengagement from the oedipal parent. The elaboration of masculinity and femininity is not completed during adolescence but "awaits final consolidation in subsequent stages." A striking example of the developmental unreadiness of ongoing, mature, heterosexual relatedness may be found among some adolescent couples who have progressed from "going together" in a sexual union and who set up housekeeping arrangements during their mid or later teens.

These situations are dramatic and almost invariably involve youngsters from troubled family backgrounds. Either their parents have abdicated their parental responsibilities or the hostile interaction between parents and adolescents has driven the youngsters away from home. In another era, a young person who was unhappy at home but not quite ready to be out on his or her own, might find refuge within an extended family. In our age of nuclear families, the "solution" appears to be to move in with one's boyfriend or girlfriend.

The following clinical material is offered in illustration. An 18-year-old girl with considerable ego strength, whose psychoanalytically oriented therapy has been supervised by me, moved in with her 24-year-old boyfriend right after she graduated from high school. This took place with the tacit approval of her parents and the active approval of his parents, who helped them find an apartment. The couple had dated for more than six months previously, enjoyed each other, and apparently felt comfortable about their sexual relationship.

The girl was raised by a depressed mother and an alcoholic father. During her childhood and early adolescence, she was cast in the role of mother to her own mother. She prided herself on being independent and adult.

To escape from her unhappy home situation, she entered a seemingly mature heterosexual relationship. She had neither freed herself from her intensely ambivalent ties to her mother, who in repetitive dreams menacingly came toward her, nor had she yet crystallized her own sense of self. Her associations went directly from her mother to her boyfriend. Through the latter, she was trying to reinforce her incomplete identity as a person. She verbalized her desire to mold herself in her boyfriend's image since her own identity was still unclear.

An early marriage was planned. After three or four months of living together, the couple decided to postpone marriage. She complained about the burdens of keeping house while working full time. She missed dating and the excitement of going dancing or to the movies. She became afraid to ask for sexual gratification for herself lest she drive him away. Her boyfriend, only slightly more mature than she, busied himself with his graduate work. He wanted a bedmate and housekeeper who would make relatively few emotional demands on him. He called her a "baby" for wanting to go out. There was little effective communication between them.

For this young woman, taking on an adult role for which she was unprepared has interfered with the development of a secure sense of identity. To try out her femininity in a continuous relationship with a man, before she felt fully secure as a woman, and before a greater resolution of her dependence on mother had taken place, has hindered mature relatedness. Several months later, when the relationship terminated, she experienced considerable bereavement and depression.

I suspect that such relationships and less dramatic versions of the same theme may have a paradoxical effect. Adolescence takes a long time. Identity formation, sexual identification, and vocational choices are all complex developmental tasks which cannot be effected overnight. Even in young people of considerable ego strength, who have had relatively nondistorted childhoods and reasonably healthy relationships and communication with their parents, these tasks must take their due course. In speeding up the process by which boys and girls experiment with sexual intimacy and commitment, try out their newly forged identities, and relinquish their old ties to their parents, the ego's integrative capacities may be strained in endless combinations of arrest, premature closure, and prolonged adolescence. When only seemingly firm love relationships are formed before one's identity is fully crystallized, there may be fewer options for subsequent growth. Ironically, this may lead to inconstant and shallow human relatedness.

References

1. Baker, R. *The New York Times,* April 20, 1972.
2. Blos, P. *On Adolescence.* New York: The Free Press of Glencoe, 1962.
3. Commission on Population Growth and the American Future. *Population and the American Future.* Washington: U. S. Government Printing Office, 1972.
4. Deutsch, H. *Selected Problems of Adolescence.* New York: International Universities Press, 1967.
5. Kantner, J. F., and Zelnik, M. Sexual experience of young unmarried women in the United States. *Family Planning Perspectives, 4:*4, 9-18, 1972. The quotation cited by Kantner and Zelnik appeared in *The New York Times,* May 10, 1972.
6. Kinsey, A. C., Pomeroy, W. B., and Martin, C. E. *Sexual Behavior in the Human Male.* Philadelphia: W. B. Saunders, 1948.
7. Kinsey, A. C., Pomeroy, W. B., Martin, C. E., and Gebhard, P. H. *Sexual Behavior in the Human Female.* Philadelphia: W. B. Saunders, 1953.

13

Sexuality in Adolescents: A Plea for Celibacy

EDWARD J. HORNICK

IN AN EFFORT TO DETERMINE whether or not we're doing a favor for ourselves, our youngsters, and our patients, I am going to make a plea for celibacy. Anna Freud described adolescence in terms of four alterations. The first, in early adolescence, she called the *quantitative increase in the drives*—the pre-genital explosion in which kids of about 11 through 13 are hungrier, greedier, crueler, more eccentric, more inconsiderate, more inquisitive, more boastful, more dirty. In later adolescents this becomes what is called a *qualitative change in the drives,* as they grow more genital-oriented and, as such, more guilt-ridden, because the temptation, of course, is to attach that drive to the earlier objects of one's life: parents, sisters, brothers, uncles, aunts.

The second stage of adolescence she described as an *alteration of an ego organization.* In *The Ego and the Mechanisms of Defense,* she cited as the two signal defenses characteristic of adolescence ascetism and intellectualization. Peter Blos, in his re-write of *Adolescence,* added a third which he found most common in American children, namely uniformism, as he called it, having to do with the child attaching himself to other peers, with the group around him sustaining him through the experience of drive release.

The third phase Anna Freud noted was the *alteration in object relations.* In short, youngsters, whether girls or boys, have to get the cathexis off the parent and onto a peer, which they do with irregular success. In this process, of course, parents have to be thrown out. There is no other way. And in the process of doing that, youngsters are terribly good at disparaging their parents and putting them down. The parent has to be able at one moment to take the damnedest insults and taunts and at the next moment to be helpful, kind, generous, and sympathetic, as the youngster demands that of him, too.

The fourth alteration Anna Freud described is the *alteration in ideals and social relations.* And she pointed out that they tend to choose first a very important person apart from the parents—a coach, a teacher, a public figure—and then gradually move that attachment into the peer group. This then becomes the ideal relationship before they go on to a single sexual object. Obviously, the tasks of adolescence are enormously difficult. It is really unfortunate that in our society not only do we ask kids to develop sexually in the period from 12 to 20, but we ask them also to get through a rather stiff academic performance, to choose a career, and to take on social and financial responsibilities for themselves. All these internal and external tasks come down on the young person at the same time. It is not surprising that very many of these tasks are left unfinished at 20 and run on to 30 or 40.

Now let us turn to sexuality. We tend to say about it, as God said to Noah, "Everything that's fastened down is coming loose." All the established values and ideals of our sexual behavior and customs seem to be changing. But instead of going over the changes, I would like to look at them from the opposite perspective, if I may. In the assorted statistics which we have, we see that by age 22 across our nation, somewhere between 40% and 60% of young people have had coitus in some form or another, depending on which sample—black or white, urban or rural—one looks at. But let us turn that around and say that 40% to 60% of these young people have *not* had intercourse. And of the ones who say they have had it, many of them have had only a single experience, and that frequently of a very poor quality, so that to really call them sexual is a mistake.

Now this low frequency of participation in those who do and this total celibacy of the many, many others who don't at 22 tells us something about what I feel is the difficulty of the task of maturing sexually.

Here are three small clinical excerpts, all from cases of boys, but these could be duplicated with evidence from cases of girls. First is Jack, who was a virgin until he turned 24. Jack is the youngest of four kids in the family and the only boy, which meant that he had four mothers—three older sisters and a mother. As such, he was both overindulged and overcontrolled, with all the good and bad of four mothers. In the early days of his treatment, whenever he went out with a new girl, it was a matter of how many hours and how many minutes he could be with her before she would remind him of one of his sisters or his mother and destroy the whole relationship. More than three years of careful treatment were necessary before he could deal with a girl and see her as separate from his original harem. At the same time, he was trying to support himself and get through college. All three tasks are for him very, very difficult. It took a lot of patience for him to stay with one girl, so that he could grow and graduate. And to grow takes time.

Our second example is Harry, perhaps still a virgin at 28. He spent five years in therapy with me while struggling through college. On only one occasion in five years of one- to two-times-a-week psychotherapy did he let loose even a fantasy. On that occasion he reported a fantasy he had had of himself as a big game hunter meeting up with Amazons and subduing them serially, quickly, and coolly. Most of the time he kept his fantasies under secure wraps, while he worked over calculus and physics and sought through intellect to match and then sluice his fear of professional things. He's now winding up his Ph.D. in another city.

I want to mention that both these young men masturbated, but they did so with such diluted contexts that they were not scared by their own masturbation.

Our third subject, Walter, has just become 20 and is a potential rock composer and star. His lyrics "explode with sexuality," but he finds the whole business of sex disgusting, dirty, and unnatural. He has never kissed a girl. Though he is a very handsome young man, he is afraid to appear undressed at a swimming pool or on the beach, because he is afraid that his flabby breasts resemble those of a girl. He is worried about control problems, terrified of unleashing the sexual avalanche from within him. He flirts with death as a way out of his problems, and alternatively with homosexuality as a way of sharing his problems with someone like himself.

This then is the cautionary note. We do well to regard these tergiversations from the sexual drive with respect. These young men did not have to be celibate, were not deprived, but yet were so laced with terror that sex was unspeakable, let alone permissible, as an act to perform. I am not now addressing the attitudes toward sex of guilt and shame that our society imposes upon young people. I am as much against those as any of you. I am speaking of the inherent developmental difficulties of growing up, of switching from the original object to a new object, and of doing this at the same time that one must do many other things.

Like the scientists in Chicago in 1943, they have to take the charcoal rods out very slowly before they can let the sexual explosion happen. When they do so, they are like one of my favorite adolescents, Stephen Dedalus, who had the most horrendous trouble both with masturbation and with the prostitute he finally slept with. After solving both those problems, he said on the day of his wedding: "I go to encounter for the millionth time the reality of experience and to forge within the smithy of my soul—the uncreated conscience of the race."* He was 27 when he achieved resolution of his problems.

---

*Joyce, James. *The Portrait of the Artist as a Young Man.* Edited by C. G. Anderson. New York: Viking Press, 1969.

14

The Effect on Ego Development of Sexual Experience in Early Adolescence

MICHAEL G. KALOGERAKIS, M.D.

A RECENTLY PUBLISHED STUDY of adolescent sexual behavior in the United States indicates that by their 20th birthday 52% of boys and girls are no longer virgins. Thirty-seven per cent have had intercourse before they are 16. Boys start earlier than girls but the girls catch up so that almost as many girls as boys have had coitus before they reach their 17th birthday (6).

The actual breakdown of age at first intercourse among the nonvirgin adolescent population is as follows:

	Boys	*Girls*
12 or under	17%	7%
13	18	12
14	18	11
15	18	26
16	12	21
17	12	6
18 or 19	5	17

These figures, the first that give a comprehensive picture of adolescent sexuality in a representative sample of the United States population, provide us for the first time with hard data to set alongside of impressions formed by clinicians and social scientists who have studied specialized groups, e.g., college students, ghetto youth, addicts, hospitalized adolescents. In the absence of any earlier basis for comparison, it is impossible to say for sure that the figures given represent any change in the sexual practices of American youth. In fact, Offer (5) firmly denies that a sexual revolution has occurred. However, other, less comprehensive surveys and the impressions of many workers in the field suggest that significant changes have occurred, largely in the *amount* of sexual activity among adolescents, as well as in the age at which they get started.

Whatever the case may be with regard to the matter of change, Sorensen's statistics make it possible to reexamine the role of coital experience in the life of the younger adolescent, particularly with an eye to its effect on developing ego functions.

Arbitrarily, I shall focus my remarks on *girls experiencing intercourse before their 16th birthday*. Three assumptions are implicit in this choice:

1. There is a significant difference between coital experience and other forms of sexual contact in their effect on subsequent ego development.
2. Coital experience affects boys and girls in different ways.
3. The age at which intercourse first occurs is a pertinent factor in assessing differences in adolescent ego development.

Though some authors have not seen fit to draw a line between sexual intercourse and heavy petting as varieties of sexual experience, the attitudes of society and, by extension, of adolescents in general in regard to virginity are still such as to warrant a distinction. This does not imply that a different level of intimacy is necessarily achieved by intercourse nor that the difference in the physical experience per se is significant, only that the *psychological meaning* given to sexual intercourse remains important in our society.

Clinical experience regularly reveals how differently boys and girls approach sexuality and how diverse may be their reactions to sexual involvement. The statistical data presented by Gagnon et al. (2) and by Sorensen (6) strongly confirm this.

That the age at which initial coitus occurs is of importance seems self-evident, for as the event supervenes in the life of the growing adolescent at different points of vulnerability, it has different effects.

Foremost among ego functions likely to be affected by sexual experience are object relations. As is well known, sex is by no means a simple human experience in which physical pleasure is the only goal. It has been described as experimentation or exploration, as exploitation and manipulation. It can be an attempt to cure loneliness or a means of self-debasement. For many girls it is the most effective available means for expressing defiance and rattling the shackles of parental authority. In such cases it may appear to be a move towards autonomy and independence.

A love relationship, the stated or implied purpose of many a sexual involvement, is an unlikely aim of adolescent liaisons and an even less likely result. This is truer when the participants are younger. Mature love as adults know it is probably quite impossible for the younger adolescent. Though there may be much *talk* of love among younger teenagers, this is often a transparent attempt to be grown-up, and older adolescents are less likely to claim love as a motive than the younger ones. The 13-year-old who insists she is madly in love and defies anyone to prove otherwise will often admit a year or two later she didn't know what love was then and maybe doesn't really know yet.

Helene Deutsch (1) is very blunt on this point: "There is no question that a too early involvement in sexual gratification interferes with the development of real, tender feelings of love and enchantment."

For Deutsch and others, early adolescence is too narcissistic a stage of development for true object relations to exist. She goes a step further and claims that early sexual involvement interferes with and postpones normal development. It prolongs the stage of narcissism which may become fixed, permanently damaging the developing personality.

The psychiatrist treating adolescents is able to confirm this in many patients. What is not clear is whether this is a result of the early sexual involvement, or whether both are *symptoms* of preexisting pathology in which a narcissistic personality organization is the major feature.

As in all instances, the clinician is open to the criticism that he is a priori dealing with the *disturbed* adolescent and that consequently his inferences can relate only to the disturbed population, with limited application to normals.

Sorensen (6) rejects the notion that "increasing sexual permissiveness and the prevalence of sex are dehumanizing the emotions of our youth and depriving many adolescents of any meaningful perception of love." His data indicate that "a new kind of love is being worked out by American adolescents in a strongly sexual context" in which mutuality and belonging are emphasized. They seem to distinguish between *transient* love and *durable* love, the latter being the kind that leads to marriage. Yet they are firm in their belief that transient love, even if only of a few weeks duration, is valid and can be quite profound.

Still others (3, 4), working primarily in the ghettos, have taken the position that coitus serves an *integrative* function in young adolescents who have nothing else going for them. When family relations are chaotic or patently destructive, when school is a total loss, when the street is a dangerous place to be, the moment of pleasure that sexual intercourse provides can be the one bright light that makes life worth living and permits the young person to keep plugging. Ladner and Hammond have described the important role of sex for the lower-class black starting from the age of five or six. In the group they studied in St. Louis, both discussion of and participation in sex were the focal points of the adolescents' lives. Sex as fun-and-games soon becomes part of the game of survival in ghetto existence. The authors state:

> Participation in sexual activities can be seen as an integrative function which provides the participants with a sense of togetherness: they share common experiences which they can discuss with each other, and the individual girl shares with the boy a sense of belongingness . . . it provides a sense of togetherness, identity, vitality, and enjoyment.

They go on to point out that in later adolescence, sex frequently becomes a form of exchange for material goods and services. It is a common means of escape from overwhelming ghetto problems. In the words of one 15-year-old:

> When I have intercourse, I get a thrill. I just forget about all my trouble. It makes you forget that you don't have the kind of things you need for school, the money to buy your lunch and clothes to wear and stuff like that.

Or, a 13-year-old girl:

> When we are hanging around the building and don't have anything else to do and boys come around, we might start playing with them and before you know it all of us are mellow (i.e., having sex).

I could add an endless number of similar statements from adolescents I have seen at Bellevue Psychiatric Hospital. There is no question that sex has many uses for all adolescents, and that these uses become more important as other aspects of life fail to provide what they should. However, the attempt to replace a disorganized life and disastrous relationships with parents by one or a series of sexual involvements is doomed to failure. One can never be a substitute for the other, least of all in early adolescence. In the attempt, the full potential of a good sexual relationship may never be realized as sex is called upon to do too much. There is little question that in the majority of instances the integrative function that coitus may seem to be serving is specious and at best short-lived.

As Deutsch (1) points out, the ego ideal of a girl is built largely on the mother—the ideal mother. Consequently, transgression of sexual boundaries is seldom real sexual freedom and guilt reactions tend to be very strong. Referring to the changing mores on sexual behavior she states: "This social progress is thus not a constructive force; one could say that the ego ideal is shattered by it."

Though one could quarrel with the universality of such a dictum—it was based primarily on work with middle-class adolescents and often seems invalid for ghetto culture—it is none the less a good basic assumption to make. The facts in a particular case may prove the exception. The adolescent girl from the ghetto often finds little in her mother with which she can establish a stable ego ideal. She is forced to look elsewhere, often to an aunt or her grandmother, at other times to an older sister or her own peers. If the role model provided by her mother is chaste but hypocritical and selfish, her sexually active girlfriend who is warm, considerate, and genuine can very understandably become the one to emulate. Her ego ideal diminishes the traditional importance society places on sexual behavior, as other values assume correspondingly greater significance.

Again I would stress that this is the exception, not the rule. The baseline that is always present and must be our constant reference point is the traditional one as defined by Deutsch. Gagnon and his co-workers (2), in their study of college youth, were able to confirm what we have always suspected: that society exacts a price for sexual involvement which is generally greater for the girl. Reported happiness and popularity decreased as the girl's level of sexual involvement increased.

Perhaps one of the most important points about early involvement in sex is that it can serve to divert interest from the important tasks of early adolescence. For example, rather than allowing the adolescent girl the opportunity to wean herself gradually from the dependency bonds of earlier childhood, it provides an outlet for displacement of these bonds. This is more likely to happen when a sexual relationship is sustained, but I have seen it also in the short-lived involvement in which the quest for the surrogate mother/father becomes an endless pursuit, a promised but elusive Eldorado.

It is safe to say that no 12- or 13-year-olds and few 14-year-olds have sufficiently resolved their dependency problem to be able to broach sex in anything resembling a mature fashion. The most it can provide is the respite from life's hassles or the fun-and-games already referred to. But does such a meaning to sex then condition the adolescent to require nothing more of a relationship as he or she gets older?

Beyond its effect on developing object relations, we must also consider what early sexual involvement does to impulse control, frustration tolerance, and other ego functions. Unfortunately, hard data on this score do not exist and impressions are contradictory.

The pursuit of objective data to answer our basic question, "Is sexual intercourse in early adolescence destructive?" leads once again to Sorensen (6). In reporting their first experience, very significant differences emerged between boys and girls. Far more often than girls, boys reported positive emotions such as excited, happy, satisfied, thrilled, joyful, mature, fulfilled and powerful. Girls, on the other hand, reported a preponderance of negative emotions: afraid, guilty, worried, embarrassed, sorry, hurt, used, and disappointed. The comparative statistics on some of these feelings are striking:

	Boys	*Girls*
Powerful	15%	1%
Guilty	3	36
Sorry	1	25
Hurt	0	25
Used	0	16

Curiously, girls 15 and younger at the time of initial coitus more frequently reported positive feelings than did older girls. The ratios were 2:1 for "excited," 4:1 for "joyful" and 1:2 for "hurt," "foolish," or "disappointed."

Negative feelings generally diminished with subsequent sexual experience for the majority of girls.

Another significant finding was that girls responded three times more often than boys that they wished they had waited till they were older before having sex for the first time.

A sociological inquiry such as Sorensen's will generally miss important data that only extensive psychological exploration can turn up. For example, the operation of defense mechanisms such as denial and rationalization, which is particularly common in the 12- and 13-year-olds, is not taken into account. What a young teenager feels about his emotional life is sometimes best learned by asking about others. Thus it is not surprising to a clinician that while Sorensen's adolescents staunchly defend their right to make their own decisions about sex, 74% agreed with the statement, "Too many young people these days are irresponsible where sex is concerned."

Similarly, this approach does not provide much information about the prevalence of psychopathology in the sample except of a gross variety, and this was noticeably lacking. One suspects, however, that a careful psychiatric evaluation would have turned up significant disturbance. (A follow-up study of his subjects five or ten years later might be very instructive in this regard.) In a hospital population such as Bellevue's, emotional disturbance is a regular finding, by definition. The same can be said of patients undergoing psychoanalysis. These samples are generally not suitable for drawing firm conclusions about cause and effect relationships between sexual activity and ego dysfunction. Possibly, trends might be identified by a comparison of such adolescents with one another. Clinical impressions, as yet unsubstantiated by hard data, indicate a far higher incidence of coercion, incest, homosexuality, and adult partners in our Bellevue group than Sorensen found in his nationwide sample. Whether this is a function of the emotional disturbance or a norm for ghetto youth is impossible to say without further study, but indications are that both factors contribute, each in its particular way.

To summarize, the present state of our knowledge permits the formulation of the following tentative conclusions:

1. Coitus, i.e., the physical act of penetration, continues to have specific significance different from other forms of sexual behavior for many adolescents but this seems limited to the first time, at

which virginity is surrendered. Subsequently, it is *physical intimacy,* with or without intercourse, that assumes importance in object relations.

2. The sexual experience must be viewed in its full psychosocial context for its impact to be understood. Of particular importance as determinants of subsequent disturbance are the existing personality organization of the subject, the relationship to the sexual partner, the presence or absence of force, the current home situation and other circumstances surrounding the sexual experience.

3. Even when such disorganizing features are absent, early sexual involvement interferes with and diverts the adolescent's attention from the confrontation of the important developmental tasks of this period of life.

4. It can be generally assumed that the younger the girl when she first has intercourse, the greater the risk of emotional trauma with its disorganizing sequelae.

References

1. Deutsch, H. *Selected Problems of Adolescence.* New York: International Universities Press, 1967.
2. Gagnon, J. H., Simon, W., and Berger, A. J. Some aspects of sexual adjustment in early and later adolescence. In J. Zubin and A. M. Freedman (Eds.), *The Psychopathology of Adolescence.* New York: Grune and Stratton, 1970.
3. Ladner, J. "Deviance in the lower class adolescent subculture." Masters Honors Essay Series, Social Science Institute, Washington University, St. Louis, 1966.
4. Ladner, J., and Hammond, B. "Socialization into sexual behavior." Presented at Annual Meeting of Society for the Study of Social Problems, San Francisco, August 27-29, 1967.
5. Offer, D. Attitudes toward sexuality in a group of 1500 middle class teen-agers. *J. of Youth and Adolescence, 1,* 81-90, 1972.
6. Sorensen, R. C. *Adolescent Sexuality in Contemporary America.* New York: World Publishing, 1973.

15

Some Effects of the "Sexual Revolution" on the Mid-Adolescent Girl

CLARICE J. KESTENBAUM, M.D.

THERE HAS BEEN A GREAT DEAL OF SPECULATION in recent years about the so-called sexual revolution. I am going to leave the job of determining the nature and the extent of the revolution, if it exists, to the anthropologists and sociologists. Is there a real or only an apparent change in sexual mores, how does it affect the young, and is the change a good thing? There most certainly has been more public talk about sex of late, more "do-it-yourself" sex manuals to add to the mass of "how to" books stacking the shelves, more openness in high school hygiene classes. Yet mere knowledge of a subject has little to do with understanding; denial and repression are powerful mechanisms. In spite of the best efforts of sex educators, there is a vast sea of sexual misinformation concerning such basic considerations as menstruation and conception.

Psychiatrists do not ordinarily see the normal adolescents in our society. We treat in depth a limited number of youngsters, all of whom exhibit some pathological adaptation. These patients, to be sure, represent the pathological extremes of a spectrum. Conclusions drawn from studying their deviations from the norm may nevertheless help us in our assessment of "normality." The youngsters in the middle of the spectrum may, for example, be symptom-free. The same pressures which produce symptoms or behavioral changes (viz., asceticism or promiscuity) in less healthy adolescents may be causing mild anxiety or depression in their somewhat healthier peers.

The adolescent is faced with the difficult task of "finding himself" that is, forging a unique personal identity and eventually a plan, among the myriad choices, for his life work. Equally important is the establishment of an intimate heterosexual partnership which should be fulfilling and pleasurable. The ability to form intimate bonds does not occur overnight. The individual mode of earlier attachments tends to repeat itself. The process of forging a more mature relationship takes time and it also takes another person. The working out of this process occurs in a trial-and-error fashion. The ability to be with another without fear of losing one's own newly established identity, in a truly mature union, occurs in late adolescence, the age of psychological maturity varying from culture to culture. In previous generations, "going steady" often implied sexual intimacy just short of intercourse. In some circles the custom is now called "living together." This usually implies sexual intercourse with an exclusive partner. It is a private matter of two people engaged in a sort of trial marriage (since none of the responsibilities of children, financial obligations, or extended families are included).

What is "revolutionary" today is merely that what was done quietly is now frequently done in the open. With mature young people this is a logical intermediate step to final commitment. Where the new pattern fails is with the group of unready youngsters who feel put upon by peer pressure. Girls, for example, often feel compelled to lose their virginity (rather than lose face!) and to engage willy-nilly in some mock-marriage arrangements. Often such experimentation has disasterous results. Out-of-wedlock pregnancy is always a situation of crisis. Even with liberalized abortion laws, abortion is a psychic trauma to both partners. Rapid change of partners can also have serious side effects, particularly if sexuality is being used as a proving-ground for genital competence, or a defense against homosexual strivings. The sexual act becomes divorced from feelings. Oftentimes, one member of the couple, usually the girl, "feels" more than the other and when the partner leaves her to seek greener pastures, she feels abandoned, rejected, and depressed. In the "sink-or-swim" atmosphere of late adolescence, young individuals have to begin to take ultimate responsibility for their own actions and choices, no matter what their degree of readiness.

What about the middle adolescent, the 15- or 16-year-old in a period of liberalized attitudes: can he stand the pressures of the "New Freedom?"

As in evaluating "normality" of any developmental stage, one looks to the previous stages for clues. Did the child make an adequate attachment, separation, and individuation? Did he master the oedipal conflict and arrive at a comfortable and appropriate kind of latency (of the sort, that is, that Peter Blos* describes so beautifully)?

The young adolescent's struggle to become an individual tends to be spasmodic: his every advance beyond his childhood object-ties is followed, in so many instances, by a regressive pull.

The sense of self is weakened through increasingly powerful drives at the same time that parental support is lessened. If the earlier life adjustment was healthy, that is, if the individual had a satisfactory latency period, he or she will not be overwhelmed by the resurgence of the sexual and aggressive drives in adolescence. By this I mean that the child who has learned to postpone immediate gratification, to sublimate instead, and who has developed cognitive skills, will have the "ego-strength" necessary to manage the powerful drives. By mid-adolescence the superego is becoming less rigid, parents are no longer superheroes and have in most cases even fallen from grace, replaced in part by peers as models. All the same, parents are needed more than ever, in spite of protestations to the contrary, as ongoing reminders of childhood models and as controlling influences.

---

* Blos, Peter. The initial stage of male adolescence. In *Psychoanalytic Study of the Child,* Vol. XX. New York: International Universities Press. 1965. Pp. 145-164.

In many cases parents, believing themselves to be "modern," abdicate their true parental role, and instead act like "pals." This puts a particularly heavy burden on the shoulders of their children. The mother who takes her 15-year-old daughter to be fitted for a diaphragm "to be ready when it happens" is giving the girl a clear message. Parents like this one frequently push their children to act out their own sexual fantasies. Lack of sexual controls results, in middle adolescence, in shallowness of relationships, or conversely, in a symbiotic clinging to a parent surrogate. Sex becomes the vehicle by which dependency needs are met. The children may experience, in their pseudoheterosexual attempts, anxiety, lowered self-esteem, and feelings of vulnerability.

The too-early sexual liaison does not allow a proper working through of the separation from parental objects. Normal adolescents spend countless hours in romantic fantasy. Masturbation is usually accompanied at first by guilt feelings, even in the most liberal homes. They fear the loss of control and incestuous fantasies, albeit unconscious ones. Normal adolescents, however, when the masturbatory fantasies are neither sadistic nor masochistic, soon learn to contain the drives. The guilt is overcome and the adolescents become familiar with the functions of their own bodies. Only when they become comfortable with their own bodies will they be reasonably secure with a partner.

Object choices at first are narcissistic and transient. Romances are fleeting. Boys often see a girl literally as part object, and use the relationship to "show off" before their friends.

It is important to remember that such experimentation must occur, better by far in fantasy than reality. The beginnings of heterosexual friendships are often pseudo-intimate. Safety is provided by distance–such as endless telephone calls. Even the dancing is a kind of mating game–pelvic gyrations without body contact. Both sexes are frightened by the idea of sexual contact. They fear the possibility of failure or rejection.

The following dreams are taken from the histories of three adolescent girls, aged 14 to 16. Two of the girls fall into the healthier "adjustment reaction of adolescence" and the third had a long history of maladaptive "psychopathic" behavior.

Linda C., a suburban professional's daughter, first came for psychotherapy at age 12 because of school examination anxiety and "panic" during summer camp, from which she was sent home early. Originally referred as a case of "middle child syndrome," after two-and-a-half years of treatment she was well on the way to normal school adjustment, had many girlfriends, and had a good relationship with her concerned parents.

> Dream 1. I was in a harem with a lot of girls. The teacher-camp director turned into a bankrobber and I was scared.

Her associations concerned the sex talk of the campers and her own wish for a sexual experience accompanied by fears and fantasies of rape. She also acknowledged her fear of growing up.

> Dream 2. I was riding on a train on my way to my session when some Puerto Rican boys started chasing me. I was scared and went to find mother.

The day residue involved her actually seeing some young boys near my office on Central Park West.

At age fifteen she developed her first "crush" and spoke about him incessantly with girlfriends, writing notes, comparing strategies, etc.

> Dream 3. I was walking on the beach and bumped into Kenny. Suddenly we were in bed together. We lay down next to each other. I was completely relaxed. We were very happy. Then it was suddenly morning and I knew I was not a virgin any more but I didn't care. I was very happy.

Her first comment after reporting the dream was a giggling, "We didn't do anything, honestly. It just happened."

These dreams are typical of healthy girls who are still far from true intimacy. Linda is now 16½ and has a few "friends who are boys" but feels she is more mature than most of her classmates.

She has still not had a sexual experience, no more than have most of her girlfriends. She is looking forward to college where she will meet older boys and has many romantic aspirations about the kind of boy she is hoping to meet. "He should be attractive but more important, kind, and he should be interested in helping people and pretty smart and, of course, should really like me."

I first saw Rima, a 16-year-old high school senior, when the principal of her private school learned that she had been present at an unsupervised "pot party" and urged that her parents have her evaluated. Actually, she had no drug problem of any kind but did suffer feelings of inadequacy. She was very bright, creative, attractive, slightly overweight, but felt she was unpopular and "on the fringe" of the social group. Her parents were fiercely modern, they even allowed her to go on weekend trips unchaperoned. "She has good sense. She can learn to take care of herself." Her naivete nearly got her raped on a Washington peace march when she accepted a ride with a "nice" older man, who only let her go when she said, "Look, I'm only fifteen, same age as your daughter," a lucky guess. She had had one sexual experience with a boy she adored, who, when she phoned him a week later to find out why he hadn't called, told her she was an inexperienced baby and too dependent. She had felt humiliated, but had a few similar encounters during the next two years, each of which left her ashamed, empty, and depressed. She felt being a woman was a sorry fate.

> Dream 1. I was eight, wiggling my front tooth. It came out and left a big hole in my gums. I was embarrassed and said to my mother, "Is there any chance of my getting a new tooth?" No one was interested.

The castration anxiety needs little comment; her anger at her mother for being unconcerned (in this case with her missing "tooth"—in real life with her dependency needs) was brought out in subsequent sessions. A few months later she developed strong feelings for a boy who totally ignored her. When he finally showed fleeting interest one night at a party, she engaged in a "one night stand" only to be disappointed once again. That night she dreamed:

> Dream 2. Richard was about to hug me. A maid came in. "Your mother said 'clean up the room'." I dropped my teddy bear in the middle of the floor. My mother had guests downstairs. I felt choked, like having a tantrum. Mother ignored me, even when I cried. I tried to turn on the light but the switch broke off in my hand. It was dark. I was afraid.

The equation between rejecting lover and rejecting mother is apparent, as is the regression in the dream to early childhood with its fears and anxieties. Although this girl displayed some neurotic features, her conflicts about her femininity, her fears of growing up, and her wishes to find a love object for herself are the most common themes in the fantasy life of mid-adolescent girls. In Rima's case success in her first year away from home in college and increased sense of self-worth eventually helped her form a happy and meaningful "first love" relationship with a young sophomore. They live in separate college dorms, spend a great deal of time together doing homework and attending campus affairs, have a sexual life limited to vacations or occasional weekends "because that's all we can hassle when we're under pressure of so much work, and besides we're not even sure this is the real thing."

A dream reported during this period was simply, "I was pregnant and had a baby. I was very happy."

The third case demonstrates severe psychopathology in a 14-and-a-half-year-old girl. Her dreams, nevertheless, show many of the same preoccupations as do those of the healthier adolescents.

Louisa, an only child of a wealthy professional man, had been "acting up" sexually since she was 11. She was considered "boy crazy," had run away from home to her 16-year-old boyfriend's house on several occasions, lost all interest in school, even girlfriends. Her parents had no control over her whatsoever. She seemed, in fact, to have run the household from day one. Her mother was obese; her father was a dapper man-about-town, clearly involved with other women; and Louisa was caught in the throes of oedipal feelings. There was a lot of walking about the house semi-nude and accidental opening of the bathroom door, Louisa attended sessions under stress, forced by the school principal. She announced one day that she was going to lose her virginity. Her mother accompanied her to the gynecologist for a diaphragm, against my advice. Meanwhile, she was dating Jim, a known "junkie" who had been dropped from school because of drugs, and "Peter," a rather shy classmate.

> Dream 1. I was in the forest. Millions of people were there in wheelchairs. I was with two girls in wheelchairs at a hospital. A doctor had to perform an operation. He cut the skin on my stomach in the shape of a square, removed the inside, and put the square patch back. The knife really hurt. I was scared.

She related this dream to thought of intercourse, which she feared, and her girlfriend's recent abortion. She felt she hated all men and wanted to get even with them.

The parents continued to allow her to go to parties unchaperoned, were out of town often themselves. Shortly afterwards, she took LSD and attempted intercourse. She was frightened and called me in the middle of the night, her parents having left town.

> Dream 2. I was in a hospital, nine months pregnant. I had horrible labor pains. The baby was Jim's. I was upset and in great pain.

Attempts to have Louisa hospitalized to prevent further acting out led to the father's "firing" me. Nonetheless, in the last sessions Louisa reported:

> Dream 3. I'm at the circus. I see a trapeze-artist holding my girlfriend's hands. He dropped her. She died.

The following day the mother telephoned to say that Louisa had gone to a party and under the influence of "some drugs" was the object of a "gang-bang" by seven boys.

Louisa's behavior finally forced the family to exercise some controls and hospitalize her. The three-year follow-up results are gratifying in that Louisa, after two years in a protected therapeutic environment, is now in college and by all reports doing very well scholastically and socially.

I have presented these dreams as a way of underlining the concept that heterosexual fantasy plays a major role in the adolescent's development but that there is a vast difference between *thinking, dreaming,* and actually *doing.*

Adolescence is no time to abdicate parental authority, not until a true sense of the self has emerged.

16

Sexual Behavior in High School and College Students

JAMES TOOLAN, M.D.

THIS PAPER IS BASED ON THE PREMISE that there has been a major revolution in the sexual mores and behavior of high school and college students. In brief, the female is behaving more as the male has behaved for centuries. The female regards herself as equal to the male in all areas, including sexual behavior. A manifestation of this equality is the so-called unisex attire of many young people. Some critics have wondered whether this attitude is a healthy one, or whether the youngsters are not in some way confusing their identity. I believe that they are identifying as equal individuals, rather than as sexual stereotypes. We have seen a similar use of attire to stress the classless society in present-day China.

Both sexes have challenged the age-old double standard of sexual behavior imposed on the sexes by our society. Since the change has been greatest in the female, I will begin with a description of her sexual behavior. It is quite apparent that sexual behavior in all forms is beginning at a much earlier age. The young female is beginning to masturbate not only at an earlier age but with greater frequency, and she no longer feels that this is a shameful act that must be kept secret from men at all costs. Like the male, she now feels a pressure to begin heterosexual activity at an earlier age. There is an urgency to lose her virginity. As a result, some females may feel coerced into sexual behavior before they are sufficiently mature to cope with its emotional entanglements. One may now encounter females who, like males, may brag about having lost their virginity when such is not actually the case. The female's sexual behavior now more closely resembles that of the male in that she may engage in a sexual liaison in a more casual fashion, without the necessity to believe that the physical union is accompanied by love in order to justify such behavior. Some girls undoubtedly still become sexually involved as the price of obtaining the boy's affections, and some undoubtedly still feel guilt for their behavior, despite their conscious denial of same. I would expect, however, that the guilty reactions will be fewer in the future as society comes to fully accept the change in female mores. The female is behaving in a less passive fashion in all areas, as well as the sexual role. It is not at all unusual now for the young female to openly initiate sexual behavior. She no longer feels that she must be "seduced" by the male.

There has been a definite pressure on the female not only to be involved sexually, but also to achieve orgasm. Not infrequently the therapist is consulted by young female college students who are very concerned about their sexual adequacy because they are unable to achieve orgasm with any regularity.

The young female accepts her responsibility for contraception to a greater degree than ever before. No longer does she rely on the male to take care of this as was the case in the past. The increased ease of obtaining contraceptive help has certainly influenced this behavior. With the easy availability of abortions, young females no longer feel that this is a traumatic procedure. The records in New York State, since the open abortion law was adopted, have revealed a surprisingly low incidence of negative emotional reactions to abortions. One can only wonder how much the guilty reactions of the past were iatrogenically induced by male physicians, who fundamentally disapproved of the procedure's being performed on the "naughty" females. It is to be expected that in the future abortions will have no more emotional connotation than contraception has today.

There has also been an increasing incidence and acceptance of bisexual and homosexual behavior on the part of the young female. This has undoubtedly been influenced by both the gay liberation and the female liberation movements. Females on many college campuses, for example, will now openly acknowledge their homosexual behavior.

There is also a much greater incidence of group sex and sharing of sexual partners among young people which is not only confined to communal living. Many of these young people question why sexual fidelity is important at all, and also question whether jealousy is a natural or a pathological reaction.

Most young males have accepted the change in the double standard of sexual behavior; very few would expect to marry a virgin. Most males no longer divide women as a group into "good" or "bad" girls and, as a result, they expect most females to be sexually available. The male will therefore tend to begin his heterosexual life earlier, and no longer need resort to prostitutes. One might anticipate that as a result of this fact the impotence of married men with their wives, due to their viewing sex as "bad" and their wives as "good Madonna figures," should lessen considerably.

The male, however, may frequently feel pressured to satisfy the female sexually. He can no longer hide behind rationalizations such as respecting the female's virginity. Many young men are threatened by the openness and assertiveness of the female in the sexual area, as can be illustrated by the young woman who called her lover one evening and invited him over, as she wished to be "indulged." Some men would take this action as a compliment; some, unfortunately, consider it a threat to their virility and potency. As a result, many young men have reacted to the new sexual behavior of females with premature ejaculation and impotency.

The male also appears more tolerant of bisexual and homosexual behavior, as well as group sexual behavior.

It is now commonly accepted that many young couples openly live together before marriage. When these liaisons break up, as they so frequently do, the result is often quite traumatic to either partner, in many ways as traumatic as a divorce to married persons.

It is also quite evident that young people do not marry for sex, as perhaps they so often did in past generations. Their marriages instead usually reflect a commitment to live together indefinitely, and to solemnify this commitment the marriage ceremony still serves the young people as a useful symbol. On occasion, however, youngsters have married because of parental pressure. Parents who could not accept their children's cohabitation out of wedlock have undoubtedly precipitated many marriages, some of which certainly have been ill-advised.

One may also note a greater number of friendships between members of the opposite sex without sexual involvement. Although such friendships have existed in the past, they seem to be much more frequent today. This would appear to support the contention that youngsters view each other more readily as persons, rather than simply as sex objects.

It would not be amiss to mention the role of the parents in the sexual revolution. As a general rule, fathers seem to be more upset by the behavior of their daughters than do mothers. At times, though, one sees a very interesting reaction on the part of many parents. These are parents who do not object to their children's being sexually active when away from home, but become very upset when the youngsters logically assume that such behavior is acceptable also at home.

Changes in Therapy

One of the fruitful results of the women's liberation movement has been our increased awareness of stereotypical thinking. We have begun to question the value of virginity in women. One might well ask why virginity in males has never been prized, or why there are no promiscuous males but only promiscuous females. This change in our thinking has made us question some of the basic psychoanalytical concepts, such as passivity in females, aggression in males, penis envy, the role that each sex is expected to fulfill, and especially the concept "anatomy is destiny."

We have begun to realize also that transference and countertransference phenomena are much more complex than as originally conceived by Freud. The question has been raised, "Can a male therapist adequately understand and treat a female patient?" This is similar to the question of whether a white therapist can treat a black patient, or vice versa. One would hope so, certainly, but I believe that to do so adequately will require significant alteration in the stereotypical thinking of most therapists.

The work of Masters and Johnson has cast new light on the female orgasm and has made the question of clitoral versus vaginal orgasm as urgent as the medieval question of how many angels can dance on the head of a pin.

If we are to be competent therapists, we must also reexamine the issues of masochism and submission on the part of the female. Such behavior appears clearly related to cultural expectations.

Perhaps the most challenging question of all might be the question of homosexuality, and whether it is per se pathological. Certainly many of the earlier studies of homosexuality are of limited value, since they consisted only of patients. Recent studies have indicated that homosexual men and women appear to function as well in general as heterosexual people.

Identity Formation

The sexual revolution has challenged our simplistic notions of identity formation, especially those conceived of as role behavior. Young males and females are tending to share activities and duties to a greater degree than ever before. Not only may they share household chores but, of greater importance, both sexes may feel equally responsible for the care of their children. It is not unusual today to encounter couples where the female may work to support the male, rather than fulfilling their more traditional roles. Both sexes now have more career choices open to them; for example, many young men are going into careers involving child care. Females, on the other hand, are moving into so-called male roles, such as surgery, with greater ease.

The young people of today are questioning the entire concept of marriage, children, and the role of each parent. Females in particular are questioning the validity of marriage, perhaps for the first time. Until very recently, most females felt great pressure to marry and have children, and in the classic tradition, the female identified vicariously with her husband's career role, rather than thinking of herself as an independent agent. Today many girls question whether they should marry at all, and if so, what role they should play in the marriage. Both young females and males are giving deep thought to the prospect of having a family, and many wonder whether they should have children at all. The female seriously questions the value to herself of the mothering role, and whether or not a woman needs to have a child in order to be a complete woman. Hopefully, the answer is no.

Another question that is being raised is whether two parents are necessary to bring up a child. For years, divorced and widowed parents (usually mothers) have raised children alone and often have done an excellent job. The next logical step, therefore, is to inquire whether a single male or female can raise a child adequately. In my opinion many single persons could do an adequate job and should not hesitate to have or adopt children if they so desire.

Object Relations

Finally, I would like to discuss some of the effects of the sexual revolution on object relations. There is considerable evidence that youngsters may be relating to each other more as individual persons than as sex objects. We see evidence of this in their unisex clothing styles and their ability to have friends of the opposite sex who are not lovers. We have, hopefully, seen the demise of the double standard of sexual behavior. Perhaps we may now see more honest and more open relationships between members of the opposite sex.

Marriage, as never before, is being threatened and challenged on all sides. Many thoughtful persons have wonderd if the traditional concept of marriage is viable. Quite a few alternatives have been suggested. One such variation is termed "open marriage," where both partners are free to enter into relations, sexual or otherwise, outside of the marital union.

There have been questions raised as to the adverse effects of changes in our sexual mores and behavior. From a traditional point of view, we hear that adolescents should be allowed to develop emotionally and intellectually, free from sexual tensions and pressures. This naive concept might be amusing if it were not seriously held by so many intelligent people. Teenagers have never been free from sexual tensions. They have tried to lessen them by means of masturbation, fellatio, and cunnilingus, all of which were designed to preserve the technical virginity of the female. These practices were usually accompanied by guilt. In addition, they were scarcely designed to lead to a healthy sexual adjustment after marriage. It is interesting to note that for centuries educators insisted that sex, by which they presumably meant heterosexual activity, was detrimental to intellectual growth and accomplishment. At the present time only the three service academies, and perhaps a few all-female and/or some sectarian colleges still support this belief. After World War II the returning veterans, many of whom were married, did significantly better academically than many of the younger single students. Not many years ago medical students and interns were expected to remain single to devote themselves to their work. Medicine has not suffered from present-day students, the majority of whom are married.

Another matter under question is why such a premium is placed on vaginal intercourse, as opposed to all other forms of sexual activity. Why, pray, should the insertion of a penis into a vagina be so significantly different from all other types of sexual contact?

It is my distinct impression that psychiatrists and psychoanalysts are among the most tradition-bound of individuals, although it will undoubtedly be shocking to them to be so labeled. Unless they are willing to reexamine their beliefs and separate myth from scientific fact they may awaken some day to discover themselves viewed in the same light as African medicine men.

17

Sexual Deviation: A Critical Review of Psychoanalytic Theory

JULES R. BEMPORAD, M.D.

THIS PAPER WILL ATTEMPT a critical and, therefore, biased review of the psychoanalytic theory of what had been called the "perversions" such as fetishism, transvestism, exhibitionism, and voyeurism, but excluding homosexuality, which is covered elsewhere. Today, the term "perversion" is deemed archaic and demeaning, and so such disorders are classified as sexual deviations or sexual variations. This may denote a salutary attitude that is less moralistic and more tolerant of uncommon sexual practices. However, as will become evident from the following exposition, a change in nomenclature does not necessarily represent an advance in understanding and the etiology of these disorders is as uncertain as ever.

Classical Psychoanalytic View

As is well known, the first step toward a psychoanalytic study of the perversions resulted from Freud's finding similar sexual aims in the psychic life of children and in adult "perverts" which led him to conclude that the possibility for sexual deviancy results from the undifferentiated nature of childhood sexuality, and the potential for regression to these immature forms of sexuality (1). As Fenichel later pointed out:

> The simple formula presents itself: persons who react to sexual frustration with a regression to infantile sexuality are perverts; persons who react with other defenses or who employ other defenses after the regression are neurotic (2).

This formulation that neurosis is "the negative" of a perversion was maintained essentially unchanged throughout a good deal of later psychoanalytic writing, despite the frequent finding that deviants often show neurotic problems as well as sexual difficulties. As Fenichel added in 1945 (2), "Actually, things are not so simple." He indicated that deviant sexuality cannot be equated with infantile sexuality since the former results in genital orgasm, i.e., its goal is genital primacy. Therefore, Fenichel (as others) postulates the hypertrophy of a pregenital component instinct whose satisfaction makes possible the achievement of genital orgasm. Therefore, the hallmark of deviation is this hypertrophy of a partial instinct which, however, allows for genital primacy. The reason for the regression to the partial instinct and the blockage of normal genital outlet was thought to be an intense castration anxiety. This early classical view was that the deviant is someone who cannot gain sexual pleasure through normal genital outlets because of castration fear and who, through his aberrant sexual behavior, attempts to deny the possibility of castration and, insofar as this denial is maintained, is able to be orgastic and obtain sexual pleasure. While a retreat from genital sexuality due to castration fear was also found in the neurotic, in this case the component instinct is desexualized and its discharge conflictual. In both the neurotic and the deviate, however, the regression to partial instincts helps to keep other internal strivings repressed and defends against the possibility of castration. In summary, then, the purpose of deviancy was to allow some sexual release while guaranteeing the repression of the oedipal complex and the dreaded castration anxiety.

This basic formulation has been applied to most forms of sexual deviation. In fetishism, for example, this theory soon supplanted the earlier adherence to the belief that the etiology of fetishism depended on a chance childhood association between the presence of a specific object and sexual excitation. In time, these childhood associations were seen as screen memories: the formation of the mental association was not the cause of fetishism but rather the effect of an already existing pathological condition. Therefore, the foot might become sexually exciting because the child, already suffering from castration anxiety, needed to find a nongenital object to serve as a substitute for the female phallus in his effort to deny the castration of females. The transference of sexual importance from the genital to the foot allowed the child to continue his belief, on an unconscious level, that the female also possessed a penis and so he need not fear his own castration. From then on, he is only able to perform sexually if the foot plays a prominent role because the fetish object serves to reassure him against castration anxiety. Therefore, most fetishes are phallic substitutes, or more specifically, representative of the illusory female phallus.

The situation in fetishism becomes more complex with the shift of interest in psychoanalytic theory to the ego and its defense mechanisms. In his paper on fetishism (3), written in 1927, Freud described the fetishist as having a "double attitude toward the possibility of castration": one part of him acknowledges the castrated female state while another part of him refuses to forego his belief in the female phallus. The fetishist does not hallucinate a female phallus, he can test reality adequately but retains the myth of female phallus by a "rift in the ego." This split in the ego as defensive mechanism was to occupy Freud in later papers and eventually to characterize most forms of pathology (4)*.

Freud essentially postulated that two conflicting beliefs can be maintained concurrently, one belief being conscious and the other repressed. Despite its alleged ubiquity, the "split in the ego" mechanism has been most frequently mentioned by post-

---

* To quote Freud: "It must not be thought that fetishism presents an exceptional case as regards splitting of the ego; it is merely a particularly favorable subject for studying the question (4)."

Freudian psychoanalysts in reference to the sexual deviations. Recently Kohut (5) has postulated a "vertical" rather than a "horizontal" split in the personality structure of sexual deviation. By this "vertical" split, Kohut intends the coexistence of disparate personalities so that these disorders resemble cases of multiple personality or disassociate states.

Transvestism was seen as a sort of compromise between fetishism and homosexuality (6). The transvestite both identifies with the mother (homosexuality) yet denies the castration of the female (fetishism) by himself becoming a woman with a penis. Various permutations around this basic theme have been proposed. Grotjohn (7) believes that the female attire itself becomes a substitute for the missing penis or that the transvestite is identifying with his own penis. The fundamental mechanism, however, remained the denial of castration by the creation of a phallic female.

In voyeurism, the individual attempts to repeat a frightening experience from childhood in which he had seen the castrated female genital. By repeated voyeuristic activity, the individual tries to reassure himself he will not suffer the same fate. Voyeurism is thus a repeated attempt to master a frightening situation much as the recurrent dreams in a traumatic neurosis. It is obvious that this disorder in which the individual actually seeks out the female genital would not fit the theory of the belief in the phallic woman and so lends itself to another model. Nevertheless, some authors have attempted to fit voyeurism into the phallic female model by stating that the voyeur truly seeks a phallic female or that he switches the importance of the phallus to other objects such as feces which serve to reassure him against castration.

Exhibitionism repeats the castration theme in that the exhibitionist is said to unconsciously wish that the female victim will show him her penis in return and thus prove that women are not castrated. Exhibitionism in the female is said to result from inferiority feelings because of a lack of a penis so that the importance of the phallus is displaced to other body parts that are then exhibited.

Sadism and masochism, while possibly being totally different from the disorders described above, were also fitted into the castration-fear formulation. At first sadism was thought of as a normal component of active sexual aims, being necessary for primal man to subdue his mate and thus perpetuate the species. Similarly, masochism was felt to be a normal aspect of feminine "passive" sexuality. With the alterations brought about by postulating a death instinct, primary masochism, and aggression as an outward deflection of instinctual forces (8), more complex formulations have supplanted these early theories. Castration anxiety in sadism was believed to be appeased by the sadist being in complete dominance, doing to others what he secretly fears will be done to him. Masochism, on the other hand, seemed to represent the individual suffering a known amount of trauma in order to avoid a greater injury (i.e., castration), although, as stated above, the hypothesis was complicated by the introduction of the death instinct (9). In general, sadism and masochism, while classified with sexual deviations, do not share some of the basic characteristics of other deviations such as the pronounced split in the ego, belief in the female phallus, displacement, and symbolization. Also, sadism and masochism very frequently accompany other deviations and may be important motivating forces. However, when seen in isolation neither sadism nor masochism appears to display the elaborate mental mechanisms seen in other deviations.

The classical psychoanalytic interpretation of deviation, then, resides in the myth of the phallic female and the reduction of castration anxiety. In addition, the extreme usage of component (pregenital) instincts serves to increase the repression of dangerous genital impulses while permitting sexual gratification. This theoretical position described by Abraham (10) in 1910 was recently restated by Hammer (11) on the basis of psychological test data of 286 male deviates. Hammer found an increased incidence of responses which he believed related to castration fears and concluded that giving discharge to infantile impulses seemed to ward off other, more forbidden and dangerous desires.

Criticism and Evaluation of Psychoanalytic Theory

Since its presentation well over half a century ago, the classical psychoanalytic formulation has been subjected to two major theoretical criticisms although no truly comprehensive theory has been proposed as a substitute.

One source of criticism has arisen from a general shift of interest within orthodox psychoanalytic circles to pre-oedipal determinants of pathology and a concomitant de-emphasis of castration as a major dynamic mechanism. The other source of criticism has come from the existential and culturalist schools of psychoanalysis. The thrust of this criticism has been more fundamental since the validity of basic postulates of classical psychoanalysis such as instinct, libidinal stages, and even the entire formulation of castration fear has been seriously questioned.

Among the authors who, while remaining in the classical psychoanalytic framework, have questioned the exclusivity of castration fear and the phallic woman theme as either the sine qua non or the major determinant of deviancy are Payne (12), Gillespie (13), Greenacre (14), Bak (15), Sperling (16), and Segal (17), to cite some of the most pertinent contributions.

In 1939, Payne (12) applied the theories of Melanie Klein to a case of fetishism. She interpreted the fetishistic symptom as a defense against an archaic wish to murder the love object. She stated,

> the component impulse which would prevail if not placed under special control is the sadistic impulse . . . It (the fetish) provides reassurance that sadistic wishes have not destroyed the objects.

In her investigations, Payne did not focus exclusively on the symptom but attempted an evaluation of the total personality.

As a result, she was struck with the latent hostility in these individuals. She concluded that the fetish represented the internalized parental images whom the fetishist symbolically controlled, rather than the female phallus. Gillespie (13) essentially confirmed Payne's views in a case study of fetishism published one year later. Gillespie described his patient as fearful of destroying his paramour while at the same time being unable to commit himself to her for fear of losing her due to external forces. The fetish reassured both fears: it was indestructible (i.e., easily replaceable) and totally controllable. It is evident that there is a theoretical shift from castration anxiety to object-relations theory, especially with reference to hostility and control.

Greenacre (14) seems to have attempted to reconcile the two views by postulating that early difficulties in the mother-child relationship hamper the successful resolution of the oedipal conflict and prevent the development of genital sexuality. Here again, early pre-oedipal events are seen as of primary importance. Bak (15) also attempted to trace the "acting out" quality of sexual deviancy to early infancy, postulating that increased excitation in infancy sets up a pattern of immediate discharge with little interference from the ego.

While these authors have been mainly concerned with fetishism, similar conclusions have been reached in the study of other forms of deviancy. Sperling (16), in presenting the analysis of an exhibitionist, interpreted the fundamental problem as separation from the mother figure. Segal (17), in his report of three homosexual transvestites, also stressed the importance of a symbiotic tie to the mother. The true anxiety in this form of pathology, according to Segal, is separation anxiety. This formulation is supported by the finding that these individuals cross-dressed when they felt alone and abandoned and that the cross-dressing gave them a sense of comfort and security.

Other studies could be cited; however, the authors quoted above indicate what is probably a general trend in psychoanalytic theory as specifically applied to sexual disorders. This trend is an overall de-emphasis of the oedipal complex and castration anxiety as the major determinants of pathology and a greater stress on early infantile experiences such as identification, individuation, and separation from the mother figure. In addition, the stages of development are viewed as indicating types of object relationships rather than the release of a specific component instinct. This shift of forces was perhaps best stated by Fairbairn (18):

> . . . it must be stressed that it is not in virtue of the fact that the genital level has been reached that object relationships are satisfactory. On the contrary, it is in virtue of the fact that satisfactory object-relationships have been established that true genital sexuality is attained.

As will be discussed in the next section, the most promising recent advances in the psychoanalytic theory of sexual deviancy have in fact come from studies of early infantile object relations.

The second line of criticism of the classical theory alluded to above is more fundamental in that its adherents have rejected a number of basic psychoanalytic concepts. The criticism of the classical theory of deviancy is thus an extension of a general overall critique rather than a specific instance of disagreement. The major critics of classical theory are the existential and cultural schools of psychoanalysis. Among the existentialists, Boss (19) has written a monograph on deviancy summarizing his point of view, and among the culturalists, Nagler's shorter work on fetishism (20) may be taken as representative.

Boss objects to the whole mechanistic orientation of classical psychoanalysis which views component instincts as actual, discrete forces. Boss feels that theory as well as therapy should be based on humanistic rather than physicalistic models. For example, he describes "perversions" as disorders of "love" and not of libido. More specifically, Boss believes that impulses or symptoms must be derived from the total personality structure rather than deriving personality from the vicissitudes of libido. In short, Boss stresses that only a consideration of the total world view of the individual can lead to an understanding of pathology; symptoms in isolation are insufficient. In keeping with this general theoretical structure, Boss describes sexual psychopathology in terms of the deviant's phenomenological point of view. He describes the deviant's world as so narrow and rigid that love can only emerge in an aberrant manner. Boss (19) asserts that

> the fullness of the loving mode of existence is limited by the mode of being as an isolated, autocratic, petty and fear-laden individual.

Because of this restricted mode of being, the deviant "can gain access to the loving core of human existence, to the love union of male-female essence" only through aberrant behavior. In his description of case histories, Boss attempts to show how the deviant behavior allowed the individual to express a drive toward heterosexual union.

While Boss' emphasis on the total personality seems salutary, his description of deviancy seems to avoid etiological factors as well as the common sporadic expression of deviant wishes in some individuals who also are capable of "normal" sexual behavior. He does not seem to appreciate the defensive use of deviant sexual behavior and thus the situations which elicit the behavior. On the other hand, his stress on deviant behavior representing the only mode through which love can be expressed is somewhat analogous to the Freudian view that deviancy is due to an overusage of a component instinct when mature libidinal release is blocked. Boss' contribution appears to be his acknowledgment of factors other than simply sexual drive as important in deviancy. The emphasis on human relationships, love, and his criticism of a mechanistic orientation seems a more realistic appraisal of the complexity of deviant sexuality.

Nagler, in a paper on fetishism, also sees deviant sexual behavior as symptomatic of a more basic psychopathology of the entire personality. Nagler states that deviancy is not produced by the fear of castration but rather by "the fear of the male social role in its entirety in the face of an overwhelming sense of inadequacy and a low self-esteem" (20). The deviant, according to Nagler, is an insecure, passive, and inadequate male "whose auto-erotic and diminished sexual activity is simply a reflection of his general inactivity." Nagler sees the development of deviancy as not simply due to a regression of instinct but as the symptomatic expression of an individual who cannot fulfill his social role and defends against the resultant anxiety and feelings of inferiority by pathological behavior. Like Boss, Nagler takes into consideration the total experience of the individual and attempts to derive symptoms from the total personality rather than from isolated instincts, etc. Furthermore, he attempts to show the influence of cultural expectations in the perpetuation of illness. However, the culturalist as well as the existential formulations are weakest in determining the actual cause of the disorder. For example, many males in our culture may feel inadequate in the face of social role expectations yet only a small number of these seem to become sexual deviants. The failure to explain symptom choice, however, is a problem with orthodox psychoanalytic theory as well. Freud, in fact, confessed that he could not explain why the sight of the castrated female should lead to homosexuality in one instance, neurosis in another, deviancy in another, and apparent normalcy in yet another.

The import of the culturalist and existentialist theories seems to lie in their consideration of nonsexual factors and in their taking into account the total personality as well as environmental and social factors.

As may have become apparent, there is as yet no truly satisfactory theory of sexual deviancy. Early experiences appear important, as do social mores and cultural expectations, in that these factors greatly influence the estimate of masculinity and self-esteem. The castration anxiety hypothesis seems to be losing its former predominance among some psychoanalysts. In the following sections some recent findings which have a direct bearing on the theory of sexual deviancy will be discussed as will some difficulties which seem to encumber an adequate understanding of this form of psychopathology.

Recent Pertinent Contributions

One of the most significant findings relating to sexual deviancy has been the clinical differentiation of the sub-group of transsexuals. As defined by Benjamin (21) and by Stoller (22), the male transsexual openly wishes to be a female and has always so desired. The male genital is viewed with disgust and hatred since it keeps him from being a woman. The transsexual shows no deviant sexual activity and apparently only wants conventional sex with a partner of the same sex. Now that change-of-sex surgery is available, it is avidly sought and, after surgery, the transsexual seeks out a nonhomosexual male and a normal relationship. The singling out of this group of individuals has important ramifications for theory. First, transsexuals do not try to be women in order to save the penis but instead strive toward change-of-sex surgery. This finding is a strong blow to the classical theory which postulated the penis as the most highly prized possession and castration fear as the strongest motivating force. Second, the causative events of transsexualism are seen to occur in the early months of life, much before the oedipal phase and the threat of castration. Stoller has found that the future male transsexual is born to a mother who has difficulty with her own sense of femininity and finds expression of her masculine strivings in the birth of a son. This mother forms an intense physical relationship with the infant, holding him for hours and excluding the father (and all others) from their symbiotic intimacy. As the infant matures, the mother condones or rewards feminine behavior in the son which has been learned through copying his only adult model.

Stoller cites as further causative factors the passivity or absence of the father and the physical beauty of the child which increases the attraction of the mother. The transsexual behavior occurs during the second year of life and is evidence of a feminine "core gender identity" which then persists through life. Stoller considers this process as analogous to imprinting in birds, so that once a core gender identity is formed it cannot be altered.*

Stoller's citing the second year of life as the first instance of

* Recently, however, Barlow et al. (23) have reported the "cure" of a 17-year-old transsexual with behavior therapy.

manifest transsexual behavior correlates very well with the studies of Money (24, 25) on hermaphrodites showing that sex assignment (i.e., gender identity) occurs very early and is a result of social expectations rather than anatomy. These findings have led Greenson (26) to offer a hypothesis reversing the classical description of gender development. Greenson speculates that the primary identification for both sexes is with the mother and that the male child must "disidentify" from her in order to become masculine while the female child can continue to model herself after the mother. Freud (27), on the other hand, had postulated that the mother was taken as a love object rather than an identification model by both sexes so that, according to his formulation, the male child continues to maintain the same-sex love object while the female child must shift her affections from the mother to the father. As is well known, here again Freud utilized the father's possession of the prized penis as crucial to the girl's turning away from the mother and toward the father. However, Greenson is not simply substituting identification for object love as central to the development of gender identity; he is also pushing the occurrence of gender choice to a much earlier stage than the phallic stage so that castration anxiety is negligible.

How do these findings alter the psychoanalytic view of transvestism? Stoller writes that male transvestites do not show a history of the close symbiotic tie seen in the infancy of transsexuals. Rather, Stoller believes that the future transvestite has a "normal" infancy—that is, forms a male core gender identity—but later in childhood is forcibly dressed as a girl, usually as punishment. In time, according to Stoller, this "punishment" becomes a source of erotic excitement. While this latter formulation is admittedly speculative, there is little doubt that transsexuals differ markedly from transvestites. Ovesey and Person (28) have attempted to differentiate the two in terms of gender disorders and sexual disorders. According to this scheme, transsexualism is primarily a gender disorder, homosexuality a sexual disorder, and transvestism somewhere in between. Ultimately, Ovesey and Person view all these individuals as suffering unresolved separation anxiety and dependency which is seen as the "nuclear conflict." In a manner similar to Segal, they view the transvestite as perpetuating a bond to the mother figure by wearing female apparel. This need to feel the security of the fantasied mother occurs after a crisis which is narcissistically damaging. The transsexual, on the other hand, has totally identified with the mother, and continuously rather than sporadically feels himself a woman. In this case the behavior is not defensive and not reparative; it may be speculated as "conflict free."

Buchner (29), in a recent survey of transvestism, also postulates a reunification with the fantasied mother as the major motive. He has found that the transvestite develops two personalities (similar to the vertical split proposed by Kohut): one personality is the male facade that is presented to the external world; the other is a female alter ego that is passive, giving, and nonthreatening. By donning female clothing, he becomes his own woman and thus escapes from the real life difficulties such as possible rejection by women or having to meet demands of an actual female partner. Buchner stresses these social "advantages" of transvestism, agreeing with Nagler's statements regarding fetishists, that these individuals cannot cope with the competitive aspects of the real world and so develop a safe, auto-erotic outlet. Freud, also, was not unaware of this aspect of deviancy, stating that "the fetishist has no trouble in getting what other men have to woo and extend themselves to obtain." One transvestite patient seen by the author presented this dual identity. He was very secretive about his transvestite practices, considering this behavior intensely private and personal. While dressed as a woman he felt his body was "like someone else" within himself and that the act of cross-dressing was like intercourse with "the me within myself." The feminine self was a kind, soft woman, in contrast to his actual critical and harsh mother. Another transvestite patient, on the other hand, who used bondage as part of his repertoire, imagined himself as at the mercy of a powerful woman, and as the powerful woman at the same time. In both of these individuals, the identification with the mother, or at least a female, appeared predominant. Another individual, described to the author by Dr. Paul Schneck, never actually cross-dressed but had, from early childhood, a fantasied female alter ego who performed all sorts of marvelous feats. In this individual the fantasy of being a woman rather than the need to concretely dress as one sufficed to bolster self-esteem.

It would appear that transvestism is a complex symptom that does not lend itself to simple formula explanations. There may in fact be many types of transvestites—i.e., homosexual, masochistic, nonmasochistic—who achieve different aims from cross-dressing. For example, while Segal's three reported transvestites all had homosexual experiences, Buchner reports that in a sample of 262 transvestites, two-thirds were married and, of these, two-thirds had children; the rate of homosexuality in the sample was less than in the general population. Despite these differences, the work of Benjamin and Stoller on transsexuals has demonstrated the importance of very early experiences and emphasized the role of maternal identification while at the same time limiting the role of castration anxiety.

As regards fetishism, the major theoretical development appears to be Winnicott's (30) description of the "Transitional Object." According to Winnicott, some familiar object is often used to ease the critical passage from infantile omnipotence (when the world is conceived of as part of the self, or at least created by the self) to a realistic appraisal of the environment as existing independent of wishes and needs. While actually supplied by the environment, the infant believes the transitional object to be created by the self (yet it is not part of the self) and the object becomes the repository for fantasies as well as a source of reassurance against anxiety. Thus the transitional object allows for a prolongation of the dwindling state of narcissism while the infant is coming to grips with frustrations of reality. In adult life, the concrete object is normally replaced by "transitional phenomena" such as aesthetic or religious feelings. Winnicott defines all transitional phenomena as "a neutral area of experience which will not be challenged"—that is, where the mind is free to dream and fantasize.

Winnicott states that there is no direct relationship between the usage of a transitional object in normal development and the adult's aberrant utilization of a fetish except when the infantile object represents the female phallus. Other authors, however, have seen similarities between these two states in that, in both, inner fantasies are projected onto a concrete object to satisfy needs. Socarides (31) reported the case of a fetishist who had used a transitional object until he was eight years old, suggesting that a pattern of utilizing a concrete object to satisfy needs had been prolonged beyond infancy and may have established a pattern that later predisposed to fetishism.

Greenacre (32) believes that a transitional object arises from a normal mother-infant relationship while an infantile fetish is the product of an impaired relationship. In the former case, the object is used to widen interests and activities while in the latter case the object serves to form an illusory union with the mother and restricts growth. Sperling (33) has taken issue with the whole concept of the transitional object as a normal developmental milestone, considering it a pathological phenomenon evidencing the mother's inability to allow the infant normal independence. However, most child psychiatrists agree with Anna Freud's position (34) that the use of a transitional object is a normal phenomenon in development which may occasionally result in pathology under adverse circumstances. Freud does not believe that the transitional object, per se, predisposes to fetishism and as evidence cites (1) the high frequency of transitional objects in children versus the rarity of fetishism in adults, and (2) the equal usage of transitional objects by boys and girls versus the almost uniform incidence of fetishism among male adults. Finally, she cites Wulff's early paper (35) stating that only when a childhood object becomes erotically stimulating (and symbolizes genitalia)—that is, after the phallic phase—can fetishism realistically be diagnosed. Prior to this period the transitional object serves phase-appropriate needs such as dependency or sadism.

While Freud's comments are undoubtedly sound, there may be a relationship between fetishism and the prolonged use of a transitional object beyond the time when it becomes transformed into intangible "phenomena," so that a concretization pattern is established and an inanimate object is utilized in lieu of human relationships. The ability to control the object and its resiliency to aggressive attacks may create such a secure outlet that later it becomes the recipient of erotic drives as well. The author, with Drs. Dunton and Spady, has reported the development of a childhood foot fetishist (36, 37). It was found that the mother's overpossessive and restrictive attitudes rewarded the patient's playing with her feet in infancy. Later these same maternal attitudes in concert with the father's punitive and competitive behavior essentially restricted the child's activities so that he was constantly near the mother and her feet. These feet served different purposes at various stages of development, eventually becoming sexually arousing at age six or seven when the child would rub and lick them while fondling his genitals. By this age, the feet had become separate part-objects and often appeared in his dreams as autonomous entities. In addition to the feet as part objects, this patient also evolved a fantasy world around detached penises (after his father told him that cold cuts hanging in a delicatessen window were actually detached penises), detached hands, and other concretized body parts as well as paper animals. It was possible in this patient to trace the evolution of a fetish, in the true sense, from an early infantile object which had served to reward him and absorb his needs throughout childhood.* In other individuals the use of a concrete object to satisfy needs may be discontinuous and may be reevoked during periods of stress or humiliation.

While the formal mechanisms of fetishism may vaguely be related to the use of a transitional object, the motive forces be-

---

* It may be of interest that this patient, now 14 years old, has lost his fetishistic behavior but continues to spend a great deal of his time in fantasy. He appears to feel totally ineffectual except when he can become so repulsive as to shock another person, usually a female. This duality between a weak child and a repulsive monster was recently portrayed in a drawing representing a two-headed person being hanged—one head was drawn as normal while the other was studded with ugly warts and scars. This drawing seemed to portray his depression as well as a dichotomy—reminiscent of Kohut's vertical split—within himself.

hind fetishistic behavior are still a mystery. Recently, more emphasis has been placed on the fetish as a safe recipient of hostility or its satisfying dependency needs (38) than as its symbolization of the female phallus. Gehard (39), in fact, relates fetishism as almost a form of sadomasochism, believing that the majority of fetishistic behavior is of a mild form and is not clinically reported. He views fetishism as basically a function of symbolic transformation quoting Whitehead's "fallacy of misplaced concreteness"—that is, ascribing all importance to the symbol rather than the actual entity so that the individual responds to the symbol just as he would to the real entity being symbolized. Gehard seems to be reviving a theory which Adler proposed over 30 years ago (40), that the fetishist, by displacing interest from a living partner to an object or an incidental aspect of the sexual partner, depreciates the partner and, by thus making her less powerful, is able to control the situation. By making the incidentals of sexual activity more and more important, the actual partner becomes less threatening (or even unnecessary) and sexual activity is possible.

Ultimately it may well be that, just as with transvestism, there may be a variety of motives that channel their way into fetishism and it may be found that the fetish may symbolize a variety of objects or individuals.

As regards exhibitionists and to a lesser extent voyeurs, the most recent literature stresses the superiority of group therapy as a treatment modality (41, 42, 43) and the need for legal reform in that most of these individuals are essentially harmless and their acts should not be considered criminal (44). Much like other deviants, exhibitionists are described as lacking self-confidence in their sense of masculinity and as having an ambivalent attitude toward women. By their exhibitionist act they hope to shock a woman and therefore feel a momentary sense of power (41). This is as far as they are able to pursue their relationships with women and, in fact, Boss (19) reported an exhibitionist who would run away in a panic when occasionally a female took his exhibiting himself as a request for further intimacy and approached him with sexual overtures. Group treatment is seen as allowing the exhibitionist to talk freely about his problem with others who will understand him while at the same time prevent him from utilizing excessive rationalization. Of greater importance, the group is said to supply masculine support and peer relationships, both of which were previously lacking. According to the reports cited, results with group therapy are quite encouraging.

This emphasis on supportive group therapy as well as occasional instances of behavior therapy (45) demonstrate a change in some therapists' approach to deviancy. There seems to be less of an effort to understand the evolution of a symptom than in finding a practical method of treatment. This echoes the previous remark that there is still no sufficient theoretical structure to explain deviancy. The recent advances have emphasized early experiences, such as infantile identification with the mother and the prolonged usage of a transitional object. Other theorists are stressing power relationships, while others are describing personality structure such as Kohut's vertical split. Attempts at generalization, however, have usually failed. There are still many obstacles in formulating a comprehensive theory of sexual deviation and the more one explores the field, the more one is struck by the complexity of these disorders that would preclude a facile interpretation.

One of the major difficulties is simply one of definition of deviancy. In the older psychiatric literature, any behavior other than genital intercourse between opposite sex members was considered as "perverse" and thus the compilation of "psychopathia sexualis" was an easy affair. With the liberalization of accepted sexual mores, however, it has become quite difficult to determine what forms of sexual behavior are deviant, if any are at all. Social relativists would argue that deviancy is an arbitrary label which depends on prevalent modes of a culture. Transvestism had apparently been accepted by certain American Indian and Siberian peoples and homosexuality was considered a higher form of love in classical Greece. Since the deviant does not "suffer" and rarely seeks treatment on his own, there is questionable justification according to the medical model for calling such persons ill. On the other hand, the thrust of the culturalist tradition in psychoanalysis has been to show that behavior is greatly shaped by society and that, as such, sick societies may sanction sick behavior, even when the citizens of such a society do not consider themselves as particularly disabled. More orthodox authors, such as Geza Roheim (46), have also tried to show that man has an essential nature, and essential needs, that transcend cultural variations. In a roundtable discussion reported by Arlow (47), an attempt was made to define deviancy by absolute rather than relativistic criteria. Devereau remarked that in contrast to normal sexual activity a perversion tends to decathect the partner and to perceive the partner as a partial object. Muensterberger stated that perversions are the result of the avoidance of mature sexual outlets and the failure to meet genital demands in a genital way. In a recent survey article Stoller (48) tried to confront the problem of social relativism using the concept of defense as a major criterion. Stoller writes:

> I am retaining the quaint word 'perversion' (rather than the more neutral terms 'variant,' 'deviation,' or 'aberration') for the habitual, preferred, compelling need to perform an erotic act when the deviant act arises from severe anxiety and the act protects the person from the source of anxiety. This implies that there are both perversions and variants—the latter not the result of such anxiety.

Stoller is forced to include "variants" since his own work on transsexuals has shown that such individuals, who would superficially appear the most disturbed, are actually quite free of anxiety if they can achieve their goal of sex transformation. His definition of perversion, however, is significant in that it is based on motivation rather than overt behavior. As such, much of "normal" genital intercourse could also arise as a need to protect against anxiety.* Similar questions may be raised against the definitions of Devereau and Muensterberger quoted above. Therefore a definition in terms of behavior may be too arbitrary while one in terms of motivation may be too all-encompassing. Possibly, the most that can be said at present is that an attitude of tolerance should prevail and that deviations be viewed scientifically rather than morally. This is especially pertinent if it is realized that many deviations are less crippling than other conflict-solving mechanisms that allow for normal sexual behavior.

Another difficulty that besets the study of deviation is that uncommon sexual practices may occur in all sorts of diagnostic entities—from comparatively normal individuals to blatant psychotics. Furthermore, there does not appear to be a positive correlation between the extent of deviancy and the general psychological health of the individual. Arieff & Rotman (50), in a survey of 100 exhibitionists, found six to be schizophrenic, 13 psychopathic, 29 compulsive neurotic, and 39 mentally retarded, plus an additional 16 in the dull normal category, and so on. No one diagnostic category fit their patients. Similarly, while most fetishists are described as shy, passive, ineffectual men, Snow and Bluestone (51) have described two fetishists who murdered older women (presumably mother substitutes) and a third fetishist who had strong homicidal impulses toward women. An especially troublesome finding is that some apparently normal individuals will begin to show deviant behavior as a result of cerebral damage. Walinda (52) reported an individual who developed transvestite behavior five years after a head injury. The deviant behavior ceased when he was given anticonvulsant medication, only to recur when the medication had to be discontinued due to side effects. Ball (53) reported the return of fet-

* A few years ago, the author proposed a tentative definition of deviancy as the compulsive use of a sexual modality to express or fulfill nonsexual needs. This definition was prompted by the observation that deviant behavior appeared to be a reparative maneuver which bolstered a threatened self-esteem. As in Stoller's case, however, this definition would encompass so much "normal" sexual behavior as to be too general and all-inclusive for practical use. (49)

ishistic symptoms which had been resolved through behavior therapy after the individual developed a left temporal lobe tumor. Mitchell (54) and Hunter (55) have reported good results in selected patients with anterior temporal lobectomy. A further correlation between deviancy and neuropathology has been indicated by Epstein (56), who reported that, of 12 cases of transvestism and fetishism seen by him, eight had abnormal EEG's, two had frank seizures, and four had clinical evidence of brain damage. In a similar series of 26 transvestites reported by Walinda (52), 12 had abnormal EEG's. These individuals raise the question of a "latent" tendency toward deviancy which is "released" by cortical damage. On the other hand, the frequent implication of the temporal lobes suggests a similarity to the Kluver-Bucy syndrome. It remains difficult to properly categorize these individuals unless it is assumed that similar dynamics as seen in overt deviants are present but strongly repressed prior to injury.

Another inconsistent element is the presence or absence of homosexuality. Freud believed that the deviations protected the individual from homosexuality by allowing him to accept a female (albeit a phallic female) as a sexual partner. However, these disturbances have been found in overt homosexuals and some theorists consider all deviants as basically "homosexual." The question of whether deviants are actually compensated homosexuals brings up the whole issue of "latent" homosexuality and the difficulties surrounding that very complex problem. Just like the types of deviancy discussed here, homosexuality is becoming an increasingly complicated spectrum of entities from the pseudo-homosexual as defined by Ovesey (57) to the overt, effeminate drag queen. The entity, or variety of entities, also seems to defy any simple dynamic formula. In a manner similar to homosexuals, sexual deviants have been lumped together into a single category as if they all had significant features in common. There appear to be as important differences between categories such as voyeurism and fetishism as between sociopathy and obsessive-compulsive neurosis.

Some of the difficulties mentioned in regard to an understanding of sexual deviancy may result from the paucity of relevant literature. Most articles consist of one or two case reports which are used to illustrate the author's specific orientation. There seems to be a need for a comprehensive, in-depth study of a large series of individuals to determine similarities and differences. When a large group was indeed studied, such as in the work of Benjamin (21) and later of Stoller (22), their findings had great relevance for psychoanalytic theory and caused basic changes in our understanding of gender identification. It appears time to duplicate the encyclopedic work of Krafft-Ebing and Havelock Ellis, going beyond their descriptive goal and utilizing the insights of psychoanalytic theory and the methodology of academic psychology to probe the still elusive genesis of sexual deviation. These disorders remain a fruitful and important area for future research.

References

1. Freud, S. Three essays on the theory of sexuality (1905). *Standard Edition,* Vol. 7. London: Hogarth Press.
2. Fenichel, O. *The Psychoanalytic Theory of Neurosis.* New York: W. W. Norton, 1945.
3. Freud, S. Fetishism (1927). *Standard Edition,* Vol. 21. London: Hogarth Press.
4. Freud, S. An outline of psychoanalysis (1940). *Standard Edition,* Vol. 23. London: Hogarth Press.
5. Kohut, H. *The Analysis of the Self.* New York: International Universities Press, 1971.
6. Fenichel, O. The psychology of transvestitism. *Int. J. Psychoanal., 11,* 211-227, 1930.
7. Grotjohn, M. Transvestite fantasy expressed in a drawing. *Psychoanal. Quart., 1,* 340-343, 1948.
8. Freud, S. Beyond the pleasure principle (1920). *Standard Edition,* Vol. 18. London: Hogarth Press.
9. Bieber, I. Sadism and masochism. In S. Arieti (Ed.), *American Handbook of Psychiatry,* Vol. III. New York: Basic Books, 1966.
10. Abraham, K. Remarks on the psychoanalysis of a case of foot and corset fetishism. *Selected Papers.* New York: Basic Books, 1953.
11. Hammer, E. F. Symptoms of sexual deviation: Dynamics and etiology. *Psychoanal. Rev., 55,* 5-27, 1968.
12. Payne, S. Some observations on the ego development of the fetishist. *Int. J. Psychoanal., 20,* 161-170, 1939.

13. GILLESPIE, W. H. A contribution to the study of fetishism. *Int. J. Psychoanal., 21,* 401-415, 1940.
14. GREENACRE, P. Certain relationships between fetishism and faulty development of the body image. In *Psychoanalytic Study of the Child,* Vol. VIII. New York: International Universities Press, 1953. Pp. 78-98.
15. BAK, R. Fetishism. *J. Amer. Psychoanal. Assn., 1,* 285-298, 1953.
16. SPERLING, M. The analysis of an exhibitionist. *Int. J. Psychoanal., 28,* 32-45, 1947.
17. SEGAL, M. Transvetitism as an impulse and as a defense. *Int. J. Psychoanal., 46,* 209-217, 1965.
18. FAIRBAIRN, W. R. D. *Psychoanalytic Studies of the Personality.* London: Tavistock, 1952.
19. BOSS, M. *Meaning and Content of Sexual Perversions.* New York: Grune and Stratton, 1949.
20. NAGLER, S. Fetishism: A review and a case study. *Psychiat. Quart., 31,* 713-741, 1957.
21. BENJAMIN, H. *The Transsexual Phenomenon.* New York: Julian Press, 1966.
22. STOLLER, R. J. *Sex and Gender.* New York: Science House, 1968.
23. BARLOW, D. H., et al. Gender identity changes in a transsexual. *Arch. Gen. Psychiat., 28,* 569-576, 1973.
24. MONEY, J., et al. An examination of some basic sexual concepts: The evidence of human hermaphroditism. *Bull. Johns Hopkins Hosp., 97,* 301-319, 1955.
25. MONEY, J. Sex assignment as related to hermaphroditism and transsexualism. In R. Green and J. Money (Eds.), *Transsexualism and Sex Reassignment.* Baltimore: Johns Hopkins Univ. Press, 1968.
26. GREENSON, R. R. A transvestite boy and a hypothesis. *Int. J. Psychoanal., 47,* 396-403, 1966.
27. FREUD, S. Femininity (1932). *Standard Edition,* Vol. 22. London: Hogarth Press.
28. OVESEY, L., and PERSON, E. Gender identity and sexual psychopathology in men. *J. Amer. Acad. Psychoanal. 1,* 53-72, 1973.
29. BUCHNER, H. T. The transvestic career path. *Psychiatry, 33,* 381-389, 1970.
30. WINNICOTT, D. W. Transitional objects and transitional phenomena. *Int. J. Psychoanal., 34,* 89-97, 1953.
31. SOCARIDES, C. W. The development of a fetishistic perversion. *J. Amer. Psychoanal. Assn., 8,* 281-311, 1960.
32. GREENACRE, P. The transitional object and the fetish with special reference to the role of illusion. *Int. J. Psychoanal., 51,* 447-456, 1970.
33. SPERLING, M. Fetishism in children. *Psychoanal. Quart., 32,* 379-392, 1963.
34. FREUD, A. *Normality and Pathology in Childhood.* New York: International Universities Press, 1965.
35. WULFF, M. Fetishism and object choice in early childhood. *Psychoanal. Quart., 15,* 450-471, 1946.
36. DUNTON, H. D., and BEMPORAD, J. R. Foot fetishism in an eight-year-old boy. *Bull. Assn. Psychoanal. Med., 9,* 53-57, 1969.
37. BEMPORAD, J. R., DUNTON, H. D., and SPADY, F. The treatment of a child foot fetishist. (In preparation.)
38. GILLESPIE, W. H. Notes on the analysis of sexual perversions. *Int. J. Psychoanal., 33,* 397-402, 1952.

39. GEHARD, R. H. Fetishism and sadomasochism. In J. Masserman (Ed.), *Science and Psychoanalysis,* Vol. XV. New York: Grune and Stratton, 1969. Pp. 71-80.
40. ANSBACHER, H., and ANSBACHER, R. (Eds.) *The Individual Psychology of Alfred Adler.* New York: Harper Torchbooks, 1964.
41. WITZIG, J. S. The group treatment of male exhibitionists. *Amer. J. Psychiat., 125,* 75-81, 1968.
42. MATHIS, J. L., and COLLINS, M. Mandatory group therapy for exhibitionists. *Amer. J. Psychiat., 126,* 1162-1166, 1970.
43. FREESE, A. L. Group therapy with exhibitionists and voyeurs. *Social Work, 17,* 44-52, 1972.
44. MATHIS, J. L. The exhibitionist. *Med. Aspects of Human Sexual., 3,* 89-101, 1969.
45. BARKER, J. C. Behavior therapy for transvestism. *Brit. J. Psychiat., 111,* 268-276, 1965.
46. ROHEIM, G. *Psychoanalysis and Anthropology.* London: 1947.
47. ARLOW, J. A. Perversions: Theoretical and therapeutic aspects. *J. Amer. Psychoanal. Assn., 2,* 336-345, 1954.
48. STOLLER, R. J. New advances in sex research. *Amer. J. Psychiat., 150,* 241-251, 1973.
49. BEMPORAD, J. R. An attempt to define sexual deviation. *Forum of the Society of Medical Psychanalysts, 1,* 2-5, 1971.
50. ARIEFF, A. J., and ROTMAN, D. B. Psychiatric inventory of one hundred cases of indecent exposure. *Arch. Neurol. Psychiat., 47,* 495-498, 1942.
51. SNOW, E., and BLUESTONE, H. Fetishism and murder. In J. Masserman (Ed.), *Science and Psychoanalysis,* Vol. XV. New York: Grune and Stratton, 1969. Pp. 88-97.
52. WALINDA, J. Transvestism. *Int. J. Neuropsychiat., 1,* 567-573, 1965.
53. BALL, J. R. A case of fetishism, transvestism, and organic cerebral disorder. *Acta Psychiat. Scand., 44,* 249-254, 1968.
54. MITCHELL, W., et al. Epilepsy with fetishism relieved by temporal lobectomy. *Lancet, 2,* 626-630, 1954.
55. HUNTER, R., et al. Temporal lobe epilepsy supervening on long standing transvestism and fetishism. *Epilepsia, 4,* 60-65, 1963.
56. EPSTEIN, A. W. Fetishism: A comprehensive view. In J. Masserman (Ed.), *Science and Psychoanalysis,* Vol. XV. New York: Grune and Stratton, 1969. Pp. 81-87.
57. OVESEY, L. The pseudohomosexual anxiety. *Psychiatry, 18,* 17-25, 1955.

18

The Psychological Impact of the Sex Revolution

HENRY GREENBAUM, M.D.

THROUGHOUT HISTORY, VIEWS ABOUT SEXUALITY have swung widely, encompassing the attitude that sex is a source of evil and sin and, at the other extreme, the conviction that sex is both a life force and a fount of supreme happiness. In Western civilization, under the influence of Judeo-Christian teachings, sex has been predominantly regarded as a necessary evil in the service of procreation. In recent years, however, sexual behavior and attitudes in this country have undergone marked change. This is popularly referred to as the sex revolution.

In a historical sense, the term *revolution* is applied to a radical change in political, social, economic, technological, intellectual, or moral conditions that is brought about for the purposes of *improving the quality of life for the individual and society*—thus the American Revolution for independence, the French Revolution bearing the banner *Liberté, Egalité et Fraternité,* and the Russian Revolution with its ideology of social justice.

Similarly, some of the attitudes and practices conceptualized as the sex revolution are truly revolutionary and will no doubt exert a profound influence on sexual mores in America. Other aspects of this sexual revolution appear to be actually counterrevolutionary; that is, they may serve to impair the quality of life for both the individual and society. It would be well to differentiate the positive aspects of this ongoing movement from the negative import of some sexual attitudes and activities it has fostered.

Liberation of Sex from its Biological Aim

Most significant perhaps among the attitudes that are influencing our sexual mores is the separation of sex for *pleasure* from sex for *procreation*. In other words, sexual intercourse has been liberated from its biological aim—perpetuation of the species—and the pursuit of sexual pleasure has been established as a legitimate and autonomous human function. Such changes have occurred in the use of other human faculties. For instance, seeing and hearing, whose original biological aims were in the service of survival, are frequently enlisted by modern man for purely esthetic enjoyment, such as viewing a Picasso painting or a sunset, listening to a Beethoven symphony, or engaging in spirited conversation.

Countless individuals have advocated and indulged in sex for pleasure, but in the past they invariably met with public condemnation. To a growing number of people today, however, this pursuit has become morally acceptable, even morally expedient in view of the population explosion and the availability of contraceptive measures. Consequently, this aspect of the sex revolution will probably endure.

Nevertheless, emotional and psychological opposition to the pursuit of sex for pleasure is still strong. Its persistence in our culture testifies to the derogation of sex since time immemorial. The biblical legend of Eve's arousal of God's wrath and severe punishment for yielding to the temptation of the serpent has left a deep impression on the psyche of Western man: sexual gratification is to be tolerated only for the sake of preserving the species; sexual activity engaged in for pleasure is a transgression of Divine Law and the source of Original Sin. This impression has been reinforced by the New Testament concept of the Virgin Birth and also by the dogma of the Immaculate Conception, which holds that the Virgin conceived without the stain of Original Sin, transmitted to mankind by Adam and Eve. Small wonder that sexuality has been permeated with so much guilt and shame and so intensely thwarted.

Legends usually reflect the moral climate and conditions that obtained at the time they were elaborated. To have elicited such severe moral condemnation of sex, conditions prevailing at the dawn of our civilization must have dictated the imposition of sexual restraints on the individual. One may speculate that this development coincided with the formation of the family unit and the necessity of establishing the authority of the father and imposing the *incest taboo.* The biblical story of Abraham bent on sacrificing his son Isaac argues in favor of that hypothesis, as does the reemergence, in the New Testament, of the theme of a father sacrificing the life of his son.*

Not infrequently, however, measures deemed desirable or necessary at one period of history far outlive their usefulness, eventually becoming a destructive force. The sex revolution, in counteracting the crippling influences just mentioned, endows human sexuality with dignity and respectability.

Sexual Equality of Women

Another major facet of the sex revolution is the struggle of women for sexual equality. For most of recorded history, they have been subjugated to an inferior position—sexually as well as politically, socially, economically, and morally. The countless legends and myths, reinforced by misconceptions and misrepresentations, that have been woven to justify and perpetuate the subjugation, have had such a powerful impact that it is now virtually impossible to differentiate the innate sexual nature of women from their culturally determined traits. Their inherent sexual characteristics will unfold only after they have achieved true equality.

The story of Adam and Eve offers forthright evidence of female inequality. The Bible recounts that the first man was created in God's image and that the first woman was formed from

---

* The same theme is also encountered outside the Judeo-Christian framework, notably in the Greek myths about Zeus and Prometheus and about Agamemnon and Iphegenia.

Adam's rib—as his extension—and cursed to bear children in sorrow and to be subservient to her mate.* Pious Jewish men still thank God in their daily prayers for having spared them from the lot of women. And Christian veneration of the Virgin reflects a further downgrading of female sexuality and the reproductive capacity. Is it surprising, then, that women have had virtually no access to the priesthood, the ministry, and the rabbinate?

In adherence to biblical precepts, women, especially those of the so-called higher social classes, have been represented as naturally devoid of strong sexual drives but passionately devoted to children and the domestic care of men. To males of all social classes, on the other hand, sexual drives too powerful to control have been attributed. Prostitution, serviced by women, has therefore been regarded as a dire necessity to protect the purity of the so-called virtuous woman.

These and many other misconceptions have so thoroughly permeated our culture that even Freud, a man of genius, was unable to extricate himself from the prevailing belief in women's sexual inferiority. Like his Judeo-Christian forerunners, Freud failed to perceive woman as a complete individual "made in the image of God," the privilege that they reserved for men. Only man is complete; endowed with a penis, he is superior to woman. Lacking a penis, she is fated to feel sorry for herself throughout life, and she suffers from the complex of penis envy, which colors her sexuality and her total psychology. This complex, according to Freud, is universal and unavoidable. In a description of the average feminine character, he states that women

> fall a victim to *envy for the penis* which will leave ineradicable traces on their development and the formation of their character and which will not be surmounted in even the

* "And Adam said, This is now bone of my bones and flesh of my flesh: she shall be called Woman, because she was taken out of man. . . . Unto the woman he said, I will greatly multiply thy sorrow and thy conception; in sorrow thou shalt bring forth children and he (man) shall rule over thee." [Genesis 2,23–3,16] (1)

> most favourable cases without a severe expenditure of psychical energy. . . . Her [the girl's] self-love is mortified by the comparison with *the boy's far superior equipment* . . . If envy for the penis has provoked a powerful impulse against clitoridal masturbation . . . the girl . . . gives expression to her entire dissatisfaction with her *inferior clitoris* * in her effort against obtaining satisfaction from it . . . Along with the abandonment of clitoridal masturbation a certain amount of activity is renounced. Passivity *now has the upper hand* . . .
>
> Thus we attribute a larger amount of *narcissism* to femininity . . . so that *to be loved is a stronger need for them than to love.* The effect of penis-envy has a share, further, in the *physical vanity* of women, since they are bound to value their charms more highly as a late compensation for their original sexual inferiority.
>
> The fact that women must be regarded as having *little sense of justice* is no doubt related to the predominance of envy in their mental life . . . We also regard women as *weaker in their social interests* and as having *less capacity for sublimating their instincts than men* . . . A man of about thirty strikes us as a youthful, somewhat unformed individual, whom we expect to make powerful use of the possibilities for development opened up to him by analysis . . . A woman of the same age, however, often frightens us by her *psychical rigidity and unchangeability.* [All italics added] (2)

The passages just cited demonstrate that one of the most brilliant minds of our era shared history's ancient prejudice against

---

* The view, widely held, that the penis is superior to the clitoris is based on an erroneous comparison. To compare them is tantamount to comparing an apple with an orange. To be valid, a comparison must be between anatomical structures and functions of a similar nature, such as the areas of maximum sensibility for sexual pleasure in each sex. These are the *frenulum preputii* and *corona glandis* in the male, and the junction of the *frenulum clitoridis* and *glans* in the female. These areas have a similar voluptuous capacity; neither one is superior to the other. Among other comparable parts of the sexual organs are the shaft of the penis and the vagina; these are comparable in the sense that they complement each other both in function and structure, like an arm and a sleeve. But here again, there is no justification for describing one as being superior to the other, apart from the fact that one is visible and the other is invisible. Although studies suggest that boys and girls are aware of their anatomical differences as early as 18 months of age, it is not certain that the invisibility of the female organ leads to castration anxiety in boys and penis-envy in girls. H. G.

women. Freud's views on the subject served to reinforce the belief in woman's sexual, social, and moral inferiority. To be just, it ought to be mentioned that Freud sometimes doubted the validity of his own observations. Referring to the statements quoted above, he wrote:

> We do not claim to more than an average validity for these assertions; nor is it always easy to distinguish what should be ascribed to the influence of the sexual function and what to social breeding. . . . If you reject this idea as fantastic and regard my belief in the influence of lack of a penis on the configuration of femininity as an *idée fixe,* I am of course defenceless. (2)

Freud's views on femininity are defied by logic and clinical observation. To be sure, many women do suffer from penis-envy and conform to Freud's description of them. It is also true that many men suffer from vagina-uterus-breast envy. Both of these conditions, however, are the consequence of a combination of pathogenic factors in the family and society at large. In families where women are treated with love and respect and accorded as much consideration as men, it is doubtful that girls grow up suffering from penis-envy and its consequences. Yet, incredible as it may seem, many astute psychoanalysts, females among them, still adhere to Freud's views on the universality and inevitability of penis-envy in women and on their inferiority.

Stoller reports on new research findings that place Freud's argument on the primacy of the penis in a precarious position:

> In mammalian species the function of cells is female in both sexes, until androgens are added in fetal life. In fact, except for the chromosomes, one cannot talk about two sexes until androgens have been added; there is only femaleness. (3)

Women's struggle for sexual equality is one of the most positive aspects of the sex revolution. Inequality of the sexes poisons human relationships by creating a master-slave atmosphere. The master cannot help but feel contempt and pity for the slave; the slave responds with hate and resentment under a façade of placation. Inequality of men and women breeds suspicion and distrust, which destroy love and inhibit the exchange of tender feelings. True love requires sexual equality.

In appealing for the liberation of the "second sex" from enslavement, Simone de Beauvoir writes:

> To emancipate woman is to refuse to confine her to the relations she bears to man, not to deny them to her; let her have her independent existence and she will continue nonetheless to exist for him also: mutually recognizing each other as subject, each will remain for the other an *other*. The reciprocity of their relations will not do away with the miracles —desire, possession, love, dream, adventure—worked by the division of human beings into separate categories; and the words that move us—giving, conquering, uniting—will not lose their meaning. On the contrary, when we abolish the slavery of half of humanity, together with the whole system of hypocrisy that it implies, then the "division" of humanity will reveal its genuine significance and the human couple will find its true form. (4)

Freedom for Sex Variations

Western societies have identified, morally and legally, with the heterosexual way of life and severely condemned those who deviated from that model. The contempt, the hatred, the suspicion, distrust, and harassment of homosexuals, transsexuals, and transvestites are well known consequences of departing from what has commonly been regarded as the "natural order of things" in sexual practices. Rejection by employers and imprisonment are more dire consequences faced by those who engage in sex variations. Their struggle for equality with heterosexuals in civil rights and against discrimination is an important aspect of the sex revolution.

There is no valid justification for the antagonism directed toward these individuals. They are found in every walk of life and their social, intellectual, and work behavior presents a broad spectrum not very different from that of heterosexuals, ranging within the polarities of low achievement and socially distasteful patterns of conduct to the highly approved behavior patterns of well-motivated business and professional people, and gifted and creative individuals in the arts and sciences.

Society has reacted toward people who depart from heterosexual behavior as if they had deliberately chosen a sexual way of life that can be changed at will. The fact is that psychosexual orientation is not determined exclusively by biological factors, such as anatomy and hormonal physiology; powerful environmental factors, such as family configuration and parental relationships and expectations during the formative preschool years, also play a part. In early childhood, feminine or masculine gender identifications and roles are so deeply established in the psyche and have so profoundly influenced the development of the personality that the sexual orientation cannot be discarded or reversed at will. To deprive people of their civil rights because they engage in sexual variations is therefore cruel and punitive and has no rehabilitative influence.

Kinsey's comprehensive survey of the sexual behavior of males (5) and females (6) suggests that there are few adults who do not, in private life at one time or another, depart from the conventional model of sexual behavior. Judd Marmor has stated:

> Even a cursory look at the recorded history of human sexuality makes it abundantly clear that patterns of sexual behavior and morality have taken many diverse forms over the centuries. Far from being "natural" and inevitable, our contemporary sexual codes and mores, seen in historical perspective, would appear no less grotesque to people of other eras than theirs appear to us. (7)

It is high time for our democratic and pluralistic society to accept the existence of variations in sexual behavior and to evolve new sexual codes and mores that would allow these variations to be practiced among consenting partners.* Such an approach would improve the quality of life in our society and have a re-

* Of course, sex variations that inflict physical injuries or threaten life are clear-cut sexual perversions of the sadomasochistic type and must not be tolerated.

habilitative effect on persons with sex deviations that cause them suffering. At the present time, many of them do not seek psychotherapeutic help in alleviating their suffering because they ascribe it to oppressive factors in society rather than to the underlying psychopathology. With the resolution of these factors, the effects of psychopathology would become obvious to them and they would become more responsive to their emotional needs and psychotherapeutic intervention.

Sex in the Arts

Sexuality has for many years been portrayed with such vagueness and pseudo-discretion in the performing arts, literature, and news media that it impressed one as a forbidden topic. And when an artist treated sexuality honestly and openly, his work was condemned as pornographic and even banned. That was the fate, decades ago, of James Joyce's *Ulysses,* D. H. Lawrence's *Lady Chatterley's Lover,* and Henry Miller's *Tropic of Cancer,* to mention a few. In recent years, thanks to the sex revolution, a breakthrough has taken place. The more frank and realistic treatment of sexuality today has the effect of a fresh breeze clearing the atmosphere.

Fear of being accused of pornography has inhibited the treatment of sexuality in the arts. The coining of the word *pornography* to denote art that causes or intends to cause sexual excitement or lust reflects a peculiar antisexual attitude encountered in our culture. No word has been created and no motivations have been attributed to art depicting violence, such as Goya's paintings of execution by garrote or firing squad. Why not call such work "thanatography" and attribute to it motivations of inciting cruelty and violence? Why has sex in the arts been singled out as more dangerous than violence?

In principle, a work of art should be judged by its esthetic and technical qualities, not by its theme, be that sex or violence. Good art elevates the human spirit; bad art leaves it unmoved. Complete freedom to deal with the theme of sexuality in the arts would represent a momentous advance in our way of life.

Negative Aspects of the Sex Revolution

After reviewing developments and directions in the sex revolution that have a potential for enhancing our lives, both as individuals and as a society, it is appropriate to point out aspects of the sex revolution that have destructive implications.

Chief among these dangers is the encouragement given to the mindless cult of sex without love. One observes a total preoccupation with immediate sexual pleasure—the pursuit of sex without affection and tenderness, without kinship or devotion, and without commitment and compassion. The poet Archibald MacLeish describes this state of affairs:

> There again the word we are talking about—love—is the great contemporary example. We've gotten it mixed up with what we awkwardly and self-consciously call "sex"—not only mixed up but inverted, the cart before the horse, if you will excuse the image. In a healthy, natural society . . . what we call "sex" was the healthy and rational consequence of love. With us it's the other way around. We start with our interest —obsession might be a better word—with "sex" and assume that what then happens is going to be love. It could be, I suppose, but the chances are against it. A couple of eighteen-year-olds—boy and girl—going to bed to exercise themselves sexually aren't going to end up with anything Catullus or Sappho . . . would recognize as love. Which is their loss. But if we follow that habit in our paperbacks and our blue motion pictures, the end result may well be that the corrupted word will corrupt the thing itself. And that would be a loss to all of us—to our humanity—to the meanings of our human lives. (8)

MacLeish grasped the importance of love in imbuing the sexual drive with a human quality. Indeed, without love the sexual drive in humans is not essentially different from the sexual drive in mammalian animals, from the lowest species on the evolutionary scale to the primates. Neuroanatomic structures, neurophysiology, and biochemistry—the biological roots of the drive—are basically constant in all mammalian species and transmitted phylogenetically.

In isolation from other human functions, the sexual drive is fundamentally a neutral force that seeks discharge without discrimination among objects and without a conscience. It can therefore take autoerotic, heterosexual, and homosexual directions and it can assume masochistic, sadistic, and random characteristics. The presently widespread practices of group sex, wife-swapping, swinging, hit-and-run relations, and adolescent sexual acting-out under a permissive parental roof are all manifestations of dehumanized sexuality.

Some persons, usually neurotics, act as if the sexual drive were essential to their personal survival. It is, in fact, only species-preservative, not self-preservative. On the scale of vital functions of the individual, sex is lowest, following respiration, nutrition, sleep, the need for protection from the elements, for interpersonal relationships, for love, security, and self-esteem. The fact of the matter is that sex is no more than a *desire.* A powerful desire, it is true, and when gratified, one that enriches life immensely. On the other hand, if the desire is unfulfilled because of environmental or intrapsychic obstacles, there is no clinical evidence to support Freud's belief that the individual is harmed mentally. (9, 10)

Freud's assumption that sexual fulfillment is essential to mental health cannot be confirmed. On the contrary, there is much evidence that mental health is a prerequisite for sexual fulfillment. Many persons known to have lived without sex for long periods of time managed their lives during these periods no less effectively, in terms of happiness, productivity, and creative achievement, than many individuals who lead an active sex life. Sexual behavior reflects general personality development but does not shape it.

Sexuality and Love

To play a balanced role in the life of the individual, sex needs to be infused with love. Sexuality without love is a chaotic experience.

According to Freud (11), love is a manifestation of the sexual instinct. This view cannot be confirmed by psychoanalytic observation. A more constructive working hypothesis is that the sexual drive and the capacity to love are separate forces reciprocally influencing each other: the sex drive gives love an erotic quality; love humanizes the sex drive. The drive is innate and transmitted phylogenetically, while love is acquired and determined ontogenetically.

A new, uniquely human phenomenon in evolutionary development, the capacity to love can be acquired only by experiencing love in the intimate interaction within a family. Once acquired, it has a lasting impact on the conduct of an individual. In the words of Balzac, "True love is eternal, infinite, and always like itself. It is equal and pure, without violent demonstrations; it is seen with white hairs and is always young in the heart. (12)"

The capacity to love has its biological and psychological roots in the prolonged, interdependent relationship between the child and his parents. To acquire this capacity, the child needs to grow up with a loving mother and a loving father—parents who love each other. That a child needs to experience love from his parents is now well understood; the crucial importance of love between mother and father is less appreciated. The literature has given little emphasis to the fact that conjugal love has a profound influence on the quality of parenthood and the capacity for the development of love in offspring. I have treated numerous individuals who had loving and devoted parents, but because the parents were devoid of love for each other and maintained a sadomasochistic relationship, the patients grew up hating themselves and their parents. The patients were unable to love.

It is true that the oedipal stage is characterized by a wish to separate the parents, but the child is not conscious of this wish. If a separation really occurs, it threatens the child's security and causes him to turn against the parents. Moreover, unloving parents in conflict cause the child to take sides, and guilt is experienced toward the parent he turns against. The conflict of loyalties exacerbates his feelings of guilt and generates self-hatred.

Individuals from disturbed family relationships devoid of love often engage in the careless and senseless pursuit of sex. There is a great danger that this cult will, in turn, further cripple the family structure. The nefarious effects of hypersexualism are well illustrated in *Couples,* a novel by John Updike, and in Bertolucci's motion picture, "Last Tango in Paris."

Love is more than an emotion. It is an ethical principle as well. In addition to feelings of tenderness, pleasure, affection, and friendship, love inspires a deep sense of loyalty, commitment, and devotion—so essential for giving the relationship between a man and a woman an enduring quality.

Moral principles and ethical strivings exert little influence if structures for their fulfillment are not available. I know of no better structure for love than marriage and family life. Of course, the attractiveness and durability of this structure, like any other, depends on the people who erect and maintain it. For individuals who do not possess the capacity to love, marriage and family life are bleak and flimsy shells, even institutions of destruction and immense suffering for those imprisoned in them. Eugene O'Neill's "Long Day's Journey into Night" provides an excellent illustration of a destructive family.

But to replace marriage with group sex and communal living, as some voices of the sex revolution advocate, is not the solution. On the contrary, such practices might well multiply the evils of an incompatible marriage and an unhappy family life. In our era of rapid technological and social change, of mass production and mass consumption, of overpopulation and congestion, pressures conducive to human alienation and impersonal relationships are overwhelming. Love in marriage and family is essential to counteract the process of alienation and give the individual a sense of belonging and dignity, an oasis that offers warmth and serenity.

Much criticism has recently been directed against the nuclear family. Its isolating and constrictive characteristics have been contrasted with the advantages of the extended family, whose members live in proximity and help one another. I believe that the latter institution is not adaptable to modern living. However, the strong emotional ties established in a good nuclear family equip us with the power to create an *emotionally extended kinship family*. In a structure of that nature, family members may be widely separated geographically but they are united through a powerful bond of love, affection, and friendship. Although they may not be able to assist one another in their daily routines, they support one another on important occasions of family joy or tragedy, thus generating a sense of family strength and security in all of the members, however great the physical distance between them.

The strength of the Kennedy family, for example, appears to be derived, to a considerable degree, from such *emotionally extended ties*. Emotional ties of kinship are also frequently encountered among Jewish families whose members are scattered over the globe, and may have been a key factor in the survival of the Jewish people in the two millennia of the diaspora.

Stressing the importance of marriage and the family structure, Lidz writes:

> A larger proportion of the population is married than ever before. It appears as if people living in an insecure world in which values and purposes are obscure have intuitively realized that meaningful values can be found in the relationships between spouses and between parents and children. . . . Despite the inevitable frustrations and even despite tangible failures, the vast majority of persons seek a more enduring happiness in firm family relationships. (13)

Sexual freedom and sexual equality serve to instill a spirit of renewal and a sense of joy and happiness into marriage and family life. Conversely, in a marital relationship animated by love, sexual life acquires an orderly, meaningful, and enduring quality. Such an integration immeasurably enriches both the individual life experience and society.

References

1. *The Holy Bible,* King James Version. Cleveland and New York: Meridian Books, World Publishing, 1964.
2. Freud, S. Femininity (1932). *Standard Edition,* Vol. 22. London: Hogarth Press.

3. STOLLER, R. J. Overview: The impact of new advances in sex research on psychoanalytic theory. *Amer. J. Psychiat., 130,* 241-251, 1973.
4. BEAUVOIR, S. DE. An androgynous world. In *The Second Sex,* translated and edited by H. M. Parshley. New York: Knopf, 1953. Pp. 682-689.
5. KINSEY, A. C., POMEROY, W. B., and MARTIN, C. E. *Sexual Behavior in the Human Male.* Philadelphia: W. B. Saunders, 1948.
6. KINSEY, A. C., POMEROY, W. B., MARTIN, C. E., and GEBHARD, P. H. *Sexual Behavior in the Human Female.* Philadelphia: W. B. Saunders, 1953.
7. MARMOR, J. "Normal" and "deviant" sexual behavior. *JAMA, 217,* 165-170, 1971.
8. MACLEISH, A. The most compelling acts of love to touch my life. *Today's Health,* February 1973.
9. FREUD, S. "Civilized" sexual morality and modern nervous illness (1908). *Standard Edition,* Vol. 9. London: Hogarth Press.
10. FREUD, S. Civilization and its discontents (1930). *Standard Edition,* Vol. 21. London: Hogarth Press.
11. FREUD, S. Instincts and their vicissitudes (1915). *Standard Edition,* Vol. 14. London: Hogarth Press.
12. EDWARDS, T. (compiler). *The New Dictionary of Thoughts. A Cyclopedia of Quotations.* Standard Book Co., 1957. P. 374.
13. LIDZ, T. *The Family and Human Adaptation.* New York: International Universities Press, 1963. Pp. 37-38.

Index